Perspectives on Strategic IQ from Practitioners and Scholars Around the Globe

"Terrifying but true! Wells zeroes in with supreme intellectual precision on the heavy price firms pay for moving too slowly on the business battlefield."

Bill Roedy, ex Chairman & CEO, MTV Networks International, USA

"Wells makes a compelling case for dramatic change for those at the helm – and suggests ways to push beyond the limits of traditional thinking and behaviours that can stand in the way of innovation."

Ron Sargent, Chairman & CEO, Staples Inc., USA

"A comprehensive compendium for any CEO trying to drive excellence in their company. John Wells masterfully links the need for a winning strategy, a smart structure and business model for flawless execution, and the kind of human capital and culture needed to sustain excellence through wrenching change. A must read for any CEO looking to jumpshift their company's performance."

Michael White, Chairman & CEO, DIRECTV, USA

"Our people, strategy and culture are what make us special. Wells offers insightful research into how these factors influence strategic intelligence and offers real world, practical advice to raise your company's Strategic IQ."

Glenn Renwick, CEO, Progressive Corporation, USA

"John Wells has created the next strategic classic. He brings the strategic, structural and human capital challenges together into a holistic view of the challenges of change and survival in an increasingly complex changing world."

Saul Berman, Global leader of Strategy and Change, IBM, USA

"The Danaher Business System is about 'doing the right things, well.' Wells' compelling book makes the case for tightly weaving a firm's strategic, operational and organizational initiatives into whole cloth before well-meaning but fractured, functional efforts cause even the most successful company to unwind."

Larry Culp, CEO, Danaher, USA

"John Wells does an enormous service to the science of strategy by categorizing and describing simple and practical measures and mental models that distinguish great firms from the rest."

John Pittenger, Senior Vice President, Koch Industries Inc., USA

"Profound and objective thoughts for all firms focused on long term success. Wells examines rigorously the role of structure and people in shaping successful cultures for long term survival."

Marcelo Odebrecht, CEO, Odebrecht S.A., Brazil

"An essential read for leaders of any organization in these turbulent times."

Charles Gurassa, Deputy Chairman, easyJet plc, UK

"Hard-hitting and stimulating, Wells' thesis carries a robust message that should make business leaders the world over sit up and think. From the sociology of wolves to the demise of Circuit City, this book is at one a diverting read and at the same time a brutal wake up call for the business establishment."

Archie Norman, Chairman, ITV, UK

"John Wells is one of the world's finest strategic thinkers. Especially during these tumultuous times, every business leader should read Strategic IQ."

David Soskin, Chairman, mySupermarket.co.uk

"As always, Wells gets to the heart of outstanding performance. Neither leadership nor analysis by themselves is enough. It's the combination that is potent. This is a must-read for anyone in a position of authority."

Gerald Corbett, Chairman, Supermarketmoney.com; Chairman, Betfair; Chairman, Britvic plc, UK

"Wells brings his famously sharp mind and uncompromising approach to a brilliant new book. Deeply researched and beautifully crafted, you will enjoy the read, but flinch at the implications."

Dan Cobley, Managing Director, Google, UK

"Always stimulating, John Wells will challenge your mindset and stretch your ambition. Strategic IQ is a powerful antidote to organizational complacency."

Luke Mayhew, Chairman, British Retail Consortium, UK

"A masterclass on strategy from a master strategist – Wells has devoted his professional life to understanding what makes successful organizations and successful managers tick; this book brings together theory and practice in a highly readable format that CEOs and senior executives will be able to apply directly to their companies. If you can only read one business book this year, Strategic IQ is the one. Wells provides busy executives with the insights and the practical 'how to' playbook that will allow them to compete in today's ever more challenging business environment."

Rick Mills, Group Director, Strategy Innovation, Alliance Boots, UK

"John Wells brings his much appreciated experience to bear on the challenges facing all leaders of businesses in today's world grappling with extraordinary times of change."

Duncan Weston, Managing Partner, Cameron McKenna, UK

"The time to read this book is before you realise that you need to! John Wells blends the fundamentals with bleeding edge insight to produce a handbook that will provoke any manager to ask searching questions about the strategic direction of their enterprise. When it comes to scrutinising a strategy, John Wells is a hard taskmaster, but in the current economic environment, that is just what most companies need."

Rupert Morley, CEO, Sterling Ltd, UK

STRATEGIC IQ

"In evolutionary systems, sustainable competitive advantage does not exist; there is only a never ending race to create new sources of temporary advantage."

Eric D. Beinhocker

The Origin of Wealth (p. 332)

STRATEGIC IQ

Creating Smarter Corporations

John R. Wells

JOSSEY-BASS
A Wiley Imprint
www.josseybass.com

This edition first published 2012
© 2012 John Wiley & Sons, Ltd

Under the Jossey-Bass imprint, Jossey-Bass, 989 Market Street, San Francisco CA 94103-1741, USA
www.jossey-bass.com

Registered office
John Wiley & Sons Ltd, The Atrium, Southern Gate, Chichester, West Sussex, PO19 8SQ, United Kingdom

For details of our global editorial offices, for customer services and for information about how to apply for permission
to reuse the copyright material in this book please see our website at www.wiley.com.

Wiley publishes in a variety of print and electronic formats and by print-on-demand. Some material included with
standard print versions of this book may not be included in e-books or in print-on-demand. If this book refers to
media such as a CD or DVD that is not included in the version you purchased, you may download this material at
http://booksupport.wiley.com. For more information about Wiley products, visit www.wiley.com.

Designations used by companies to distinguish their products are often claimed as trademarks. All brand names and
product names used in this book are trade names, service marks, trademarks or registered trademarks of their
respective owners. The publisher is not associated with any product or vendor mentioned in this book. This publication
is designed to provide accurate and authoritative information in regard to the subject matter covered. It is sold on the
understanding that the publisher is not engaged in rendering professional services. If professional advice or other
expert assistance is required, the services of a competent professional should be sought.

Library of Congress Cataloging-in-Publication Data

Wells, John R.
  Strategic IQ : creating smarter corporations / John R. Wells.
      p. cm.
  Includes bibliographical references and index.
  ISBN 978-0-470-97828-3 (hardback)
  1.   Strategic planning. 2.   Organizational effectiveness—Management. 3.   Organizational change. 4.   Success
in business.   I. Title.
  HD30.28.W383 2012
  658.4'012—dc23

                                                                                                2012003409
A catalogue record for this book is available from the British Library.

ISBN 978-0-470-97828-3 (hardback) ISBN 978-1-119-94278-8 (ebk)
ISBN 978-1-119-94279-5 (ebk)   ISBN 978-1-119-94280-1 (ebk)

Set in 11/13pt Calibri by Thomson Press
Printed in Great Britain by TJ International Ltd, Padstow, Cornwall, UK

Contents

Preface

This book reflects my 35 year intellectual journey in search of strategy. Along the path whenever I reached a crossroads, I turned in whatever direction interested me most, and so my route has been a diverse and varied one.

In total, I have spent 15 years in academia, studying, researching case examples and teaching. In developing cases, the focus of attention is typically on successful companies since few failures wish to lift the corporate veil on their problems for public consumption . . . and so, in the process, I became a student of success.

In contrast, for ten years I was a strategy consultant and the reverse held true. Few companies hire strategy consultants when things are going well – it is normally to address major challenges . . . and so I became a student of failure.

And I spent ten years in management practice myself, running large firms and small, making strategy happen and, in the process, generating my own personal set of successes and failures.

And along the way, I always promised myself that I would one day sit back and reflect on what I have learned and share it broadly with practitioners. I wrote this book not in the hope of generating something stunningly new . . . the latest intellectual insight or quick fix. Indeed, many of the fundamental principles of good business practice have been around for generations. Rather, I wanted to collect my thoughts and integrate them in a useful way in the hope that leaders might gain these insights more quickly and at lower cost than I incurred on my journey. If not, I hope at least that it makes an interesting read.

I have many to thank for this work and only myself to blame for its shortcomings. I would like to mention my colleagues at Boston Consulting

Group who revealed to me nearly 35 years ago how rigorous economic analysis can help make strategic choices; my colleagues at Monitor Company who demonstrated how to turn choices into action; my colleagues at Unilever, PepsiCo, Thomson Travel Group, Energis and IMD who helped me to change and execute strategy in the real world; and my colleagues at Harvard Business School who patiently provided feedback on my work. During my three teaching stints at Harvard, several thousand MBA students and over a thousand experienced executives have provided me with insights and feedback on my work. It was a privilege to work with them; there is no better way to really understand something than to try to teach it. I have also worked with executive teams at nearly 100 companies to solve business problems, and learnt much myself in the process. I thank them for the opportunity. I must also pay tribute to the rich literature that has inspired my work; I list a few examples in the bibliography that have consciously influenced me. I apologize profusely to any I have inadvertently left out.

Nor do I mean to offend when I give special thanks to a few. To Michael Porter, my thesis supervisor, who first invited me to teach at Harvard Business School and work with him on *Competitive Advantage*. To Chris Argyris, the most profound influence on me, both professionally and personally, who opened my eyes to the impediments to individual and organizational learning and how to overcome them. To John Clippinger who introduced me to social mechanics. And finally to Manoj Badale and Charles Mindenhall, founders and owners of Agilisys, a fast-growing UK-based, IT services and outsourcing company. As the company name suggests, they live by the principles I espouse in this book. They inspired me to write it and helped fund my early research.

I also want to thank my research and editorial team. Travis Haglock, Elizabeth Raabe and Carole Winkler worked with me on many of the cases; Rob Wiseman was a knowledgeable and expert editor; and Carole Winkler provided research and editorial support throughout. Together, they added tremendous value to both the text and my thinking; indeed, they helped me to rediscover the pleasure of writing which is so easily lost in today's tweet and SMS-driven world. Finally, a very special thank-you to Rosemary Nixon of Wiley and her team. A year ago, she reviewed my first 500 page draft and told me frankly that I would have to cut it by half. I hope that the latest version is more acceptable, in no small measure to all the help I have received. To the extent that it falls short, the fault is mine alone.

My research for this book would not have been possible without the generous financial support of the Division of Research at the Harvard Business School and the Research Department at the International Institute for Management Development (IMD). I am deeply grateful.

As I sit writing this, I know my intellectual journey is incomplete. The more I learn, the more I realize I do not know. Had I discovered this many years ago, I might not have had the courage to continue, but now the prospect excites me. My career has been very varied because I have always followed the most exciting intellectual path, and I will continue to do the same, even though I now know there is no end.

But as I reflect, I must also look at the cost of this journey. I have always been consumed by my work, and this has been a great strain on my family; I was not always there for them. My eldest son is recovering from a near-fatal illness which struck him just before the holidays. I need to take note. I do not need to travel so fast because there is no end to the journey. Instead, I must make sure I take time to enjoy the precious fruits along the way, and there are none so precious as my three sons. And so, I dedicate this book to them.

To Charles, James and Matthew

Wollerau, Switzerland, January 2012

Introduction

Why do Successful Companies Fail?

No financially successful firm wants to believe that failure could just be around the corner. But successful firms fail all the time and they fail dramatically. It is a common pattern: years of stellar profit growth and then sudden collapse.[1] It does not appear to be confined to particular sectors or geographies. It happens to high-tech firms and low-tech firms, manufacturing businesses and service businesses, across all sectors of the economy and all around the world. It seems to be part of the price paid for success.

Once firms hit the wall, it is difficult to recover. Turning round a large corporation takes great leadership, huge resources and a good deal of serendipity. A few, like technology leaders IBM[2] and Hewlett Packard, come back from the brink and re-establish their leadership. But many, such as word processing pioneer Wang Laboratories, instant photography king Polaroid and minicomputer pioneer Digital Equipment Company, quickly disappear, going bankrupt or being absorbed into more successful enterprises. Some try hard to turn round but finally succumb: Circuit City and Kmart, both leaders in their retail sectors, went bankrupt seven years after their first major profit declines. Others limp along for decades. Photography giant Kodak[3] and fashion supremo Gap[4] both suffered material profit declines during the 2000–2002 recession. Kodak finally failed in early 2012, a decade later, while Gap continued to struggle.

Why does this happen? It is tempting to blame major external events like the financial collapse of 2008. Sometimes it's true. Northern Rock in the UK was a well-run company that perished when its access to capital markets was choked off. But for many the financial meltdown compounded their existing problems and accelerated a decline that had begun long before. General

Motors had been in trouble for decades before it went bankrupt in 2009. English retailer Woolworths drifted along for years with no clear strategy until it was forced into administration in 2008. Circuit City had long wrestled with change after losing its leadership position to Best Buy in discount consumer electronics. These companies went bankrupt during the economic meltdown, but the crisis merely hastened their demise.

Inertia — A Fatal Disease

A closer look at these failures suggests they were self-inflicted. The victims did not adapt to a changing competitive environment. They succumbed to the fatal disease of inertia.[5] As Jack Welch, former chairman of General Electric, once said, *"I'm convinced that if the rate of change inside the institution is less than the rate of change outside, the end is in sight. The only question is the timing of the end."*[6]

Like many fatal diseases, this one can be slow to incubate. Sales and profits may continue to grow for many years after the initial infection, lulling the firm into a false sense of security while it hurtles towards a precipice. By the time the organization is looking over the cliff at the rocks below, it is too late – the firm's fate is sealed. Companies with many years of financial success under their belts might do well to ask, "Are we already dead?"

In this book we identify three types of inertia (Figure 1) that can kill if left unchecked for too long. **Strategic inertia** is the failure of companies

Figure 1: Types of Inertia

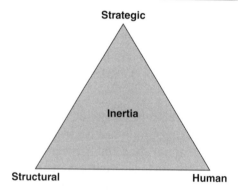

to change their strategies in a timely fashion. **Structural inertia** is suffered by firms that know they need to change but their structure gets in the way. **Human inertia** is the reluctance of individuals and groups to change.

In Search of Strategic Intelligence

To deliver superior sustainable performance, firms must position themselves well within the competitive environment, choosing attractive places to compete and building competitive advantage in order to be able to win. That is the goal of business strategy. But the world is always changing, so firms looking for long-term success must be prepared to retool their strategies. At a minimum, this requires agility – the capacity to change – but mindless movement leads nowhere. Firms must steer purposefully in a winning direction and this requires strategic intelligence.

There are different levels of strategic intelligence. The least intelligent don't realize they need to change or cannot change even if they do. Smart firms react and keep pace with external changes, but the very smartest change even faster, shaping the environment to their advantage. When the environment is not changing much, smart firms will gain ground on their less intelligent competitors. When times are volatile, they are more likely to be able to weather the storm, adapt and survive.

When companies first face profit pressures in the marketplace, most don't recognize it as a strategic problem; nor do the financial analysts who follow them. Their first instinct is to try harder. Ironically, this often improves short-term results even though they are heading in the wrong direction. The insidious thing is that this convinces the firm that its current model of success is right, blinding it to the need to change.

This reminds me of an experiment with a pigeon.[7] Put the pigeon in a cage with two feed hoppers and it will peck around for food. Put grain in one of the hoppers and the pigeon will soon figure out where the food is and happily eat away. But if we switch the food from the first hopper to the second, the pigeon will continue to peck at the first hopper until it dies of starvation. The problem for pigeons is that once they have learnt something, they cannot relearn. So why is it that highly intelligent executives grouped together into a company behave with the intelligence of a pigeon?

When trying harder doesn't work any more, some firms turn to overhead cost reduction programmes. The logic here is to *do the wrong thing more efficiently*. It works for a while, but the overhead soon grows back and meanwhile the underlying problems get worse. Other companies opt for reorganization – *doing the wrong thing more effectively*. Kodak did this in the face of the digital photography threat – a total of seven reorganizations in ten years.[8]

Overhead cost reductions and reorganizations may improve short-term results, but they focus firms inwards rather than outwards, where the real problems lie, and make them even more blind to the need for strategic change.

As pressure mounts, some companies resort to playing games with their accounts, using financial engineering to create the illusion of profitable growth, creating a false sense of security before the inevitable collapse. Meanwhile, the organization drifts further and further from a winning strategy until only a Herculean effort can save it.

When the company finally implodes, shareholders are hammered and many members of the management team lose their jobs, along with large numbers of unsuspecting employees. And often, the new management team takes a huge financial write-off, building reserves in the balance sheet to feed back into the P&L later. This creates the illusion of a dramatic recovery and heralds the next inevitable collapse. Surely there is a better, more responsible way to run an enterprise? Our jobs as leaders are not just to get great results while we are around and to heck with whoever comes after us. Our responsibility is to build enterprises that will last for generations. So how do we avert these self-inflicted crises and build more sustainable businesses?

That is the subject of this book. We identify ways to help companies act more intelligently. In **Part One: Smart Strategy,** we show how firms can overcome strategic inertia to develop winning strategies, stay ahead of the competition and shape the environment to their advantage. In **Part Two: Smart Structure,** we address structural inertia and describe how firms can design structures that support or even drive rapid strategic adjustments. **Part Three: Smart Minds** tackles human inertia and shows how firms can harness the infinite desire for personal growth. In the process, we examine different levels of strategic enlightenment as firms climb the ladder of strategic intelligence (Figure 2).

Figure 2: Climbing the Strategic Intelligence Ladder

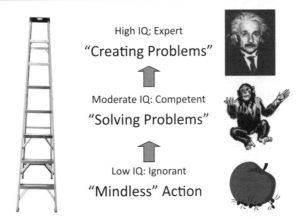

High IQ; Expert
"Creating Problems"

⬆

Moderate IQ: Competent
"Solving Problems"

⬆

Low IQ: Ignorant
"Mindless" Action

Smart Strategy

In **Part One: Smart Strategy** we focus on firms suffering from strategic inertia. This warrants a low Strategic IQ and the goal is to improve the score. But changing is hard if you don't know what you are doing, so **Chapter 1.1: The Need for Smart Strategy** provides an overview of what strategy is and why it needs to change.

Developing and implementing strategy is hard work, so it is no wonder that successful firms are reluctant to change. But the problems are often more fundamental than this, as discussed in **Chapter 1.2: Low Strategic Intelligence**. Firms can be **strategically blind** in a number of ways. The **blissfully ignorant** have never had a strategy, don't know what one is and don't much care. Those playing **let's pretend** use all the jargon, but they don't really know what they are talking about. Firms with **strategic amnesia** once had a good strategy but have forgotten it and are running on autopilot. None of these companies know what their strategy is, so it is tough for them to change. **Chapter 1.2: Low Strategic Intelligence** will help open their eyes.

The next rung on the ladder of Strategic IQ is the peculiar behaviour of **strategic denial**. These firms have a clear strategy that has worked for them in the past but they refuse to give it up despite the fact that they can see the need for change. The **wilfully blind** must confront their strategic problems and accept that they will die if they don't correct them. To do this they must apply the basic principles of competitive strategy. This is the purpose of **Chapter 1.3: What is Strategy?**

Once firms have recognized the need for strategy, they must learn how to develop and implement one. Many companies struggle for years trying to improve their performance but expend their efforts while caught in tactical traps rather than addressing the strategic issues. This is **strategic incompetence**. It is tempting to turn to consultants, but that won't solve the long-term problem. In a world where changes are often needed, it merely builds dependence. To move from low to moderate levels of Strategic IQ, firms must develop the competence to formulate and execute strategy effectively themselves. This is a complex and difficult journey, especially the first time, and firms must develop a wide range of knowledge and skills along the way. **Chapter 1.4: Moderate Strategic Intelligence** provides a step-by-step guide up the ladder of increasing Strategic IQ.

Once moderate Strategic IQ is achieved, firms are ready to tackle the next rungs on the ladder to high Strategic IQ. But there is a natural temptation to relax and stick to their newfound winning strategies for as long as possible. Don't give in – you will merely slide back down the ladder! As time passes, the competitive environment changes and the strategy falls increasingly out of step with reality. The hard-won knowledge and skills to get back on track are slowly forgotten. Once five years have passed, it is like starting all over again.

Moderately strategically intelligent companies execute their strategy until they feel the need to change it. For them, the critical question is when to change. For firms of superior strategic intelligence, this question is not relevant; they are always changing.

Chapter 1.5: High Strategic Intelligence describes how high IQ firms are never satisfied with their current model. They're always looking to improve. They are driven by lofty and inspiring goals to deliver higher performance, always enhancing their present strategy while setting aside time and resources to test radical new approaches. These companies generate many strategic options and develop superior decision-making processes for choosing between them. They seek to align their organizations continuously by focusing on measures correlated with strategic success and rewarding those who deliver it. They operate on the cutting edge, the state of the art in strategy, always prepared to change and learn from experience.[9] They shape their environment to their advantage and force others to catch up.

But where do the resources for all this change come from and how do leaders find the time? Strategic change processes are complex and expensive, but like all complex processes they benefit from learning.[10] By applying the process of formulation and implementation more regularly, firms travel down the learning curve quickly, reducing costs and time and delivering better results. Eventually, the distinction between formulation and implementation disappears – firms learn to think and act at the same time. Moreover, firms that delegate some strategic decision-making throughout the organization – distributed intelligence – create more capacity for strategic change and achieve better and faster results.

Smart Structure

To implement a strategy effectively, firms need the right structure; and when the strategy changes, at least some of the structure must change also. Often companies know what they need to do, but their internal structure gets in the way. These firms suffer from structural inertia. They must overcome this and build a smarter structure that adapts easily to changes in strategy, even driving it. **Part Two: Smart Structure** examines the pathology of structural inertia and discusses how firms can overcome it.

To recognize what causes structural inertia, it is important to understand what structure is. It is more than a simple organization chart; large organizations are enormously complex.[11] This is discussed in **Chapter 2.1: The Need for Smart Structure**. Firms are limited in their ability to change by the **assets** they have invested in. Once these commitments are made it is hard to throw everything away and start again.[12] Hence, the current asset base influences strategic choices and impedes change. **Chapter 2.2: Smart Asset Management** shows how assets can be made more flexible.

The **formal architecture** defines the way a firm's assets are organized to work together to create value. This is made up of many interrelated elements. We focus on the organization chart, which defines who does the work; business processes, which describe how the work is done; the recruiting and training systems, which put the right human assets in place; the measurement and reward systems, which maintain alignment; and the information and communication systems that tie everything together. Each element is difficult to change. Taken together, the inertia is formidable. **Chapter 2.3: Formal Architecture – Navigating the Architecture Labyrinth** describes how formal structure can be designed to be more flexible and shaped to drive strategic change.

As if the complexity of formal architecture is not enough, we must consider the **informal architecture**, social networks and informal processes that do most of the work. It is even tougher to shape this because it is undocumented and largely invisible. The key to fast change lies in harnessing the informal architecture. How can the natural capacity of the human species to self-organize[13] – social mechanics – be harnessed in the service of strategic change? We explore these exciting possibilities in **Chapter 2.4: Informal Architecture – Leveraging Social Mechanics**.

Firms with a **low Structural IQ** contain elements that are inconsistent with each other, so the structure is at war with itself. We also examine internally consistent structures that are at odds with the strategy. This forces companies in unintended directions, even to self-destruction.

Moderate Structural IQ requires a formal architecture and asset base that is consistent with the strategy and design rules that make it easier to change.

The most intelligent structures created by firms with **high Structural IQ** align formal and informal architecture to drive strategic change.

Chapters 2.1 to 2.4 identify each of the elements of structure important to effective strategy and change, discuss why they create inertia and describe how this can be overcome. **Chapter 2.5: Towards Smarter Structure** then pulls all of these elements together to provide an integrated approach to increasing Structural IQ.

Smart Minds

Ultimately, the capacity of a firm to make strategic changes is limited by the ability and willingness of its people to change. Unfortunately, most people don't like change. As individuals, we avoid anything we find unpleasant and procrastinate at will. In groups, this effect is often magnified. How can these behaviour patterns be so common in a species that is so intelligent? In **Part Three: Smart Minds** we examine the drivers of human inertia and how to overcome it.

In **Chapter 3.1: The Need for Smart Minds** we identify the remarkable inertia shown by the human species both as individuals and as groups and make the case for smarter minds. In **Chapter 3.2: What is a Mind?** we learn that the root cause of the problem lies in the way our brains have evolved. Over millions of years, we have inherited a wide range of individual and social behaviours that are programmed into our genetic make-up and over which we have little conscious control. These behaviours appear to satisfy a set of needs, some of which are quintessentially human and some more characteristic of our reptilian ancestors. Our more primitive instincts drive us to fear change while the more sophisticated help us see it as an opportunity to satisfy our curiosity and learn new things. In this way they often conflict; and unless our more primitive needs are met, we find it difficult to think on a higher plane.

Firms that display low Human IQ are wrestling with fiercely individualistic reptilian minds, fighting to satisfy their most basic needs. Those with a moderate Human IQ are working to satisfy the lesser mammalian mid-brain, providing social satisfaction and esteem in ways that reduce resistance to change. Firms with a high Human IQ have satisfied these needs and are tapping into the insatiable desire of humans to seek out common purpose, to learn more, to achieve more and to help others to do the same.

But not everything we do is hard-wired, driven by our genes. Much of our behaviour is learned, nurture rather than nature; indeed, the human brain has an enormous capacity for learning.[14] This is good news because change invariably requires learning new knowledge and skills. But the way we learn is again driven by our genes, often making us blind to what we know and making it difficult to change.

How can companies overcome human inertia? One approach is to pick the right people. **Chapter 3.3: Hiring Smart Minds** identifies profiles that help firms to sustain superior performance. And what can firms do to shape the internal context to make everyone more open to strategic change? **Chapter 3.4: Addressing Basic Human Needs** discusses how to reduce the pain of change while **Chapter 3.5: Harnessing Insatiable Human Needs** reflects on how companies can leverage the infinite human desire for personal growth.

The Holistic View

Inertia is a complex phenomenon and purposeful intelligent change even more so. There are no simple answers. In this book, we look at strategic, structural and human intelligence separately, but they are highly interrelated.

Introduction

A great strategy requires an equally great structure to implement it, and they both rely critically on human behaviour. Separating the three is a false trichotomy, but it helps to break the problem down to make it easier to solve. Look at each part of this book as a different perspective on the same phenomenon; the strategist seeks smart strategy, the organizational designer smart structure and the social psychologist, smart minds. But leaders must integrate the three to raise strategic intelligence (Figure 3). There is no smart strategy without smart structure; and this takes smart minds.

Figure 3: Climbing the Ladder of Strategic Intelligence

	Strategic	Structural	Human
High IQ	• Distributed intelligence • Synched thinking-acting • Mind-set of change	• Harnesses social mechanics • Drives strategic change • Designed to change	Neopallium (superior brain) dominates
Med. IQ	• Debating when to change • Competent to change • Clear model of success	• Ignores informal architecture • Top-down mind-set • Aligned, tough to change	Paleopallium (intermediate brain) dominates
Low IQ	• Incompetent • In denial • Strategically blind	• Aligned the wrong way • Structure fighting itself	Archipallium (reptilian brain) dominates

Notes

1. Sull (2003).
2. Austin and Nolan (2000).
3. Gavetti, Henderson and Giorgi (2004) describe the challenges at Kodak. Tripsas and Gavetti (2000) analyse it in depth.
4. Wells and Raabe (2006).
5. Inertia in many guises is discussed extensively in the literature. For instance, see Kuhn (1962); Rumelt (1995); Burns and Stalker (1966); Christensen (1997); Teece, Pisano and Shuen (1997); Gavetti (2003); Henderson and Kaplan (2005); Henderson (2006); and Seth (2007).
6. Chester Barnard and Philip Selznick first portrayed business organizations as complex technical, political and social systems adapting to survive. See Barnard (1938) and Selznick (1948).

7. For the sake of the pigeon, I hope this story is apocryphal and discourage anyone from trying to repeat the experiment.
8. Gavetti, Henderson and Giorgi (2004).
9. Garvin (2000).
10. Wright (1936).
11. Hall (1972); Mintzberg (1979).
12. Ghemawat (1991).
13. Clippinger (1999; 2007).
14. Gladwell (2008).

PART ONE

SMART STRATEGY

1.1

THE NEED FOR SMART STRATEGY

Why Strategy?

Without a goal in life, it is tough to achieve much. Mindless wandering rarely delivers great results. As the Cheshire Cat said in Lewis Carroll's *Alice's Adventures in Wonderland*, "If you don't know where you are going, any road will get you there." [1]

The goal of any business is to deliver **superior sustainable performance**. "Performance" means return on investment; firms are in business to make a profit. "Sustainable" means profit over the long term rather than to meet the next quarterly earnings targets. It's easy to deliver a short-term burst of profits by failing to invest for tomorrow and stealing from future performance. Delivering a sustainable stream of income is much harder. "Superior" means better than competitors; firms who always strive to win are less likely to be blindsided by competition, and more likely to survive and prosper. Winners also gain better access to resources (e.g. people, capital), increasing sustainability.

To deliver superior, sustainable performance firms need a *good* strategy. This requires good strategy formulation: the integration of choices on where and how to compete. It also depends on good strategy implementation: the marshalling of resources and integration of actions to deliver the strategy. Formulation and implementation both require good leadership to ensure that the right choices are made, the right assets are deployed and the right actions are taken.

Why Smart Strategy?

There is no such thing as strategy in isolation; it must be consistent with the competitive environment. This is always changing, so strategy must change too. Firms must constantly be steering purposefully in a winning direction; this is the definition of Strategic IQ. Those with moderate IQ keep up with the pack, but the smartest firms don't simply react to change; they drive it, shaping the competitive environment to their advantage. To do this, they need *smart* strategy.

Firms that fail to change their strategies in a timely fashion put themselves in grave danger. The longer the delay, the bigger the strategic problems become and the harder they are to fix. The more a firm invests in tactical responses that do not address the underlying strategic problems, the more resources are diverted from much-needed strategic change and the more the firm is distracted from the strategic issues it should be addressing.

It is easy to get caught in this trap. Sales and profits can continue to grow for many years before strategic weaknesses show through. Firms become complacent and defer expensive and painful changes until later. But once financial results collapse, shareholders have little patience with investing heavily in solving long-term problems; they want a quick fix. It becomes very difficult to make the necessary changes and the firm struggles on, squeezed between impatient investors and an increasingly hostile competitive environment until it finally fails. Far better to diagnose the disease early and treat it before it becomes critical; better still to avoid catching it at all. **Part One: Smart Strategy** of the book aims to help firms to do this.

In this chapter, we provide an overview of **Part One**. We examine the pathology of strategic inertia and identify a number of levels of Strategic IQ. We start with firms demonstrating low IQ: they either don't know what strategy is or are incapable of changing it. This begs the question "What is Strategy?" We address this briefly. We then move on to firms with moderate IQ, which have recognized the need for strategy and are developing skills in strategy formulation and execution. Finally, we identify those with high IQ, constantly striving for better strategy. The remaining chapters in Part One examine each of these topics in more detail.

Low Strategic Intelligence

Developing and implementing a strategy is a non-trivial task, so it is not surprising that firms are reluctant to change once they have discovered one that works. But for some the problem is deeper than this; they've never had a strategy and don't know what one is; they deliver profitable growth without really knowing why. They are the **strategically blind, blissfully ignorant** and sit at the bottom of the Strategic IQ ladder.

It may seem amazing to some that firms without a strategy can do well, but it is often easy to grow sales and profits when there is little competition; all ships rise on a rising tide. When competitive pressure rises, the need for strategy becomes more apparent, but the blissfully ignorant don't know how to deal with it. And when profits are suffering, it is harder to invest time and money in figuring out what to do. **The time to develop a strategy is before you realize you need one.**

There are other forms of strategic blindness. Some firms play **let's pretend** and fool themselves that they have a strategy, using all the jargon, but what they are doing has precious little to do with building and sustaining competitive advantage. Then there are those with **strategic amnesia**; they once had a good strategy but have forgotten it and are now running on autopilot. All of these firms are strategically blind; they don't really know what their strategy is, so it is tough for them to know when to change it or how to do so. The challenge is to open their eyes to the need for strategy and build commitment to developing one.

The next rung on the ladder of low Strategic IQ is the peculiar behaviour of **strategic denial**. Such firms are wilfully blind; they have a clear strategy that has worked for them in the past and they refuse to give it up despite the fact that they can see the need for change. Some try to ignore the data, like the proverbial ostrich with its head in the sand; others accept it but do nothing, awaiting their fate like a bunny in the headlights. Others exhaust themselves with tactical diversions such as overhead cost reductions and reorganizations in order to drive short-term profits rather than fix the long-term problem. Firms caught in denial must be encouraged to confront the fact that they have a strategic problem and accept that they must now move on to survive. They must also put mechanisms in place to prevent this behaviour from being repeated.

Strategically incompetent firms are one rung up on the IQ ladder from those who are in strategic denial, because they admit they have a strategic problem but they don't have the competence to solve it. Some firms are **lost in the dark**; everyone can "feel" the problem, but they don't know what it is. Others find themselves **squabbling** because there are a wide range of strongly held views on the issue and no real agreement on how to proceed. Some cannot agree on the problem, others on a solution. In either case, this is probably just as well since incompetence leads to poorly framed problems and ineffective solutions. In the absence of understanding and alignment, all these firms continue with the old strategy, or invest excessive effort in tactical palliatives. The firms in greatest danger are those that agree on the problem and on the solution, but don't really know what they are doing. They march off in the hope of victory even though they are headed in the wrong direction.

There is a temptation amongst the incompetent to hire consultants to develop a strategy for them. In a changing world, this doesn't solve the long-term problem because the strategy will soon need to change again. It merely creates dependence, effectively **outsourcing to advisors** the critical decisions on how to compete. Strategically incompetent firms must commit to building the processes and the skills needed to formulate and implement strategy for themselves. Making this commitment is the first step to moderate strategic intelligence.

The challenges of low Strategic IQ and how firms can move towards moderate strategic intelligence are discussed in more detail in **Chapter 1.2: Low Strategic Intelligence.**

What is Strategy?

To commit to building strategic competence, firms must recognize that strategy is important and understand what it involves.

The objective of strategy is to deliver superior sustainable performance. Firms that achieve this attract more and better resources (e.g. people, investment). This makes them even more sustainable – a virtuous circle. Those that do not deliver this often wither and die. The importance of the distinction should not be lost on any firm committed to longevity.

The principles of how a company intends to deliver superior sustainable performance are captured in its strategic business model (Figure 4).[2] This summarizes the choices the firm has made about where to compete, what competitive advantage it seeks, what assets and activities it will invest in to deliver that advantage (its internal scope) and how it intends to organize these assets to do so.

The choice of where to compete is important because some businesses and business segments are more attractive than others. Firms must pick the right battlefields.[3]

Figure 4: Elements of a Strategic Business Model

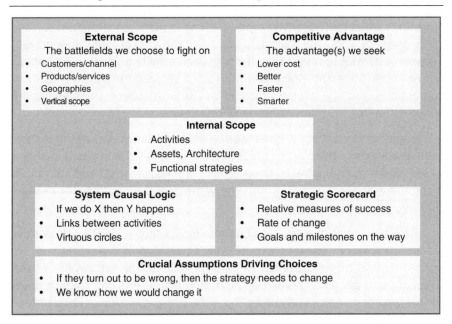

But wherever they compete, they are likely to come across competitors, so they must make sure they build an advantage that will help them to win, to deliver superior profits. The two most important static advantages are lower cost and differentiation.[4] For firms with lower costs, it is relatively clear why they can make more money. Differentiation is more subtle; it means better, as defined by the customer. And to make more profits, it must also support a price premium that exceeds any extra costs involved.

Faster and smarter are two dynamic advantages. Firms that are faster to reposition to attractive battlefields or increase static advantages have an edge.[5] They can make superior profits until the competition catches up. Smarter companies look to exploit the inertia of competitors and do things that are harder to copy.[6] They also look for pathways that give them more options for the future.[7]

A firm's ability to build advantage will depend on the assets it has at its disposal and how it organizes these assets.[8] It may choose to invest in some activities and let third parties perform others. The objective is to configure to deliver the best returns.

The strategic business model documents the causal logic of the strategy, explaining the linkages between the drivers of advantage and the level of advantage expected. For instance, a doubling in plant scale might drive unit costs down by 15%. The logic also identifies the critical interdependencies between activities to reveal the effects of each activity on overall advantage. For example, for many years, Wal-Mart used to spend more on IT than its competitors, but the overall effect of this was to reduce costs because it brought the cost of many other activities down.

In addition to the logic, firms require strategic metrics[9] showing the size of their advantage relative to competitors, the rate at which this is changing to see who is changing faster, the goals the firm has set itself and milestones along the way. Metrics help to test the veracity of the model and to ensure that everything is on track.

Ideally, the logic of a strategic business model should incorporate positive feedback loops or "virtuous circles", driving ever-greater advantage.[10] For instance, a firm might cut prices to increase volume. The extra volume helps to reduce cost per unit. This allows the firm to cut prices further, which drives further volume and more price cuts. This is the virtuous circle that has sustained Wal-Mart's strategy for 50 years. It is critical to Wal-Mart's business model. The more virtuous circles in the system, the more effective the strategy. Conversely, firms should avoid negative feedback loops or "vicious cycles". For instance, cutting quality to improve profits might have short-term benefits, but if it reduces volume and increases unit costs, then the benefit is short lived.

Finally, the model identifies the crucial assumptions on which the strategy is based. These are assumptions that drive strategic choices and require a change of strategy if they turn out to be wrong. Firms that know their crucial assumptions and are tracking them are more ready to change when circumstances demand it.

Chapter 1.3: What is Strategy? explains the principles behind strategic business models in more detail. **Chapter 1.4: Moderate Strategic Intelligence** shows, step by step, how to develop and implement one.

Moderate Strategic Intelligence

The first step on the road to moderate Strategic IQ is for a firm to make a real commitment to developing skills in strategy formulation and implementation as one of its core assets. The goal is a high level of competence. Hiring consultants to develop a strategy does not suffice. This may provide a quick and very necessary fix, but it doesn't prepare the firm for the next time it needs to make a change, or put it on a path towards high Strategic IQ where it must constantly strive for better strategy.

Developing high strategic competence is a long and challenging journey for any firm. While individual journeys differ, firms pass through various stages of strategic enlightenment as they add strategic knowledge and skills. The earlier stages typically focus on building expertise in formulating strategy while the latter are more concerned with strategy execution. But making a commitment is the first step on the journey.

And what is the path to competence? Picture a ladder from moderate to high Strategic IQ. What state is a firm in as it stands on each rung and what skills does it take to climb to the next? At the bottom, firms recognize they need a strategy and are committed to building one, but don't know how; the **"incompetent but committed"**. The first few steps for them focus on strategy formulation. They must learn to conduct a rigorous **external strategic review** to identify the range of opportunities offered by the competitive environment and an **internal strategic review** to test the firm's ability to exploit these opportunities. This helps build strategic awareness, but novice firms often become **"lost in the maze"** – overwhelmed by the detail and not knowing what to do. To climb to the next rung, they must learn how to synthesize all this information into viable *strategic options*. A range of options is helpful, but it means the firm must now make a clear choice. Many firms get caught **"dithering"**, not sure which path to take. They must build capacity to **make strategic decisions**.

Once the choice is made, the firm is ready to implement but some firms often forget to tell their people – the **"secret strategy syndrome"**. The first implementation step requires **sharing and declaring**, communicating the strategy and explaining the logic behind it. This builds commitment to action and prepares everyone for change. But a **strategic change programme** is then required to redeploy assets and realign the organization, otherwise firms find themselves **"waiting for change"**. The challenges of such programmes are discussed more fully in Part Two, but we focus on a few critical steps here. To avoid **"flying blind"** firms need a **strategic scorecard** with new metrics and milestones. And firms must also beware of **"unintended consequences"** that occur when the reward systems are not aligned with the new strategy. Once everything is working well, some firms become complacent, reluctant to change; they get "**fat and happy**". Others become "**convinced we're right**" and refuse to change. Firms must commit to a **rigorous revision cycle**, repeating the whole formulation and execution process to keep their strategy fresh and their skills well-tuned. The firm has then reached the top of the moderate Strategic IQ scale.

A firm gets strategically smarter as it climbs the ladder (Figure 5) but the benefits grow exponentially as it rises. Good formulation is nothing without good implementation. And like all skills, firms get better with experience; the more revision cycles, the better, faster and more cost-effective they become. But there is no resting place at the top of the scale; the natural tendency is to decline. It is too easy to become complacent and slide back into incompetence, denial or even blindness. **Chapter 1.4: Moderate Strategic Intelligence** describes the climb to the top of the ladder and the challenges of staying there.

Figure 5: Climbing the Strategic IQ Ladder

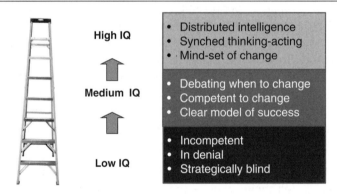

High Strategic Intelligence

Many firms that reach the top end of the moderate band still view strategy as a one shot deal. The goal for them in developing a strategy is to spend a short time thinking intensely about what they should do, make the changes as quickly as possible and then switch off their strategic minds and focus on execution. If things don't turn out quite as planned, they take a quick time-out to make a correction and then get back to work. Strategy for them is a commitment to a particular course and any deviation is a distraction, an admission of their failure to develop a good strategy in the first place. Hence, they only change the strategy if they really need to.

But making steadfast commitments in a rapidly evolving environment is foolhardy. The environment is always changing, so firms must change too. Moderately strategically intelligent companies execute their strategy until they see the need to change it. For them, the critical question is *when* to change. For firms of superior strategic intelligence, this question is not relevant; they are always changing.

Firms in this **mind-set of change** see strategy as a dynamic, on-going process rather than a one shot deal. The distinction between formulation and implementation disappears, and everything is addressed strategically. The firm is always looking to increase advantage, thinking and acting at the same time.[11] The processes that drive better strategy are developed as a cherished asset and embedded in the architecture of the firm. Firms develop a fast, efficient and effective process for strategic change and work tirelessly to improve it. They allocate resources to the change process and are financially disciplined in their approach, always expecting a payback from their efforts. And they measure, reward and celebrate change and rate of change of key strategic metrics.

High IQ firms are never satisfied with their current model. Everyone in the organization is looking for strategic improvement. They are driven by lofty and inspiring goals to deliver higher performance, always seeking to improve their current model while setting aside time and resources to test radical new approaches. They generate many strategic options and superior decision-making processes for choosing between them. They seek to align their organizations continuously by focusing on measures correlated with strategic success and rewarding those who deliver it. And they operate on the edge, always prepared to change and learn from experience.

For a top management team that insists on driving all strategic changes from the top, the concept of a continuous search for better strategy is daunting. Even when reviewed every few years, strategy absorbs a lot of top management time; doing it more frequently can quickly overwhelm the top management team. However, this capacity constraint can be relieved by integrating everyone down to the front line in strategy, **distributing strategic intelligence** throughout the organization. This dramatically increases the number of people on the look-out for strategic threats and opportunities, shaping options, making choices, developing metrics, executing change.

Properly organized, distributed intelligence provides more change capacity and leads to more timely, efficient and effective changes. But it requires a business model that distributes strategic decision rights, training and reward systems to make sure that decisions are made in the best long-term interests of the firm and information systems that support the distributed decisions and allow top management to track what is going on in order to reassure shareholders that everything is under control.

Chapter 1.5: High Strategic Intelligence describes in more detail how a firm that has developed strategic competence can break through into the upper echelons of the Strategic IQ scale.

Notes

1. Carroll (1865).
2. Magretta (2002) emphasizes the importance of a business model to success; once competition is included, it becomes a strategic business model.
3. Porter (1980) provides a robust framework for identifying attractive battlefields.
4. Porter (2004) identifies lower cost and differentiation as the key sources of competitive advantage and describes how they are built.
5. Stalk and Hout (1990).
6. Yoffie and Kwak (2001).
7. Luehrman (1998).
8. The resource-based view of strategy specifically addresses the firm's assets and how they can provide competitive advantage (Hamel and Prahalad, 1989; Montgomery and Collis, 1998).
9. Kaplan and Norton (2000).
10. Casadesus-Masanell and Ricart (2007).
11. Paparone and Crupi (2002).

1.2

LOW STRATEGIC INTELLIGENCE

What does it mean to have low Strategic IQ? This chapter identifies the tell-tale characteristics (Figure 6) and describes how firms can climb the IQ ladder to reach moderate levels of strategic intelligence.

Figure 6: Low IQ Responses to Strategic Challenges

Blissful ignorance   **Ignore it**   **Get caught in tactical traps**

Amnesia   **Freeze**

- Try harder
- Overhead cost reduction
- Re-engineer
- Re-organize
- Financial engineering

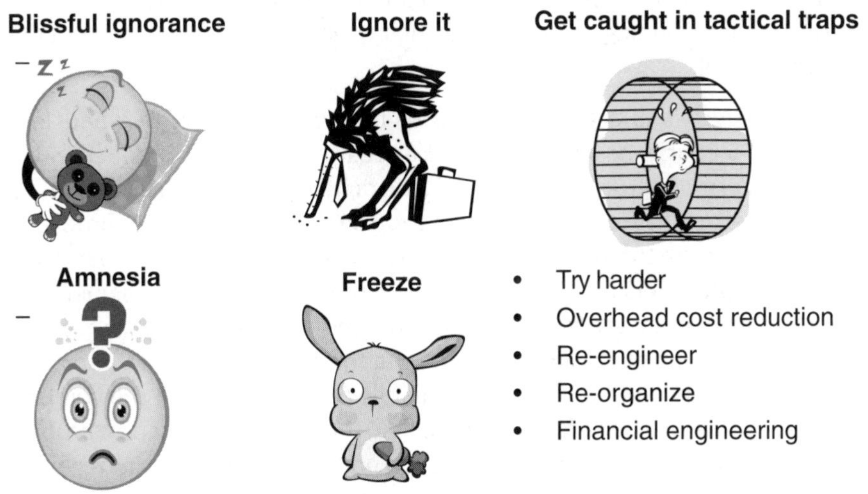

Level One: The Strategically Blind

Businesses often do not respond to strategic challenges because they cannot see them – they are strategically blind. In a famous experiment on cognition, when subjects were asked to focus on a number of specific aspects of a short video clip, they failed to notice a person in a gorilla suit walking by.

Their world didn't include gorillas; they were focusing on another problem, so they simply didn't see it.

Of course, focus has its benefits. When we focus on what we think is important, we can become very good at it. But when the world changes and something that we once thought unimportant becomes critical, we simply cannot see it. This is often the root cause of company failures.

The Blissfully Ignorant

There are a number of causes of strategic blindness, but the lowest rung on the Strategic IQ ladder is occupied by firms that have no idea of what strategy is. These are the **blissfully ignorant**. Ironically, firms without a strategy can still be financially successful for a time. When markets are growing fast and there is not much competition, everyone does well. The problems arise when competitors appear. Many entrepreneurial start-ups experience this phenomenon. They achieve impressive financial results initially by serving a new or emerging market, but begin to suffer when competitors with greater scale, better innovations or lower costs enter their arena. Without finding a solution to their strategic challenges, these companies will fail.

Ben & Jerry's is a good example of this phenomenon. Ben and Jerry bought a $5 course on how to make ice cream and started production in a one-time Vermont gas station.[1] They made rich ice cream with large chunks of filling and strong flavours. The flavours were a result of Ben's sinus problem – he could only taste them if they were extra strong – but consumers loved them; sales and profits grew rapidly, and the super-premium ice cream segment was born. Profits masked the questionable economic logic of making ice cream in Vermont and shipping it all over the USA. But for the company, commitment to Vermont farmers and the local community was important and the company thought this was a true differentiator. At first, the high costs weren't a problem because consumers were prepared to pay a premium for this delicious new ice cream. But when competitors jumped in, it wasn't so clear to Californians why they should pay extra for the services of Vermont cows, and profits suffered.

When profits faltered, Ben and Jerry were at a loss as to what to do, but the professional managers they hired to help couldn't seem to fix the strategic problems either. Instead they spent their time on tactical fixes, improving marketing and rationalizing the product line instead of addressing the inconsistencies in the firm's strategic business model. The long-term survival of the business was in doubt, but luckily for Ben and Jerry, the firm was rescued when it was acquired by major rival Unilever.

Blissfully ignorant firms are prone to attribute the wildest things to their success – Vermont milk for instance – and find it very difficult to change their minds. They must recognize that strategy is necessary, and the time to develop one is before the crisis hits, because by then it may be too late.

This book is a wake-up call for readers whose firms are doing well without a strategy. Do you have a strategic model of success that anyone in the firm can explain to a stranger in two minutes?[2] Is the logic well understood? The metrics clear? The key assumptions identified? If not, your firm is in grave danger.

Let's Pretend

Some firms are more aware of the need for a strategy but play **let's pretend**. They deserve some credit for acknowledging that strategy is important, but they don't really know what it is, so they dress up what they are currently doing as a "strategy" and hope that no one will notice.

The goal of strategy is superior sustainable performance and this requires a relentless pursuit of competitive advantage. But firms often delude themselves that they are seeking competitive advantage. They discover the jargon and apply the buzz words with no real idea of what they are talking about. For example, in Chapter 1.1, we discussed Porter's three generic strategies: differentiation, low cost and focus.[3] Companies often latch onto these terms to rationalize what they are doing. They claim they are differentiated because their product is unique, but if this uniqueness is not valued by the customer, then it doesn't provide a competitive advantage. And the real measure of a differentiation advantage is that customers are prepared to pay a price premium that exceeds any extra costs involved. Differentiation requires strict economic discipline.

Firms also delude themselves with a low cost strategy. There are many low quality players out there with average costs generating miserable profits. The goal is to be *lower* cost than competitors in order to win. And if a firm has to offer a discount because it is also lower quality, then the discount must be less than the cost advantage to deliver superior profits.

So does your firm track its relative cost position and know what price premium its products can support?

Then there are companies which think that focusing on a segment of the market is going to make them safe only to find that they are outgunned in this focus strategy by competitors enjoying the scale benefits of a broader base. Airborne, the package air freight company, fell into this trap. It focused on business-to-business accounts because the cost of picking up and delivering larger numbers of packages was lower, so it could price more aggressively.[4] Meanwhile, Fedex and UPS were guilty of "average pricing", charging the same price for business-to-business and consumer accounts even though consumers were much costlier to serve. But once Fedex and UPS removed the consumer subsidy and adjusted their prices to match underlying costs, Airborne's apparent advantage in the business-to-business niche was negated. Airborne could no longer compete with its much larger rivals and was eventually forced out of business.

Some strategically blind companies are convinced they have "distinctive competencies", a term coined by Professors Prahalad and Hamel.[5] But when pushed, they are often at a loss to describe what they are, how they can be measured, what advantage they provide or how this advantage translates into superior long-term profitability. There is no question that some firms have distinctive competencies that give them a genuine and sustained competitive advantage, but merely using the labels confers little benefit.

Some companies are hoping that a "Blue Ocean" strategy is the answer: invent new markets where there is no competition.[6] But economic discipline is required. Customers' willingness to pay must exceed the costs of serving them to establish a viable business – an issue that many dot.com start-ups failed to remember. Moreover, firms which discover viable opportunities would do well to consider how they are going to stop competitors from entering if they turn out to be successful. Friendster and MySpace both appear to have had difficulties in this area.

The latest version of "let's pretend" seems to be laying claim to network effects.[7] When they truly apply, network effects can be a very powerful driver of advantage, even leading to monopoly, so it is not surprising that companies would like to have them. During the various dot.com booms of the last 15 years, network effects have often been used as an excuse to build large market share using business models that generate no revenues in the hope that a revenue model can be found once the monopoly is established. But not all businesses enjoy network effects and for those that do, it is no panacea. Wild claims are not the answer. The focus must be on understanding the sources of advantage that they provide, building them and defending them.

So is your company's strategy based on sound economic logic or does it smack of flavour of the month?

Strategic Amnesia

On the next rung of the ladder are firms suffering from **strategic amnesia**. They had a successful strategy in the past, but the logic of what they are doing has long been forgotten and everyone is now simply repeating past behaviour without understanding why. The causal link between choice and outcome has been lost and the model has become implicit. "This is what makes us successful. This is the way we do things around here." If outcomes fall short of expectations, no one knows why. Therefore it's difficult to change, and the firm simply tries harder.

This behaviour is similar to the expert's dilemma, and we all suffer from it. As we become increasingly proficient at a task, we think less and less about how we do it and begin operating automatically on autopilot. Indeed, control is handed over to a different part of our brain to free up conscious thinking for new challenges.[8] And forcing ourselves to relearn what we know is very hard, as anyone who has tried to improve their golf swing will attest! We must learn to play the game again. This feels awkward and is embarrassing because scores typically get worse before they get better.

When many people are involved in a process over a long period of time, it is even harder to remember the logic. Managers and staff change positions; new team members learn behaviours from old experts largely through imitation, so they don't really know why they do what they do. The logic is lost; they just get on with it. With such collective blindness, the "way we do things around here" can take on almost religious proportions; anyone who questions it is seen as a deviant working against the best interests of the firm. We would be wise to remember this when we are faced with sceptics or anarchists in an organization. In the right proportions, they are very healthy. Constructive dissent provides critical information that is vital for companies which want to win in the long term. Companies that are internally too harmonious are in danger of falling off a cliff. Some have argued that this was what contributed to Lehman Brothers' demise.[9]

Just as some firms mindlessly cling to their old model when conditions change, once a strategy has been forgotten it is easy to drift from it and chase new growth opportunities. Kmart, once the US's leading discount retailer, did this.[10] Kmart's original model of selling quality well-known brands at a discount made eminent sense: "Stock the best, to heck with the rest." The consumer could see they were getting a bargain so sales volumes rose, giving Kmart purchasing power to buy at lower cost and offer even bigger discounts – a virtuous circle. With this model working well, CEO Robert Dewer expanded Kmart's offering to low quality, private label clothing. The consumer was confused because it was difficult to compare prices, and the poor quality earned Kmart the nick-name "the polyester palace". Kmart's brand image was diluted and its management distracted from its original course.

The lessons for firms in danger of forgetting their strategy are clear; they must be sure to document their strategic business model, laying out the logic and assumptions clearly so that they can be tested regularly. By taking time out on a regular basis to review and challenge what they are doing, companies will remain connected and aware of their strategies.

When did you last lay out your strategy and test it?

For those that have fallen into this trap and forgotten, try to go back in history to when the original strategy was developed and review why it made sense at the time. Then list what has changed in the competitive environment in the interim that would warrant a strategic change. This reintroduces strategic logic into the firm's consciousness, opening eyes to the drivers of past success and building commitment to future change.

Another useful way of building awareness is to map out the current strategy based on the firm's behaviours to discover what the underlying logic might be. It is always useful to compare what a company claims its strategic model to be – its "espoused strategy" – with what it is actually doing – its "strategy in use". This helps to make the strategy explicit rather than implicit; declared for all to see rather than hidden in the depths of the corporate subconscious.

Level Two: Strategic Denial

Often companies facing strategic problems have plenty of data to show they are in trouble, but they fail to respond. They are wilfully blind, and there are none so blind as the wilfully blind![11] Rather than responding to the signals that their strategy should be reconsidered, they ignore the facts, or recognize them but do nothing, or busy themselves with other activities that distract them from the main issue. But strategic denial only makes things worse in the long run.

Ostriches and Bunnies

When Kodak first saw the data showing it was losing market share in the US film market, its executives argued that the data were wrong rather than acting to stem the decline.[12] Like the ostrich with its head in the sand, the company denied the problem in the hope that it would go away. When the truth is too distasteful, it becomes unthinkable and some firms stop thinking.

Others see the problem but simply do nothing about it. In the early 1990s Circuit City, the leading US consumer electronics retailer, expressed concern each year in its annual report that aggressive discounters such as Best Buy were gaining share.[13] They could see in published accounts that Best Buy's operating metrics, including sales-per-square-foot and sales-per-employee, were superior. But they stuck with their old model, expanding geographically and delivering growing sales and profits until they suddenly "hit the wall" and collapsed in 2001. After seven painful years of trying to turn the company around, the 2008 financial crisis finally forced Circuit City into bankruptcy. Once a company hits the wall, it is often too late to save it.

Tactical Traps – The Hamster's Treadmill

Other firms distract themselves with tactical improvement programmes rather than addressing the strategic issue. But maintaining the performance improvements gets harder and harder in the face of declining competitiveness, and firms find themselves running flat out to stand still, like a hamster on its treadmill.

We discussed a number of common tactical responses in the introduction to this book, and will now take a closer look.

Frequently, the first tactical reaction to a drop-off in performance is to exhort everyone to "try harder". This costs very little and, ironically, often works. Profits improve in the short term and this convinces everyone that there is nothing wrong with the old model. But the profit improvement is short-lived because the deterioration in strategic position starts to show through.

Some firms then opt for an overhead cost reduction programme – "doing the wrong thing more efficiently". It is more painful than simply trying harder because it requires tough decisions and makes management unpopular, but it is still relatively inexpensive compared to big restructuring efforts. It is normally a fairly blunt instrument. Top management often demands similar cost reductions from everyone on the argument that this is "fair". This is a naïve, expedient choice because the potential for savings typically varies from one activity to the next. Managers who have been running a tight ship resent it because they are asked to take the same cuts as the less efficient. In the long run, this encourages them to add a little fat for the next round of cuts. The result of across-the-board cuts is also shaped by politics. The politically strong parts of the organization take fewer cuts than the weak. The impact of overhead cost reduction is also relatively short-lived. In most instances, the overhead grows back again within a few years.

The focus on overhead cost reduction to fix a shortfall in profits is easy to understand. Overhead always has a tendency to grow, so it is an obvious place to look to improve short-term results. However, it is easy to cut overhead to the point where it can no longer support the proper running of the firm. Good cost management is essential, but "good" must be defined in strategic terms. Overhead should be structured to support the current strategy and ensure its renewal rather than simply be cut to meet short-term financial targets. Overhead cost reduction programmes also reduce capacity for change by focusing employees on internal issues rather than the competitive environment, accelerating the process of decline.

Firms willing to make the extra investment will try reorganization to improve profits. This is "doing the wrong thing more effectively". It is a more complex, expensive, time-consuming and debilitating response to a fall-off in profits, so firms tend to try overhead cost reduction first. As with an overhead cost reduction, employees become more focused on internal issues. Well-structured organizations and efficient processes are essential, but only in support of strategy. However, many reorganizations and business process reengineering exercises do not have a strategic target in mind. Instead they are done to fill a short-term financial performance gap. Worse still, they are used to justify one-off "below-the-line" restructuring charges that obscure declines in long-term competitiveness.

One-off restructuring charges are a common example of financial engineering. Earnings smoothing is another. This involves understating profits in good years by hiding some of them in the balance sheet and scraping them out in bad years to boost operating results. This helps to smooth a volatile earnings stream (and make the stock look less risky). But if profits are extracted from the balance sheet to try to make a long-term decline look like a growing profit stream, the amount that needs to be scraped out each year quickly grows. It isn't too long before there is nothing left to draw upon, and then reported profits suddenly collapse.

There are other forms of financial engineering that can distract management from driving underlying profitability. Coca-Cola acquired bottlers and sold them to its own bottling company at a profit.[14] IBM switched from a leasing business model to a sales model in its mainframe computer business, and showed big gains in sales and profits from selling old, fully depreciated machines already installed in its customers' premises.[15] This boosted IBM's apparent performance in the mainframe business when, in reality, it was suffering competitively. Such clever financial engineering may fool the shareholders, but it often fools the management team too. Certainly, by the time IBM collapsed it was in a sorry state, and only survived because of the legendary turnaround engineered by Lou Gerstner.[16]

The problem with tactical responses is that every delay in fixing the underlying strategic problem makes it harder and more expensive to solve. The old proverb "a stitch in time saves nine" springs to mind. If strategy were adjusted more often, the change needed would be smaller and the process would cost less. And waiting too long is life-threatening. Once the firm has collapsed financially, it is very difficult to restore it to its former glory; the strategic challenges have become enormous, the company's reserves depleted and the shareholders' interest in investing in new business models much diminished. The company struggles on trying to find a quick fix until it eventually fails. Kmart finally went bankrupt in 2002, about seven years after the first big profit collapse. So did Circuit City. Few firms are as lucky as IBM.

Drivers of Denial

Denial is a common problem and the final fall is seldom in question. Many disasters are "predictable surprises", as Max Bazerman and Michael Watkins cogently argued in their book of the same name.[17] The characteristics of such situations are familiar. The leadership can see the problem and it is getting worse – it is clearly not going to solve itself. Unfortunately, the solution demands immediate pain in return for a future gain whose timing and size is uncertain. And the pain is not spread evenly – some interest groups have a strong reason for maintaining the status quo and will work assiduously to do so. Add the fact that human beings are born procrastinators, quick to put off painful actions until tomorrow, and we have designed a model that almost inevitably leads to crisis.

Several things reinforce this behaviour. Firms that have enjoyed a very successful strategy find it difficult to convince themselves that they must change. Their strategic business models take on almost religious significance and become belief systems that it is "wrong" to question.

Another thing that blind-sides companies is that some minor new ideas don't really look like a threat at the start, even though logic would argue that they could eventually become one. These dangers are too easily dismissed. This is a common pattern identified by Clayton Christenson in his book *The Innovator's Dilemma,* where he describes the impact of disruptive technologies.[18] They start out much more expensive and lower quality, but costs come down and quality rises to the point where they take over. Disruptive new business models can evolve in the same way.

Finally, there is the thorny issue of what top management is paid for. When the threat is ten years away, members of the top management team know they will all have passed on by the time it arrives, so what incentive do they have to take the pain for future generations? I once asked a major division head why his business was doing so well. He jokingly replied that he didn't know, but why should he care because he would be promoted before he found out. Never a truer word said in jest!

Circuit City versus Best Buy

Let's revisit the sad tale of Circuit City, which is a classic case of inertia. The strategy that helped Circuit City to become number one in consumer electronics retailing was undoubtedly a good one.[19] Discounting popular brands led to fast stock turns which more than made up for lower margins through higher productivity and delivered a superior return on investment. Higher volumes meant more purchasing power and bigger discounts from suppliers. Passing these lower costs on to consumers created a virtuous circle. The key was to be bigger than the competition and thereby offer lower prices.

But there was more to Circuit City's strategy than purchasing economies. Its operating philosophy was established in the 1980s by CEO Alan Wurtzle, the founder's son, and "embodied in its five guiding principles, known as its Five S Policy: Savings, Selection, Service, Speed, and Satisfaction."[20] These were clearly declared in Circuit City's annual filings.

Savings were core to the proposition – discounts on branded consumer electronics to draw people into the store. The discounts were also backed up with a 30-day guarantee. If the consumer could find the same product on offer cheaper, they would get their money back with an additional 10% bonus into the bargain!

A wide **selection** ensured that the store had what the customer was looking for. To support this broad offering and make sure product was always in stock, 50% of each store was set aside as warehouse space to accommodate this inventory.

Service was a very important aspect of Circuit City's philosophy and covered a number of aspects of the operations. Knowledgeable salespeople offered advice on new products and helped the consumer to identify what they should buy. Service and repair stations reassured customers that they could get their products fixed if anything went wrong. This was an important issue in the early 1980s when product reliability was much lower than today. Point-of-sales systems provided information on what was in stock. And the products were delivered to a convenient loading bay for the consumer to pick them up.

Circuit City considered **speed** an important part of its service offering. Point-of-sales systems provided data quickly on what was in stock and signalled the warehouse to pick items that had been purchased and get them to the loading dock fast.

The first four S's were all meant to drive the fifth S: customer **satisfaction**.

The model showed keen insight into consumer behaviour. When buying expensive durables, consumers like to shop around and compare different prices and brands; the challenge is to get them to decide what they want and commit to making a purchase while they are in the store. Circuit City deftly achieved this with a combination of three things: pushy commission-driven sales personnel who were always on hand to help identify needs and aid the consumer in making a choice; extensive stock so the consumer's needs could always be satisfied; and a 30-day money-back guarantee. Why delay? Why buy anywhere else?

Starting in 1980, this model drove 35% annual sales growth and 40% profit growth for over a decade. This is enough to turn any operating philosophy into a belief system.

In the 1980s Best Buy copied the Circuit City model but because it was much smaller, it didn't get the same purchasing discounts. This is the worst form of strategy: copy what others are doing even though they have a significant advantage. Best Buy's gross margin was 5% lower and its operating margins 2% compared to Circuit City's 7%. By the late 1980s its growth had stalled while Circuit City was expanding at over 30% per year, widening the competitive gap. This was not a recipe for success; Best Buy had to change.

But Best Buy realized that Circuit City's model involved certain trade-offs – all good strategies do. Pushy sales staff encouraged consumers to buy but they added to Circuit City's costs, and Best Buy's research found that consumers hated them. Circuit City's wide product offering and huge in-store inventories ensured they had what the consumer wanted in stock, but were also expensive. In response, Best Buy switched to a low service model, eliminating commissions and many of the salespeople.[21] It narrowed its product line, turned the warehouse into store space and added more product information on the product labels so that the consumers could choose for themselves. The low service model took almost 10% out of selling and general administration costs, providing a significant advantage in a business where low prices are critical to success. Moreover, Best Buy decided to stick with 2% operating margins to keep its prices really low.

The new low price, low service model proved very popular with consumers and Best Buy grew rapidly, passing Circuit City in size in 1996 and negating its purchasing scale advantage. By 2001 when Circuit City's profits began to collapse, Best Buy was nearly 20% bigger and widening the gap rapidly. By 2005, Best Buy was almost triple the size. For Circuit City, the game was over. With a significant purchasing scale disadvantage and a higher cost operating model, it was only a matter of time before the company failed.

Circuit City's profits initially collapsed in 2001, the year after Richard Sharpe stepped down as CEO after 14 years at the top. In fact, 2001 proved to be an unusually profitable year (Figure 7), with operating margins rising from 3% to 5%.

Figure 7: Circuit City Operating Profits ($ millions)

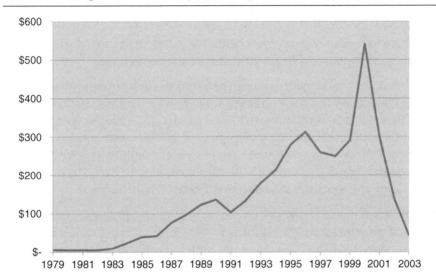

Circuit City's Denial

What was going on at Circuit City that contributed to this drama? Top management could clearly see that the deep discounters were gaining ground and would eventually overwhelm the company. The problem was clear, it was getting worse and it wasn't going to solve itself. Why did they not respond?[22]

Faith in the Five S's may have played a part. Blind faith is a dangerous condition. To continue with its service model, Circuit City was making the implicit assumption that consumers were prepared to pay a 10% premium for it. Had Circuit City revisited its strategy to understand its strengths and limitations, had it made clear the trade-offs it was making and tested this implicit assumption, which turned out to be fatally flawed, the outcome may have been quite different. Instead it appears to have clung to old beliefs and died.

Circuit City may have been blind-sided by Best Buy's disruptive business model. When it first appeared, it didn't appear to be much of a threat. Suppliers complained of the poor service and support and many brands withdrew their products. Margins were also very low; the model didn't look as if it could make money. But the model was classically disruptive. At a small scale, it didn't look like a threat, but as it grew, big suppliers returned for fear of losing share to competitors, and it appeared very different. If Circuit City had chosen to test the model in a few stores, it would quickly have established its superior economics, but it didn't. As is common in such circumstances, it may even have been bad-mouthing the new idea, which would make it doubly difficult to test it at the same time.

Circuit City may simply have been deferring the immediate pain of change. Things were going so well, it seemed a pity to rock the boat. Between 1991, when Best Buy began switching to its new model, and 1996, when it matched Circuit City in size, Circuit City's sales grew at 29% per year and its operating profits at 24% per year. Who would want to mess with these results? Circuit City's operating margins were 5% of sales compared to Best Buy's 2%. Who would ever countenance changing to a lower margin strategy?

There were also a number of vociferous key constituencies at the time that had an interest in the status quo. Would the analysts and the shareholders really have welcomed a major drop in profitability? Why would the top management team take the risk? And why would they want to face the howls of anguish from employees facing job losses in a low service model?

The pain of change was abundantly clear while the gain was still a long way off and not in such vivid focus. In fact, in the early 1990s Circuit City top management had an alternative view of the future. They still had many more regions of the USA to expand into and had factored this into their healthy growth projections, but they also calculated that their big box concept would be saturated by the year 2000. The plan was to build out their old model and then switch to something new, so they began looking for other retail concepts to apply their strengths. They settled on Car Max, second-hand cars! This only distracted them from their base business.

The last question that must be asked is what impact did executive compensation have on behaviour? Richard Sharpe stepped down as CEO in 2001 after 14 very successful years and left his successor Alan McCollough with some major problems. When McCollough took over he said, "I believe, absolutely, this is a great time to be at Circuit City." History would not bear him out.

Best Buy's Continuous Change

While Circuit City was steadfastly executing its old strategy, Best Buy was continuously reinventing itself.[23] The success of its low service concept catapulted the chain into the lead in 1996, but rather than stick with this winning formula, that year it changed, adding many more software SKUs. This drove the business to new heights; by 2003, it was twice the size of Circuit City. But then Best Buy changed again. New CEO Brad Anderson was convinced Best Buy could do better, and equally convinced that he would only have the flexibility to change when things were going well. He argued that high technology companies were allowed to test new ideas and fail – this was called R&D – but retailers had to absorb such costs in operating G&A. This was not possible when margins were tight.

Anderson felt that complacency had crept into the top team at Best Buy, and to overcome this, he set about creating a "burning platform"[24] to catalyse action. He arranged for video interviews with customers leaving Best Buy stores empty handed and asked why they had bought nothing. He identified numerous instances where sales were lost because of poor decisions made at corporate headquarters. He showed the video at a senior management conference to show that Best Buy was nowhere near as good as it thought it was. When senior executives squirmed, he showed the video again. This was the beginning of a new "customer centricity" model at Best Buy which involved inverting the organization and giving much more discretion to the stores. By the time it was fully implemented in 2007, Best Buy was three times the size of Circuit City.

Preventing Denial

We can draw a number of lessons from the history of Circuit City and Best Buy:

Beware blind faith. Revisit your strategy on a regular basis and review the logic and key assumptions. Track measures of competitiveness frequently to identify threats.

Be paranoid. Take every new idea as a potential threat. Treat each with respect and model it at full scale to see what level of threat it might present.

Self-cannibalize. Add new business models to your portfolio and cannibalize yourself in an orderly manner rather than let the competition do it at will.

Create a burning platform. It's hard to change unless the leadership team agrees that it is necessary. Creating a burning platform before a real crisis hits is important because waiting for the crisis is often fatal.

Invest in change when things are going well. Make changes when profits are good because you often don't have the option when they are bad.

Commit to future generations. Ultimately, for a leader, denial is an act of irresponsibility. The role of a CEO is not just to deliver great results while in office but to leave a secure base for future generations. Commit to this and get the board to commit to it too.

We will return to some of the issues that drive denial in more depth in **Part Three: Smart Minds**.

Level Three: Strategic Incompetence

Many firms are well aware that they have a problem but they don't know how to solve it. They are the strategic incompetents.

Lost in the Dark

Some incompetents are **lost in the dark**. They can feel they have a problem; and they know it is pretty fundamental because competitive pressure is building and it is difficult to sustain past success; but they simply don't know what to do. They are in ferocious agreement that they don't know what the problem is and they don't know how to solve it.

These companies face a number of dangers. They can consume an awful lot of time and energy **jawboning**, discussing the problem without making any headway. Like all well-meaning amateurs debating how to fix a complex problem, they are earnest in their efforts, but ignorance does not support meaningful debate or lead to effective action.

The other danger for those lost in the dark is that they revert to tactical responses to keep themselves busy, to provide a short-term palliative and to distract themselves from the real challenge. The flawed strategy remains unchanged.

For those lost in the dark, they must commit to investing the time in learning how to formulate and implement strategy.

Squabbling

Some incompetent firms are more active in their internal debates on what the strategy should be. Some firms cannot agree on the problem.

Others think they agree on the problem but cannot agree on the solution. Whatever the case, the company spends its time squabbling as opposed to defining the problem and solving it.

It is not uncommon for a top management team to genuinely disagree on the problems a firm faces. This is because we all have cognitive biases. Each member of the team is working on a partial model of reality reflecting their own responsibilities and experiences, so they will often "see" different things when they look at the same data. They selectively focus on the data they believe to be relevant, they infer meaning from the data, draw "obvious" conclusions from them and then advocate their position as if it were the truth. And because they are expert at it, they do this automatically without consciously realizing what they are doing. They are thus blind experts, talking past each other, equally convinced that they are right and everyone else is wrong.

The only real way to overcome this is to develop skills in structuring dialogue such that everyone learns from it. Only then is there a chance of a common point of view. It is an issue of balancing advocacy with enquiry.[25] Individuals must state their case in a style which encourages others to question it, and provide data and reasoning to support it. This helps those listening to learn, but it also helps the person making the case to do so as well. When we are expected to support our case with data and reasoning, this forces us to reflect on what we really know, and encouraging questions really puts this knowledge to the test.

Structuring dialogue is a great way of helping those with genuine misunderstandings to resolve them, but doesn't help so much in instances where executives are deliberately advocating a case for self-serving reasons; for example, they may be out to avoid unpleasant change, maintain a position of power that is threatened or blame others for the firm's situation. However, it is much harder to defend a position if it must be backed up by data and reasoning, so structured dialogue does drive more honest communication too.

While structured dialogue helps to create a common view, it doesn't substitute for knowledge and skills in strategy. If the structured conversation is based on ignorance, it is still incompetent. Hopefully, by working more effectively together, squabblers will agree that they don't know enough and commit to learning how to formulate and implement strategy effectively. If they do not, they will continue to squabble, and, in the meantime, tread the path of ultimate failure.

Outsourcing to Advisors

There is a temptation amongst the incompetent to hire consultants to do the work for them. In an emergency this may help, but it doesn't solve the long-term problem. Consultants seldom help firms to build competence in strategy, and some would argue it is not in their economic interests to do so. The next time strategic change is required, the incompetents will need to turn once again to their advisors, generating more valuable income for them. And because the world is always changing, it is not too long before they must call the consultants back. The result for the firm is dependence rather than competence. In effect, it has outsourced its critical decisions on where and how to compete, abdicating one of the key responsibilities of the top management team.

There are many difficulties to the outsourcing approach. When is it time to call the advisors in again? Presumably, top management must decide, but they are not competent to do so. Blind to the risks, they may delay too long, or, worse still, ask their advisors who have a vested interest in selling more work. Moreover, strategy consultants, whatever they might claim, tend to focus on strategy formulation and leave the majority of the implementation to their clients. The separation of the two[26] often leads to poor formulation because consultants don't know the firm's assets and architecture or the competitive environment well enough. It also results in ineffective implementation because employees don't fully understand what they must do to deliver strategic success and are not motivated to do it.

Strategically incompetent firms must commit to building the processes and the skills needed to formulate and implement strategy for themselves. Making this commitment is the first step to moderate strategic intelligence.

Committed

The most dangerous state of incompetence is the executive team that agrees on the problem and on the solution, but doesn't really have any idea what it is doing. Unlike firms playing "let's pretend", the committed really believe in what they are doing and think it makes strategic sense even though their reasoning is fatally flawed. Such firms actually make changes in their strategic direction, convinced of victory even though they face certain defeat. Remember Alfred, Lord Tennyson's poem, *The Charge of the Light Brigade*. During the Crimean War, on October 25, 1854 in the Battle of Balaclava, 637 British light cavalry charged into the Valley of Death and were blown to bits by Russian guns on each side. There was no doubt they were committed, but they were headed in the wrong direction![27]

Committed firms typically have a bias for action. Fire-Aim-Ready! There is little danger in paralysis through analysis! The challenge is to maintain a balance. Thinking doesn't take much time compared to undoing the mistakes made by taking a wrong turn. A little thought followed by action is very helpful; and then a little more thought to reflect on how things are going. And the first step is to learn how to think strategically.

But spending time on defining problems is a luxury not open to firms facing a genuine crisis. It is better to avoid this situation and start early, as Brad Anderson did, investing in change before the crisis hits. Indeed, if firms are always looking for a problem to solve, always in problem-creating mode, they are less likely to ever experience a crisis and always prepared to deal with one.

Dealing with Incompetence

There is no quick fix for strategic incompetence. It requires learning – learning how to formulate and implement strategy. In an emergency, it is tough to think about learning new skills, so the time to learn is when things are going well. What to learn is the subject of **Chapters 1.3: What is Strategy?** and **1.4: Moderate Strategic Intelligence**.

Summary

Firms which fail to react in a timely fashion to changes in their competitive environment have a low Strategic IQ. But there are multiple reasons for this and each suggests a different level of IQ.

At the lower end of the spectrum are the strategically blind. For some, the problem is that they don't know what strategy is and don't much care either. They are blissfully ignorant. Others are playing "let's pretend"; they say they have a strategy but it has nothing to do with reality. Others have contracted strategic amnesia; they have forgotten their strategy and are running on autopilot or in pursuit of other goals. For those firms suffering from strategic blindness, **open your eyes** and build awareness (Figure 8). For the blissfully ignorant, it is awareness of the importance of strategy; for those playing "let's pretend", it is finding out what strategy really is; and for those who have forgotten, it is a matter of remembering. They must then commit to building strategic competence.

Figure 8: Escaping Low Strategic Intelligence

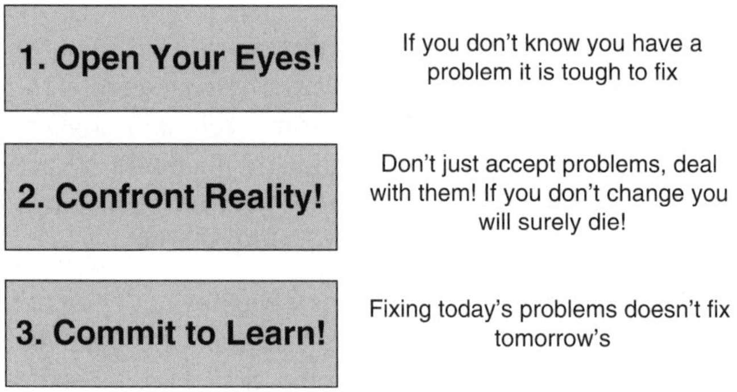

1. Open Your Eyes!	If you don't know you have a problem it is tough to fix
2. Confront Reality!	Don't just accept problems, deal with them! If you don't change you will surely die!
3. Commit to Learn!	Fixing today's problems doesn't fix tomorrow's

We then have firms in strategic denial. They all see the need for strategic change, but some, like the proverbial ostrich, ignore it in the hope that it will go away; others are frozen like a bunny in the headlights, seeing the danger but not doing anything about it; and there are those that distract themselves with tactical moves to solve the problem, like the hamster on a wheel running ever harder to stand still. The good news is that those in denial know what strategy is; the challenge is to get them to **confront reality** (Figure 8), the fact that their strategy no longer works.

Finally we have the strategically incompetent, lost in the dark, squabbling, outsourcing to advisors or fiercely committed to the wrong answer. There is no easy fix. As with the blind and those in denial, there is no substitute for learning how to develop and implement strategy well (Figure 8).

Notes

1. Collis and Conrad (1996).
2. Collis and Ruckstad (2008) propose a simpler model that focuses on goals, scope and advantage.
3. Porter (1980).
4. Rivkin and Halaburda (2007).
5. Prahalad and Hamel (1990).
6. Kim and Mauborgne (2005).
7. For a discussion of direct network effects, see Katz and Shapiro (1985). For an explanation of indirect network effects, see Econimides and Salop (1992).

8. Rettner (2010).
9. Joni and Beyer (2009).
10. Wells and Haglock (2005).
11. "Who is so deafe, or so blynde, as is hee, that wilfully will nother here nor see?" John Heywood (1546) *Dialogue of Proverbs* ii. ix. K4, quoted in Simpson and Speake (2009).
12. Gavetti, Henderson and Giorgi (2004).
13. Wells (2005), "*Circuit City Stores, Inc.*"
14. Coca-Cola Company 10K (1993) p. 162.
15. Austin and Nolan (2000).
16. Gerstner (2002).
17. Bazerman and Watkins (2004).
18. Christensen (1997).
19. Wells (2005) "*Circuit City Stores, Inc.*"
20. This is a direct quote from Circuit City's 1988 Form 10-K, p. 3.
21. Wells (2005) "*Best Buy Co., Inc.*"
22. These recommendations are based on discussions with executives as to their interpretation of the Circuit City case. Wells (2005) "*Circuit City Stores, Inc.*"
23. Wells (2005) "*Best Buy Co., Inc.*"
24. The burning platform metaphor is based on the tough choice oil platform workers faced when trapped on the burning Piper Alpha platform on July 6, 1988 in the North Sea, just northeast of Aberdeen. Stay and burn to death or risk almost certain death by diving 75 feet into freezing water and flaming debris. Many jumped and survived. The logic? "I'd rather meet probable death than certain death." No guarantees of survival, but if you don't change, you are definitely dead!
25. Argyris (1990).
26. Martin (2010) emphasizes the importance of taking an integrated view of strategy formulation and implementation.
27. Tennyson (1854).

1.3

WHAT IS STRATEGY?

The goal of any business is to deliver superior sustainable performance. To do so, it must develop a good competitive strategy. A strategy is made up of an integrated set of choices about where and how to compete. They are captured in a firm's strategic business model (Figure 9).

Figure 9: Elements of a Strategic Business Model

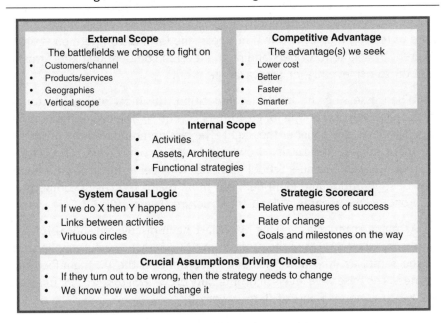

In this chapter we identify the principles behind strategic business models. In **Chapter 1.4: Moderate Strategic Intelligence**, we describe how to develop one.

External Scope

Some business opportunities are intrinsically more attractive than others, so the first strategic choice a firm must make is the battlefields it wishes to fight on. The profit potential of a business is shaped by the gap between customers' willingness to pay, and the firm's cost to supply. Businesses that create a lot of value for customers offer more potential, so good strategy starts with a deep understanding of customer needs and their willingness to pay to meet them.

But costs to supply are also important. Understanding the basic economics of satisfying customer needs and how these costs are likely to evolve over time is essential in assessing profit potential. If willingness to pay does not exceed costs, then the business is in trouble as many players in the dot.com boom and bust found out. The maximum price achievable in a business is the full value of the product to customers but they rarely need to pay this. The actual price is driven by the level of competition in the business. Low competition and the price approaches the maximum; lots of competition and the price falls, even to the point where it is below a firm's cost to supply. Businesses have different levels of competition which makes them more or less profitable. Within a business, the level of competition is often different by segment. Understanding the level of competition helps firms to position to achieve higher than average profits.

When assessing the level of competition, the most obvious factor to focus on is rivals competing for customers' attention. The bigger the number of competitors, the tougher they fight. The less differentiated the products, the more intense the rivalry. However, in his seminal work, *Competitive Strategy*, Harvard Business School professor Michael Porter[1] took a broader view of competition and identified four more major sources of competition for profits in his analysis of industry structure (Figure 10).

As many companies serving Wal-Mart have discovered, powerful customers can extract most of the profit from a business. Powerful suppliers can do the same, as Intel and Microsoft have done in the PC manufacturing business. The miserable levels of profitability drove IBM to sell its PC business and HP to announce an exit (later reversed).

But even if there are few rivals and suppliers and customers are weak, profits will still not last very long if it is easy for new firms to get into the business. To achieve good profitability in the long term, barriers to entry

Figure 10: Sources of Competition for Profits

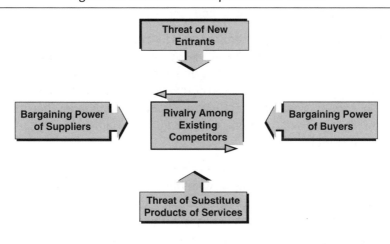

Source: Michael E. Porter (2004), *Competitive Advantage*, p. 5

must be high. And last but not least, substitute products put an upper limit on the price a customer will pay and therefore the profits a firm can make.

Careful assessment of Porter's five forces indicates the level of profitability the average firm can expect from a business opportunity. It also indicates ways in which the firm can position to achieve above average returns, such as choosing to serve less powerful customer segments. The trick is to pick the right businesses and position carefully within them to achieve higher than average profits.

Porter's five forces framework has proven to be a simple and effective tool for decades but it hasn't stopped the search for the sixth force; some have suggested that this is complements. A complement makes a firm's product more valuable; for instance, computer software makes a personal computer useful.

In some respects, the existence of complements increases the attractiveness of a business; the more software available for a given type of PC, the more attractive the PC becomes. But in other ways complements are a source of competition for the consumer's dollar.[2] They only have a certain amount to spend and if the price of the complement is high, this leaves less to spend on your product. Ideally, firms would like to see high competition in complementary businesses so that there are lots of cheap complements about, thus making the firm's product more attractive. For example, pirated music comes for free and makes iPods more attractive.

There have been many other proposals for the sixth force. In reality, there are many factors that shape the attractiveness of the competitive environment: technology, regulation, politics, macroeconomics, environmental concerns, demographic trends and social norms to name but a few. But sometimes they can have a positive effect on profitability, sometimes negative. To understand which, we can refer back to Porter's framework. This is what makes it so useful.

The dynamics of profitability over time are also important. Trends in the five forces provide an indicator of whether average profitability is going to rise or fall. Smart investors look to invest in businesses where profits are likely to increase in the future and buy into them at a discount. Equally, they look to sell out of businesses at a premium where they think profits will decline in the long term.

When evaluating a business, it is also useful to take a broader view of the total value system, looking upstream at the supply chain, downstream at the distribution channels and sideways at complementary products. The objective is to identify where profits are currently made in the value system and how this will change in future. For instance, in the music business 25 years ago most of the profits were made by the major record companies.[3] Ten years ago, an increasing share was being captured by large discount retailers. Today, digital distribution is destroying the retailers and putting even more pressure on the record companies. Digital downloading services are doing well, but, as already noted, the availability of pirated music at zero cost is making complementary digital music players such as the iPod more attractive.

Finally, rather than simply being reactive, the five forces framework can help firms to identify how they can shape the competitive environment to their advantage. This might include reducing direct competition through consolidation or more product differentiation, encouraging new customers or suppliers to enter to reduce negotiating power, building barriers to entry or increasing switching costs to protect against substitutes.

Competitive Advantage

Whatever markets a firm chooses to address, the chances are it will not be alone in making this choice; it will be up against competition, so it needs to build an advantage in order to deliver superior long-term profits. One way of doing this is to seek a price premium by delivering greater value to customers. As long as the price premium exceeds any extra costs involved, the firm will make higher profits. This is a *differentiation* advantage.

Differentiation is not merely about being different or unique; it is about being better, better as defined by the customer. And the acid test of a better product is that, placed side-by-side with the competitor's offering, the customer will pay more for it. If the price is the same, the product should be gaining share. Differentiation requires strict economic discipline. The firm must be able to calculate the extra value it is creating for customers and be able to demonstrate this to them convincingly. It must also know its relative cost position and only add to its cost base where it knows it can achieve a price premium that will cover the extra costs involved.

Differentiation is the pursuit of price premiums, but firms can also seek to build a *cost* advantage over competitors. This often means that they offer lower prices to make up for a less valuable product, but as long as the discount is smaller than their cost advantage, they make more money. Pursuing both a differentiation advantage and a cost advantage at the same time is often difficult and herein lies the second major strategic choice a firm must make. How does it expect to win in its chosen segments? Which advantage does it seek?

The profit potential for the firm is therefore made up of three components: intrinsic average profitability of the business; the incremental profit from finding attractive segments within the business; and the size of competitive advantage compared to others who are competing in the same segment.

Generic Strategies

The selection of battlefields defines the breadth of external scope of a strategy; the choice of advantage identifies how the firm aims to win. Porter suggests that this leads to three generic strategies: **low cost**, the broad-based pursuit of a cost advantage; **differentiation**, the broad-based pursuit of differentiation; and **focus**, selecting a niche to serve (Figure 11).[4] However, simply selecting a niche does not endow a firm with a right to win; it must have an advantage in serving the segment over anyone else who chooses to do so. This can often be a challenge when broad-based players enjoy scale economies from their broader positioning. It is only when large players face

Figure 11: Porter's Generic Strategies

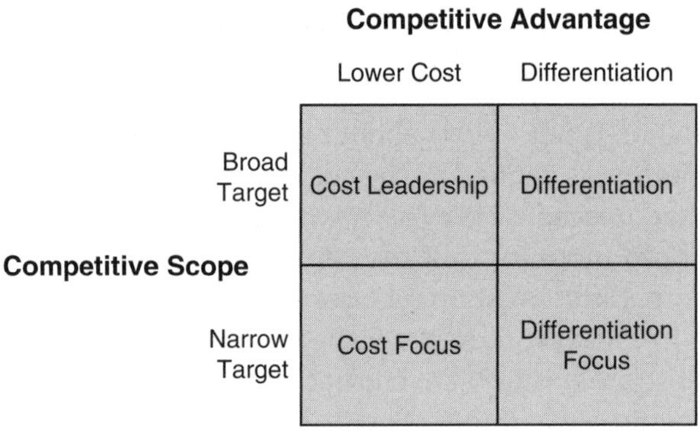

Competitive Advantage

	Lower Cost	Differentiation

		Lower Cost	Differentiation
	Broad Target	Cost Leadership	Differentiation
Competitive Scope	Narrow Target	Cost Focus	Differentiation Focus

Source: Michael E. Porter (2004), Competitive Advantage, p. 12

tough trade-offs which make niche markets unattractive to them and other small players find it hard to get in that the focus strategy is sustainable.

Beyond Static Advantage – Faster and Smarter

Differentiation and lower cost are relatively *static* advantages. There is always the possibility that competitors will replicate the advantage and catch up, or even surpass it. The economic value of the advantage is a function of how long it is likely to last. If firms are *faster* than competitors in implementing strategic moves, they will have longer to enjoy the superior profits that the new strategy provides. The capacity for speedy strategic change is also a measure of advantage.[5]

But it is important to be fast in smart ways. Strategic moves that open up a larger competitive gap are obviously more attractive. But the value still depends on how long the advantage lasts, so it helps to select moves that competitors will be slow to copy. This could be because they don't notice them for some time or they are reluctant to copy them or even that they simply cannot do so. The frequency of strategic innovation also provides greater advantage – firms which can identify more attractive moves will do better. Companies which pick moves that create more options for the future, creating new platforms and avoiding blind alleys are also better off. In short, these firms play *smarter*.[6]

Capital One, the fourth largest credit card issuer in the USA in 2011, is unquestionably faster at generating new ideas than its competitors, and it generates a lot more of them. It runs more than 50,000 new product or market segment tests each year in its quest to drive the net present value of the firm higher. In the process, it has built a valuable proprietary database (an average of one hundred pages single spaced on every adult in the USA) that also makes it smarter in seeking out new profit opportunities.[7]

Differentiation and lower cost are not enough in a fast-moving world. Firms must be agile and intelligent enough to play a faster, smarter game (Figure 12).

Figure 12: The Four Sources of Competitive Advantage

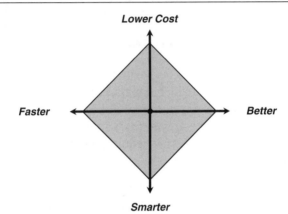

Dynamic Positioning

Capital One has long pursued a "stay-ahead" strategy – a dynamic rather than a static strategic positioning. When it entered the credit card market in the late 1980s, it was much smaller than its major competitors and would have been hard-pressed to survive offering the same products; but it introduced a series of new ideas that gave it higher margins. The competitors took time to react, and when they finally copied, Capital One dropped the old ideas and launched new ones.[8] This stay-ahead strategy required constant innovation, which was why they built their innovation machine.

Dynamic positioning (Figure 13) is common in many fast-moving environments. Take, for instance, consumer electronics. Some firms, such as

Figure 13: Dynamic Positioning for Competitive Advantage

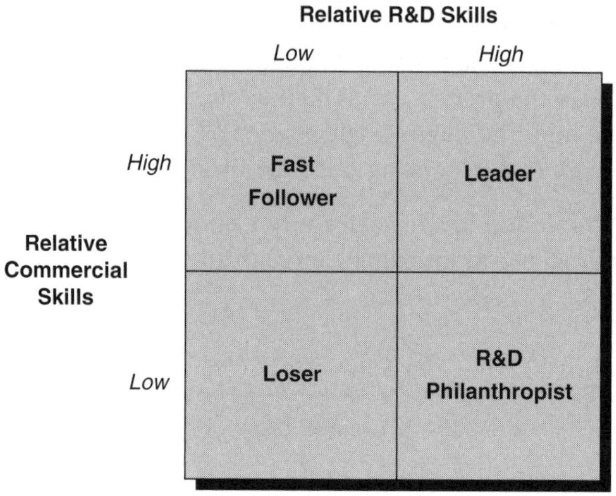

Relative R&D Skills

	Low	*High*
High	Fast Follower	Leader
Low	Loser	R&D Philanthropist

Relative Commercial Skills

Sony, have historically striven to be pioneers, coming up with a wide range of leading-edge ideas and charging premium prices to cover the extra costs of pioneering. To win playing this game, firms must be faster and smarter at playing a differentiation game. This requires both superior research and commercial skills.

Others, such as Panasonic, have tended to be fast followers, adopting successful ideas quickly; while the average price realization of this positioning is lower than for pioneers, some of the costs are avoided. Such firms concentrate on being faster rather than smarter and aim to be lower cost than pioneers rather than differentiated. The level of research skills required is not as high, but commercial skills are still essential.

Finally, there are the "me-too" players who enter late when products are well established and simply produce very high volumes at lower cost. Superior manufacturing scale is typically the key requirement. Korean companies used to play this role in consumer electronics but now firms such as LG and Samsung have moved closer to the pioneering positioning and the Chinese have taken up the "me-too" mantle. The "me-too" game is focused squarely on cost advantage.

The challenge of dynamic positioning is how to manage the product lifecycle, when to let go of old ideas and commit to new ones. Firms will often have several generations of products in the marketplace at once to manage this process, as we see with the current versions of the Apple iPhone.[9] It is a game of constant self-cannibalization which can be very painful, especially if there is a long inventory pipeline involved. Getting out too soon leaves profits on the table and may provide insufficient funding for pioneering. Too late and firms may find themselves dedicating resources to fights they cannot win against lower cost players and failing to innovate enough.

Competitive Dynamics – Anticipating Competitors

It should be clear from the preceding discussion on positioning and advantage that strategy cannot be constructed in isolation; it depends on what competitors do. Firms are continually adjusting their strategies. How have competitors acted in the past? What does this tell us about how they are likely to act in the future? How are they likely to react to any move we might make?[10]

When a firm makes any major strategic move, its goal is to improve its advantage over the competition. Taking actions that competitors can copy quickly and do more effectively makes no sense. Smart strategy seeks to exploit the weaknesses and inertia of competitors.[11] The ideal move is one where it will be very costly for the competitor to react and where they will be unable to beat the firm's advantage once they have done so. For instance, in the United States telecommunications market many years ago, MCI built a simple network with a few sophisticated switches that allowed it to vary price depending on the number dialled. This enabled MCI to offer discounts for frequently dialled calls to friends and family.[12] The service proved very popular but AT&T, the market leader, was slow to react because it had a much more complicated network based on old technology that did not allow price variations. To match MCI, it would have had to make a massive investment. Instead it delayed until MCI built up a 25% market share.

If competitors can copy fast, but the move puts them at a disadvantage, then this is still strategically desirable for the firm (Figure 14). Problems only arise when the competitors end up better or lower cost as a result of copying. It might still be worth making a move against them just so long as they are slow to respond, but firms must find other ideas once more powerful competitors copy – a "stay-ahead" strategy as illustrated by Capital One.

Figure 14: Anticipating Competitor Reactions

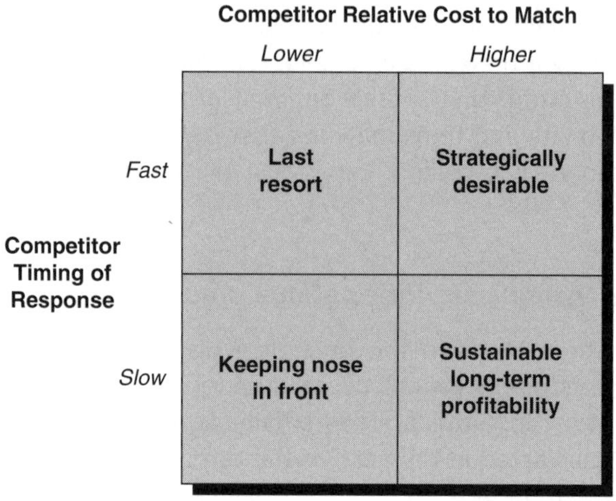

Competitor Relative Cost to Match

		Lower	Higher
Competitor Timing of Response	*Fast*	Last resort	Strategically desirable
	Slow	Keeping nose in front	Sustainable long-term profitability

While the competitors are getting their act together, the firm is free to enjoy the extra profits from its new advantage until the laggards catch up.

The most dangerous innovation is an idea that the competition can copy fast and easily and which extends their competitive advantage when they do so. This undermines a firm's strategic position and threatens its survival and should be avoided. Thus, not all innovation is good. Firms should focus not on innovation per se, but on *innovation for advantage*.

The discussion above focuses on the actions and reactions of direct competitors but it applies to all players who might compete for profits. For instance, how might customers react to a firm if it integrates forwards and begins to compete with its own customer base? Will they continue to buy from the firm or switch to a competitor? Firms must always consider how their actions are likely to affect the competitive environment.

Network Effects and Competitive Advantage

The competitive advantage bestowed by network effects has become of increasing interest over time, especially with the growth of e-commerce. A direct network effect is created when the value of a product to a customer increases as more customers buy it (Figure 15).[13] The classic example is the

Figure 15: Network Effects

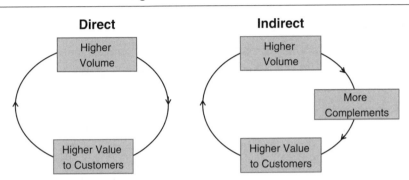

telephone. When only one person has a phone, it is not very useful, but the more people there are on the network, the more valuable it becomes. When there are a number of network suppliers, customers are prepared to pay more to be on the larger network and the cost to serve each of them is lower.[14] Under these circumstances, expanding market share is very attractive and encourages firms to invest in doing so. The ultimate goal is to get big enough that it is not worth a customer joining any other network and establish a monopoly. This is obviously very attractive from a competitive point of view. Only if a competitor can bring in a better network to attract customers over will the monopoly be broken.

Indirect network effects[15] work because of the existence of complements (Figure 15). This is most easily illustrated with an example. Microsoft's operating system is not very useful without software. The more software that is written for the operating system, the more attractive it becomes to buy it. And the larger the share of market Microsoft has, the less economic sense it makes for software producers to develop versions of their software for other operating systems. The benefits of market share work indirectly through the complements rather than directly, but the result is the same – monopoly.

It should come as no surprise that firms seek out network effects. However, the scope of the network effect is often exaggerated. For example, early claims of powerful network effects in online auctions argued that eBay would become a world standard, but since most transactions take place within local markets, many national champions have sprung up to serve local needs.[16] Rigorous review of the phenomenon is always essential.

Internal Scope, Assets and Architecture

Internal Scope

Once a firm identifies what advantage it seeks, it must make a choice as to how it will capture the value it creates. What scope of activities should it invest in? This is another critical strategic choice.

For example, consider a company aiming to differentiate itself by designing longer-lasting bearings. It might choose to produce the bearings in-house and sell them at a higher price. Alternatively, it may choose to subcontract manufacturing to a firm with greater scale and lower manufacturing cost, but maintain control of the design and the customer relationships. It could equally well decide to expand its scope and bundle the bearings with a maintenance contract to capture more of the savings in fitting costs. The firm could also narrow the scope of its internal activities and license its technology to other bearing producers, focusing all of its efforts on design. There are many ways of configuring to capture the added value with different investment profiles and different levels of strategic control.

The same holds for firms pursuing a cost advantage. They may choose to avoid investing in activities where there are plenty of low-cost suppliers and a lot of competition and outsource such products or services in the marketplace. The firm may also choose to joint venture in certain activities where other firms have advantage and seek exclusive relationships to stop competitors gaining access. But activities that are critical drivers of relative cost position are higher priorities for investment. Again, the choices are many for configuring activities. The goal is to pick a configuration that maximizes advantage and provides a sustainable position.

Assets

When a firm chooses to invest in an activity, it does so with a view to creating an asset. Assets normally require up-front investment but promise to deliver a stream of cash flows into the future. The net present value of this cash flow stream is the value of the asset.

Assets can be tangible, such as plant and equipment, or intangible, such as technology or know-how to operate a plant more effectively. Whether tangible or intangible, assets can offer competitive advantage. Larger scale equipment can contribute to lower unit costs; superior technology can provide higher quality; better operating skills can provide both. Processes to combine all three create a potent asset providing a strong source of competitive advantage – a distinctive competence for the firm.

Most firms invest in a wide range of assets over time (Figure 16), some of which provide competitive advantage. Because the money is already spent, a firm's assets often shape the choices it makes about which battlefields to fight on and what advantages to pursue. Firms seek out business opportunities that are intrinsically attractive and where they have distinctive competence. However, new opportunities often require some new assets to be developed and some old assets to be discarded.

Figure 16: Classes of Assets

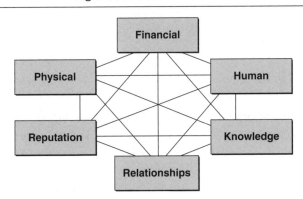

Architecture

When a firm has chosen where to compete and what advantage it seeks, it must configure the internal environment to be consistent with these choices; it must develop an architecture that organizes its assets to work together to create value. We use the term *architecture* to convey the fact that this involves much more than an organization chart. Such charts summarize the roles, responsibilities and reporting relationships in the firm and help to define who does the work. But firms also need processes to define how the work is done. They need human asset management systems to define what skills are required and how they should be recruited and trained. Measurement and reward systems are needed to motivate behaviour and track results. And finally, information and communications systems are required to hold everything together (Figure 17).

Figure 17: Elements of Formal Architecture

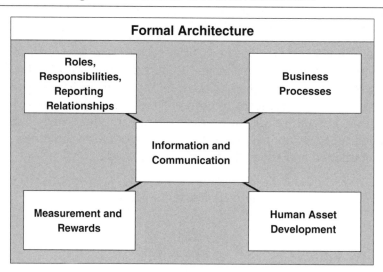

Firms typically organize individual businesses along functional lines. Each function consists of a set of highly interlinked activities, and each of these activities incurs costs and helps to create customer value. But to deliver on the firm's overall objectives, it is important to take a holistic view, reflecting the relationships between activities and functions. For instance, it may make sense for a firm pursuing a lower cost strategy to spend more on IT than its competitors because this reduces the costs of many other activities to provide an overall cost advantage. In this way, each function needs to define a functional strategy that is consistent with the overall strategy. Functions cannot be left to optimize locally in functional silos. They are part of a complex system working together to win in the marketplace.

System Causal Logic

Developing a strategy requires making a clear set of choices. The causal logic of the strategy can be captured by mapping these choices onto their expected effects.[17] This can be captured in a system diagram. Since the choices are interrelated, the cause-and-effect loops help to illustrate the impact of each choice on the company as a whole. The diagram also helps to identify positive feedback loops – "virtuous circles" – that drive greater competitive advantage. These are a good idea. Conversely, firms should avoid negative feedback loops or "vicious circles". For instance, cutting quality to improve profits might have short-term benefits, but if it reduces volume and increases unit costs, then the benefit is short-lived.

Systems diagram mapping is best illustrated with an example. Figure 18 shows four important choices made by Wal-Mart and the effects of these choices. As the figure shows, the choices are mutually reinforcing and create virtuous circles.

Figure 18: Wal-Mart Dynamic Business Model

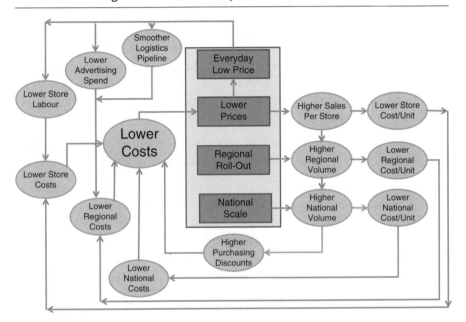

1. Offer the customer lower prices because this will increase volume and allow the firm to take lower gross margins and still cover its costs. It will also provide more purchasing power.

2. Reassure customers that the company offers everyday low prices (EDLP) to make a basket of goods lower cost than shopping at stores that promote particular items at very low prices ("loss-leaders"). EDLP lowers in-store labour costs because there is less work in setting up promotions

and changing prices. It also requires less advertising and provides a smoother supply pipeline which lowers costs.

3. Roll out stores regionally to share advertising, warehousing and logistics costs and increase overall purchasing power.

4. Expand nationally to provide greater purchasing power and sharing of purchasing department costs, national advertising (if any) and general overhead.

In addition to the systems diagram, each cause-and-effect relationship should be quantified. For example, an average price reduction of 1% might be expected to increase store throughput, but by how much? What is the impact on sales per square foot and sales per employee? And how does this affect overall store profitability? The reason for this quantification is that the model can then be rigorously tested. The effects expected from the choices are merely hypotheses. When the model is executed, it is important to check that these hypotheses hold true; if they do not, then the problem may be operational deficiencies which must be corrected or the model itself may need to be modified.

Quantification of the logic helps to identify some of the metrics that companies should track in their strategic scorecard (overleaf).

Systems diagrams also show the role of each function and activity in driving overall performance. Without this understanding it is easy for function heads and activity managers to slip into local optimization rather than total system optimization and do what is best practice for their area rather than for the company as a whole. For example, a company positioned as a fast follower should not be dedicating the same resources to R&D and marketing as a leader. While the marketing department might want to generate new product ideas, their job is to test the best ideas being developed by the competition and get them to market fast.

One of the key benefits of documenting the logic of a strategy and revisiting it on a regular basis is that this makes it more difficult to forget it. And firms are very forgetful. Responsibilities for executing different parts of the model are distributed across the organization, so it is only too easy for everyone to get on with their part of the job and "forget" why they have chosen to do it that way. Once the logic is forgotten, it is hard to improve on it or make changes. It simply becomes "the way we do things round here".

The original logic of Circuit City offering service and repair centres to its customers in the 1980s was very compelling; in those days, consumers wouldn't buy products unless they could get them fixed easily when they went wrong. But as new product reliability has increased, the power of this logic has waned.

Strategic Scorecard

Strategic metrics measure how well firms are doing against the competition. Without such metrics, companies cannot gauge their own performance or be ready to respond to competitors' moves.

A strategic scorecard measures the competitive advantage a firm has achieved and the drivers of that advantage. It compares this with the goals the company has set itself and the milestones on the way.

The Importance of Relative Cost Position and Relative Customer Value

Whether a firm chooses to be lower-cost or differentiated, to calculate the size of its advantage it must know its relative cost position. This information is difficult to extract from published accounts. It is better for the firm to look at the cost of every activity it engages in and to build a model of how each of these costs behaves (e.g. impact of scale of operations, type of technology, location of plant, etc.).[18] With this understanding of cost behaviour, the firm should then ask the question, "What would our costs be if we were to operate exactly the way our competitors are operating?" This provides a reasonable estimate of relative cost position (Figure 19) and also helps to identify how the firm must adjust each of its activities to build a cost advantage.

Whatever advantage firms seek, they must also be able to estimate how much customers value their products compared to competitor offerings. This helps determine the price premiums they can sustain or the discounts they must offer. To do this, firms must have deep knowledge of customer needs. For instance, many ball bearing customers are prepared to pay more than double the price for bearings that last twice as long. This is because they not only have to buy half as many bearings, but they also save on fitting costs – the total lifetime cost is what matters. In such industrial markets, a thorough understanding of customer economics provides insights into what price

Figure 19: Estimating Relative Cost Position

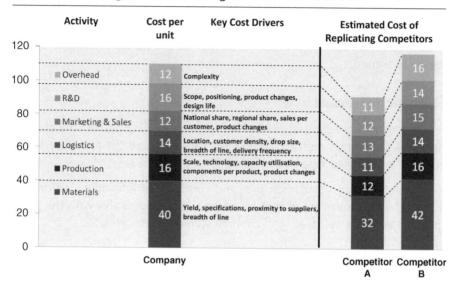

| Activity | Cost per unit | Key Cost Drivers | Estimated Cost of Replicating Competitors |

premiums the market will bear. In consumer markets, it is more difficult but there are statistical techniques for estimating the value placed on different product features.[19] These help to shape pricing strategies that reflect the firm's chosen strategic path.

Short-Term Profit versus Net Present Value

Many firms build their metrics around profitability, but short-term profits are not a good indicator of long-term strategic health. Strategic metrics should be linked to long-term performance – the goal is to increase the net present value of the firm (NPV). If everyone in the organization focuses on driving NPV, they are more likely to adjust the strategy to changes in the competitive environment. Capital One, for example, rewards employees for seeking out high net present value customers.[20] Since the NPV of a company is equal to the sum of the NPV of each of its current and future customers, Capital One's approach drives employees to seek out the most attractive strategic direction at any point in time. This has allowed Capital One to transition rapidly to different customer segments over the economic cycle, delivering sector-leading returns, while some of its less agile competitors have foundered.[21]

Measuring Drivers of Advantage

Measuring the drivers of advantage helps those managing activities on a day-to-day basis to execute the strategy well. For instance, a firm seeking a price premium from customers may need to offer a combination of better product quality, faster speed of delivery and bigger advertising spend. These factors are typically under the control of different managers in the firm and each requires a measure over which they have control to show how they are contributing to advantage. Remember, meaningful metrics motivate!

Many firms track metrics that drive relative cost position and price realization. Retailers use stock turns, sales per square foot, contribution per square foot and sales per employee; airlines track aircraft utilization, load factor and revenue per available seat mile; most firms monitor customer satisfaction. However, these measures do not become strategic metrics until they are tracked against competitors and linked to measures of advantage; i.e. how much extra profit can the firm expect for every extra unit of relative score? As already discussed, it is important to compare the advantage achieved with the drivers of advantage to make sure the company is getting the benefits it expects from its efforts. If not, the causal logic of the model may be flawed, or the firm may be executing ineffectively.

Market share is often used as a measure of competitiveness. Certainly, in fast-moving consumer goods it drives advantage; market leaders often enjoy a price premium because of the quality and assurance their brands offer; and higher volume drives unit costs down. Again, however, the critical measure is not market share but relative market share, since this determines the size of the advantage. And how much extra profit should each extra share point deliver?

But market share is not always correlated with competitive advantage. In some businesses, such as less-than-truckload shipping, large operators are no more cost-effective than small ones because scale economies are small. This makes it easy for a low overhead new entrant to get into the business with one truck and offer rock-bottom prices, which undermines industry profitability. Hence, those players aiming to build a larger share of the market are lining up to take a larger share of the losses.

Similarly, in the health club business, there are few advantages in operating nationally. However, there are costs that can be shared locally and operating a chain of health clubs in a local area allows the clubs to charge a premium for multi-club membership. Hence, local market share is more important than national share, so successful firms look to dominate a region rather than spread outlets too thinly. Indeed, 20% of the San Diego population are members of clubs run by leading health club operator 24 Hour Fitness.[22]

It is important to track metrics over time to assess strategic health. While a higher relative score may be a good sign, if the relative score is declining then this bodes ill for the future. Smart firms track the rate of change; how quickly the gap is closing or opening.

Part of Kmart's failure was its failure to track competitive benchmarks or even measure its own productivity effectively. Kmart's early focus was on driving sales, and it wasn't until the early 1980s that the focus shifted more to sales per square foot. It was even later, in the mid-1990s, that the firm began to look more seriously at relative measures. Had it done so fifteen years earlier, it would have discovered that Wal-Mart, while only one-tenth of Kmart's size, was already more productive.[23] Unlike Kmart, Nucor, which entered the US steel business in the early 1970s in the face of huge competition from established steel producers and dozens of new mini-mill entrants, was passionate right from the start about benchmarking against competitors and has grown to be the second largest steel producer in the USA in 2010.[24]

The goal of metrics is to drive everyday behaviours that contribute to long-term competitive advantage. If a company only gets data infrequently or chooses to look at them only during annual planning cycles, then it can fall behind in a fast-changing business environment. Successful firms identify short-term metrics that drive long-term success and track them on a regular basis. 24 Hour Fitness measures customer retention (a key measure of the long-term success of a club) every month.[25] Best Buy store associates meet each day to discuss how much economic value-added they created the previous day and how they can improve performance.[26] They focus on simple metrics they can affect, like the percentage of customers who actually made a purchase, the number of items they bought and the number that were satisfied with their visit, but these are all correlated with long-term value.

Crucial Assumptions

Crucial assumptions in a strategic model are deal-breakers – if the assumption is wrong, then the strategy must change. To ensure its model remains robust, a firm must test these assumptions regularly and track the results in the strategic scorecard. Companies should also identify what actions they will take if their crucial assumptions no longer hold true. This form of contingency planning makes firms more responsive to key changes in the competitive environment.

Laying out the logic of a strategy helps to identify the crucial assumptions that drive the choices being made. Take, for example, Zara, the largest fashion retail chain in the world. It is part of the Inditex Group based in Galicia, Spain.[27] Zara is known for its fast fashion; it responds quickly to the latest trends and restocks its stores twice weekly with hot-selling lines. This helps avoid costly markdowns at the end of the season, the bane of the fashion trade. Zara achieves this fast response time by producing a fair proportion of its clothes in-house in Spain and subcontracting out to North African and European manufacturers. This is more expensive than sourcing from the Far East but it is much faster, and the reduction in mark-downs more than covers the extra manufacturing costs.

Note Zara's crucial assumption! It is worth incurring higher local production costs because Far Eastern suppliers are too slow. Their whole business model is based on this. But in recent years, suppliers like Li & Fung have dramatically reduced their response times, spawning many fast fashion competitors at Zara price levels. Zara would do well to revisit its business logic.

Extending the Strategic Business Model to Competitors

In the same way that a strategic business model must take into account the effects of interactions between activities within the firm, we now see that it must also consider the effects of interactions over time with the competitive environment. Putting up a plant twice the size may lead to a competitive advantage in the short run, but if competitors can be expected to do the same thing in response, then the advantage is transient. This makes the model considerably more complex.[28]

Strategic business models are necessarily simplifications of reality.[29] Indeed, it would be impossible to build a model that explained everything. Good strategic models incorporate the critical variables that explain how the competitive environment works, how the firm is positioned and how it expects to create competitive advantage, how competitors are positioned, and how they are likely to act and react. What is included in the model is a matter of judgment. Too much causes confusion – the objective is to help the firm focus on key priorities rather than overwhelm with detail. However, this simplification creates a dilemma. When the competitive environment changes, then some of the variables may become obsolete while others, not considered important in the past, become more important. Hence, regular review and testing of the model is essential.

Many of the causal links in the model are also hypotheses rather than proven "facts". Only by testing actual outcomes of choices against the predicted effects can a firm build a more robust model. In this respect, strategy is a continuous learning experience.

Notes

1. For a detailed discussion of the Five Forces framework to analyse industry structure, see Porter (1980) *Competitive Strategy,* Chapter 1, pp. 3–33.
2. See Brandenburger and Nalebuff (1996) for an in-depth discussion of "coopetition". Yoffie, Casadesus-Masanell and Mattu (2003) describe the coopetition between Intel and Microsoft.
3. Wells and Raabe (2007).
4. Porter (1980).
5. Stalk and Hout (1990).
6. See Yoffie and Kwak (2001) on using an opponent's strength against them.
7. Wells and Anand (2008).
8. Wells and Anand (2008).
9. From http://store.apple.com/us/browse/home/shop_iphone/family/iphone Apple shop, downloaded October 17, 2011.
10. For a framework for competitor analysis, see Porter (1980) *Competitive Strategy,* Chapter 1, pp. 47–74.
11. Yoffie and Kwak (2001) discuss how to use a competitor's inertia against it in *"Judo Strategy"*.
12. Introduced in June 1991, Friends and Family was a huge success, adding 2 percentage points of share and $1.2 billion in revenues in 1991 alone (see Rosenfeld, 2011). My explanation of AT&T's slow response came from a telecommunications engineer and has not been confirmed by AT&T.
13. For a discussion of direct network effects, see Katz and Shapiro (1985).
14. When the value of a product rises with the number of customers who purchase it (i.e. a direct network effect), this is often called a *demand-side*

economy of scale. When the cost per unit falls with output, this is called a *supply-side economy of scale*.

15. For a full explanation of indirect network effects, see Econimides and Salop (1992).
16. Oberholzer-Gee and Wulf (2009).
17. Casadesus-Masanell and Ricart (2007).
18. Rivkin and Halaburda (2007).
19. Revealed preference techniques are based on analysing actual customer purchase data. Discrete choice techniques offer customers bundles of features and ask them which they would prefer. Conjoint analysis then provides an estimate of the value of each attribute. See Collis (2011).
20. Wells and Anand (2008).
21. Wells (2005) *"Providian Financial Corporation"*.
22. Wells and Raabe (2005) *"24 Hour Fitness"*.
23. Wells and Haglock (2005) *"The Rise of Kmart"*.
24. Ghemawat and Stander (1992).
25. Wells and Raabe (2005) *"24 Hour Fitness"*.
26. Wells (2005) *"Best Buy Co., Inc"*.
27. Ghemawat and Nueno (2003).
28. Casadesus-Masanell and Larson (2010).
29. See March and Simon (1958) for a discussion of the cognitive limits of rationality.

1.4

MODERATE STRATEGIC INTELLIGENCE

Many firms acknowledge their strategic problems, but do not know how to fix them because they lack even moderate strategic intelligence. The term "moderate" is not meant to downplay the considerable challenges involved in developing a strategy – one of the most demanding intellectual tasks in business. It is merely intended to distinguish between the strategically competent and the expert, smart enterprises which we discuss in Chapter 1.5.

Strategic competence requires both formulation and implementation skills. Strategy formulation is the *integration of choices* – where to compete, what advantages to seek and how to deliver these advantages. Strategy implementation is *the integration of actions* – redeploying assets and resynchronizing actions to execute the strategy.

In this chapter, we go step by step through the process of strategy formulation and implementation, applying the principles of competitive strategy outlined in **Chapter 1.3: What is Strategy?** We identify the challenges faced along the way and how firms can overcome them to reach the upper end of the Moderate Strategic IQ scale.

External Strategic Review

The path to strategic competence begins with a fresh, dispassionate examination of the competitive environment. The task is complex, the data voluminous, ambiguous and uncertain, and it is easy to get lost in the maze. So don't lose sight of the goal, which is to identify viable strategic options that will deliver superior sustainable performance. After each bit of analysis ask, "So what? What issues does this raise? What opportunities might this offer? What actions would it require?"

Global View

Begin by taking a *global view*.[1] At the broadest level, try to identify what might affect the firm's competitive arena. Consider all factors – political, social, macro-economic, technical and environmental change. What does the rise of China mean; the Arab Spring; the erosion of the dollar as a reserve currency; the greying of the population; the growth of mobile devices; the rapid development of social networks; the increasing burden on the world's water supply; volcanic eruptions? Does your list provide any exciting opportunities for players in your industry or pose any dangerous threats?

Take care not to dismiss any issues as irrelevant too quickly. The human mind is a vicious censor; it eliminates ideas even before we have had time to consciously think about them. Later in this book we list creativity tools and techniques that help suspend judgment long enough to examine the data through different eyes. Be sure to list those low-probability, high-risk events that could destroy the firm.[2] The impact of the eruption of Iceland's volcano, Eyjafjallajökull on European business travel in 2010 was a wake-up call for many. Had the eruption lasted for over a year, as it did in 1821, then many industries would have been in trouble. (The teleconferencing, high-speed rail and shipping industries, however, would have been ecstatic.) What opportunities and threats do these predictable surprises represent?[3]

Industry Structure

Next, focus on *industry structure*.[4] What does a Five Forces analysis suggest are the major sources of competition for profits? How do these vary by each product, geographic and customer segment? How are these likely to evolve over time? Are profits moving upstream or downstream through the value system? In the past, which segments of the business were more attractive, and how is this likely to change? Answers to these questions help to make the first critical choice in strategy, which is where to compete; some battlefields are more attractive than others.

Competitive Advantage

But position is not enough. Firms often find themselves competing for the same segments, so they must build *competitive advantage* to win. What does it take to deliver a superior value proposition to the customer? What price premium are they likely to pay for it? This requires a thorough understanding of customer needs and how they are changing over time.

What does it take to build a cost advantage? What activities are required to satisfy needs? What is the cost of each activity per unit of output? What are the key drivers of cost, e.g. scale, capacity utilization, run length, regional market share, technology, location, etc.?

Understanding sources of advantage helps make the second key choice in strategy, which is to identify the type of advantage sought. Broadly speaking there are only two sources of advantage – differentiation and lower cost – but in practice the array of options these two fundamental advantages spawn is large.

For instance, differentiation means "better" from the customer's view-point, and there are a myriad of ways of achieving this. Product quality is one; it may be valued by customers for emotional satisfaction – a high-quality cashmere blazer to improve the self-image – or because it saves money by lasting longer. Faster delivery and shorter response times can delight customers and save them money. Greater variety allows one-stop shopping, saving customers time and transaction costs. The many dimensions of differentiation are not all mutually exclusive, but it is often possible to generate a huge number of combinations and permutations – bundles of value. At this stage the goal is to identify the many ways in which a competitor could "play the game". This helps in developing viable strategic options at a later stage.

In principle, the lower cost game aims to deliver superior profits by delivering the same bundle of value at lower cost. In practice, lower cost strategies do not always work like this. Lower cost players typically offer less value, focusing on a few things that really matter to the customer and delivering them at really low cost. Some customers are prepared to compromise on their full range of needs and accept such an offer as long as they get a discount. As long as the discount is lower than the cost advantage, the firm generates more profit.

The scope of advantage is also an important choice. Does a firm take a narrow focus and only serve one segment or a broader focus and serve many? Broad scope can help reduce costs (e.g. sharing a bigger plant or brand advertising costs) but not always, and it creates a good deal of complexity. Narrower scope provides the benefits of simplicity – the focus strategy – but it is important to ensure that narrowing scope doesn't undermine competitive advantage.

Dynamic Advantage

Lower cost and differentiation advantages are static in nature. Smart firms can also pursue dynamic advantages. Some win through strategic innovation, coming up with new ideas for improving competitive advantage better or faster than competitors. Strategic innovation can be applied to cut relative costs or increase levels of differentiation. Strategic innovators are first to introduce ideas and increase advantage, but once the major competitors have copied, some move on to the next idea – the "stay ahead" strategy. This works well when a small, nimble firm is competing with larger competitors which enjoy greater economies of scale. Some are simply faster at coming up with new ideas. Others are shrewder, selecting paths that the competitors are reluctant or slow to follow. Some players copy quickly – a "fast follower" strategy. Others enter later in the product lifecycle and produce at very low cost – the "me too" strategy.

Configuring for Advantage

The number of strategic options is increased even further by the fact that there are many ways to deliver each advantage. In what ways can activities and assets be combined to do so? Look at current competitors as a guide, but there may be other ways to deliver an edge which might be more attractive for the firm to try, given its particular strengths and weaknesses.

The models competitors use can be wide-ranging and they often involve trade-offs. As we discussed in Chapter 1.3, Zara, the world's leading fashion retailer, sources a lot of its clothes in Europe even though Far Eastern suppliers are cheaper. This allows the company to respond faster to market needs and reduce costly end-of-season mark-downs. It trades off higher manufacturing costs for lower mark-downs. US-based Gap, the world's number two speciality clothes retailer, does the opposite, accepting higher mark-downs in return for lower cost.[5] Hong-Kong-based Li & Fung has a very different way of playing the game.[6] It supplies retailers with clothes using its very fast response pipeline and extracts a price premium for the superior speed, capturing some of the profits of fast fashion retailers without investing in retailing. It subcontracts all of its manufacturing to over 15,000 small suppliers, making sure it buys a large share of each supplier's output so that it gets low prices and shares in the manufacturing profits. Consequently, Li & Fung enjoys the profits of a retailer and a manufacturer without investing in risky assets.

Competitor Analysis

There is no such thing as strategy in isolation; it all depends on where competitors are positioned and what they are likely to do, so a review of the external environment must include an analysis of each major competitor in the industry. If there are hundreds of competitors, divide them into groups that are strategically similar to each other. How well are the competitors doing financially? How well are they doing on more strategic measures of success like relative market share, relative customer satisfaction? What segments do they serve? What advantages do they enjoy? What is their relative cost position, price realization? Are they faster than the competitors to build advantage? Are they smarter in doing things that it is tough for competitors to copy? What configuration of activities and assets have they used to build advantage? What do they claim their strategy is – their espoused strategy? Based on their actions, what strategy do they appear to have been following – their strategy-in-use? What does this suggest for their future moves? How are they likely to react to industry trends? How are they likely to react to any moves we might make? What might they ignore, find it difficult to react to? What are their "hot buttons", moves likely to solicit a violent response?[7]

Firms should then analyse themselves in the same way, developing a dispassionate view on the firm's competitive position and the strategy it appears to be executing. Role-play is useful for this, asking top management to become a competitor to look outside-in at the firm. This can be fun and highly enlightening.

Displaying Resolve

Analysing the competitive environment is hard but don't give up. It is very much like detective work, piecing together snippets of data to form an overall picture. There are many players involved and a lot of variables to consider, so the task is complex. Data are often poor and involve lots of estimates and more than a little guesswork. Detailed information on competitors is tough to find. Market research on customers can be ambiguous or misleading because customers often don't know what they need, they simply voice what they want. Different data sources often disagree. Luckily the human brain is good at such integration work, and the more we practice, the better we get.

Managing Uncertainty

We are also dealing with a dynamic environment which has evolved over the past and could take many paths in future. The picture is constantly changing. To reduce the complexity, take a number of snapshots over time; what were the Five Forces like five years ago, ten years ago, fifteen years ago, compared to today? How far back to go is a matter of judgment, but certainly it is important to go back far enough to when the firm was successful and use the analysis to explain its past success. Then, by focusing on what has changed in the interim, it is easier to understand why the old strategy no longer works and why change is needed. This helps firms to bridge from the past to the future.

But the future is uncertain; the macro environment, competitors, suppliers, customers could change in a myriad of ways. Taking a range of scenarios for every key variable generates millions of possible future worlds which would take an eternity to analyse. The danger is paralysis through analysis. Simplify to provide insight! Move ten years forward and paint a few positive scenarios; feasible, internally consistent pictures of what the world could look like that would be favourable to the firm. Then imagine you are in the future and look back at the major factors that triggered these scenarios and identify how the firm could make them more likely. Repeat the exercise for a few unattractive scenarios and identify how the firm could reduce the probability of such outcomes. This helps to build more robust strategies.

Internal Strategic Review

Assets

In parallel with the external review, firms need to conduct an equally thorough review of the internal environment to identify the opportunities this offers and the limitations it imposes on future action. Examine the assets the firm has at its disposal and the way it organizes these assets to create value. These are part of the **structure** of the firm (discussed further in **Part Two: Smart Structure**).

Firms invest in a wide range of assets over time (Figure 20). The review should put them to the test. Are they the right ones for delivering the current strategy? Do they provide a competitive advantage? Are they becoming obsolete, turning into liabilities? Do they get in the way of changing the strategy, creating structural inertia? Are there other opportunities for using them?

Figure 20: Classes of Assets

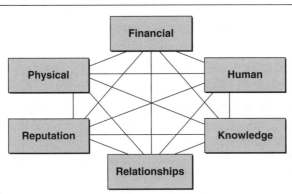

Physical assets, including plant and equipment, research laboratories and retail outlets, can offer clear advantages; for example, larger scale plants and the latest technology typically provide cost advantages. With a good knowledge of what drives costs, a firm can estimate its relative cost advantage.

Financial assets include cash in hand and a strong balance sheet. Superior financial strength provides companies with more staying power and more capacity to invest in new business opportunities. This can usually be assessed from public data.

Reputation assets are less tangible than physical assets but are often no less important. Brand is an obvious example. In fast-moving consumer goods, a strong brand will often support a significant price premium. As long as the cost of supporting the brand is lower than the premium it supports, it is a source of competitive advantage. But there are other reputation assets. P&G is known for aggressively defending its position, so competitors avoid it, allowing freer rein to make profits.

Knowledge assets range from formal patents to informal know-how. Patents can help cut costs, drive price realization or prevent others from competing. Know-how can provide measurable learning curve benefits.

Relationships can be assets. Loyal customers are very valuable, and valuable relationships can be built with channels of distribution, key suppliers, producers of complementary products and research departments of universities. The challenge is always to measure the advantage they bestow. If competitors have relationships with the same entities, this may negate the advantage, but not always. For instance, a firm that buys a large share of a manufacturer's output is likely to get lower prices than smaller customers who are often the firm's competitors. In this way large firms can get competitors to pay for some of their inputs. This is why Li & Fung aims to take between 30% and 70% of each of its 15,000 suppliers' output.

Firms often claim that their people are their most important asset, but few of them can measure the size of advantage this bestows. Companies track morale because it is correlated with business performance, but the direction of causality is not clear; does the performance drive the morale or the morale the performance? Value-added per employee is a useful measure, but it depends on the level of capital invested. A few firms work hard to measure the true value of their people. US credit card issuer Capital One estimates the net present value of its employees and compares this with the cost of developing them.

Formal Architecture

After assessing assets, we turn to architecture – the way in which assets are organized to deliver value. This too can be a significant source of advantage.

The elements of architecture (Figure 21) must also be put to the test. Are they internally consistent or is the organization at war with itself? For instance, does the firm pay its people to do one thing but expect them to do another? Are all of the elements aligned with the current strategy? Do they provide a competitive advantage?

Roles, responsibilities and reporting relationships, often summarized in an organization chart, identify who is responsible for what in the firm. Are these aligned with strategic objectives? And how easy is it to change? Complex multi-layered hierarchies and multi-dimensioned matrices have

Figure 21: Elements of Formal Architecture

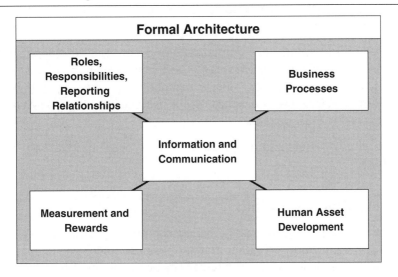

slower response times than decentralized structures. However, it is difficult to get independent units to work together to exploit scale economies or serve large global accounts. Where this is important, larger hierarchies may make more sense.

Processes define how the work is done and make firms more efficient. How good are the processes that drive strategic success? For instance, a firm pursuing a stay-ahead strategy must have an excellent innovation process. Are they being driven down the learning curve, continuously improved to provide a competitive advantage? Superior processes deliver higher productivity, faster response times, quicker development efforts and better-designed products. And there is a lot of know-how embedded in them, which is hard to copy and provides long-lasting advantage. Measuring this is not always easy, but published data can assist. For instance, retailers often publish sufficient data to compare stock turns, sales per square foot, sales per employee and same-store sales growth. These are driven as much by process efficiencies as by superior competitive positioning.

Human asset development processes include hiring, developing and firing people. These are singled out for special attention in Figure 21 because of the critical role people play in the success of a firm. Are they aligned with the strategy? Are they competitively superior?

Measurement and reward systems align people to execute strategy effectively, so they are critical to success. Does the firm measure the right things? Reward the right actions?

Finally, information and communication systems tie everything together and help deliver significant advantage. Do the systems help drive strategic success? Do they do it better than the competition? For example, Li & Fung would not be able to execute its fast response manufacturing model without superior information systems.

We discuss assets and architecture in more detail in **Part Two: Smart Structure.**

Defining Strategic Options

The next step in the process is building coherent strategic options for the firm. A strategic option is a viable strategic business model (see Chapter 1.1). It defines three clear choices: the target positioning within the industry, the type of competitive advantage sought and the configuration of activities and assets to deliver the advantage. It should also document the causal logic for why the model should work, the crucial assumptions on which the strategy is based and the timing and size of the advantage sought.

The most obvious strategic option is "more of the same". Evaluate this first to demonstrate the impact of continuing with business as usual. But don't assume that profitability will stay the same under the "do nothing" strategy. That is a dangerous trap! If competition is increasing, profits are likely to fall, and vice versa. Be sure to incorporate all external changes into the "more of the same" baseline. This becomes the minimum standard against which the other options must be compared.

Next, identify a number of alternative strategic options for the firm. The review of the competitive environment should already have identified a wide range of ways of playing the game based on different positioning choices and ways of creating competitive advantage. Now is the time to whittle the list down, identifying those for which the firm is best suited. But take care not to eliminate ideas too quickly or good options may be eliminated too early. Our brains unconsciously apply implicit criteria to ideas before they enter our conscious minds and eliminate them before they are even considered. (To read more on this phenomenon, go to **Part Three: Smart Minds.**) Before rejecting an option, ask the question, "If I were forced to pick this route, how could I make it work?" This extra effort helps to surface counter-intuitive ideas that may have considerable merit.

For each option, be sure to identify the logic behind the strategy and the crucial assumptions on which it is based. For example, as discussed in **Chapter 1.3: What is Strategy?**, part of Spanish-based Zara's business logic is that it is worth spending more on fast, local production because the savings on end-of-season mark-downs more than offset the extra costs.[8] The critical assumption is that the lower-cost, Far-Eastern supply chain will remain slower. Smart firms know what their crucial assumptions are, test them regularly and know what to do when they are no longer valid.

Develop each option in sufficient detail to make a well-informed choice between them. The level of detail is determined by the criteria used to select between the models to which we now turn. When the time comes to choose, it is often necessary to revisit the high potential options and add more detail to help facilitate the choice.

Making Strategic Choices

Individuals find tough choices hard to make, and groups find them even harder. Firms are often not very good at making big decisions.[9] The process takes much longer than necessary, too many bad choices are made and action to correct the mistakes is too slow. Smarter firms aim to make better choices faster in order to win. This is not to suggest that faster is always necessarily better; many decisions made in haste are regretted at leisure. The goal is to make informed and timely choices in an efficient and effective way.

Making good strategic choices requires clear options, clear criteria and a clear decision process.

Criteria

The criteria used to evaluate strategic choices help to define what information is required to make sure the choice is clear. Since the objective is sustainable profitability, then a measure of the net present value of the projected cash flows from a new strategic option compared to continuing on the current course is important. Cash flow forecasts are therefore required. This means estimating the size and timing of competitive advantage to indicate profitability relative to competition. While these measures are only guesses, the financial modelling forces a discipline of consistency on the whole process.

The cash flow calculations should include all the costs and risks of any structural changes required. This inevitably introduces inertia into the system and biases the firm towards continuing on its current course. Reducing the impact of this structural inertia is the subject of **Part Two: Smart Structure**.

Due to the short time horizon of stock markets, firms should evaluate the impact of each option on reported financial performance. Some economically attractive strategies involve up-front investments which create short-term reported losses. Before embarking on such a path, firms need to convince shareholders of its merits or they may find that important strategic initiatives are stalled. On numerous occasions Kmart failed to do this; it began store refurbishment and upgrade programmes, but halted when short-term profits were hit.[10]

The options a particular strategy creates are also important. Some strategies open the door to valuable new business opportunities and these must be factored into the economic assessment.

Understanding risk is crucial when evaluating options. Different levels of risk can be evaluated by using different discount rates in the NPV calculations. In addition to NPV, firms should evaluate the downside risk of each option. For example, if two options have the same NPV but one option is twice as likely to end up in bankruptcy, then this is best avoided.

There are many other criteria firms might apply to a strategic option. Does it fit with the company's vision or values? Does it help the local community? Some of these criteria may be implicit and some explicit. Individuals tend to reveal their implicit criteria during the decision process when they argue for options without clear logical support. The most common example of this is the decision on where to locate the company head-quarters. Although it is seldom mentioned explicitly, the most important driver is where the CEO wants to live. It is best to try and make all criteria explicit in order to make sound and well-informed choices.

Decision Processes

Developing clear choices and establishing criteria for evaluating them makes the decision process easier, but there must be a well-engineered decision process in place to make the final choice. Think of the management team of a company as a decision factory; how well is the factory engineered? Most production plants operate at 90% efficiency or above. This would be tough to claim for most decision factories!

Rather than approach major decisions in an ad hoc manner, firms must devise a clear decision process and always look to improve it. Who has decision rights? Who should be consulted? How should the decision be made? How should it be communicated?[11]

Decision rights are a particularly important issue. Beware the fallacy of consensus. At its best consensus is too slow; at its worst, it can lead to decision paralysis. I once had a conversation long ago with Carrie Van Loon, who was then Chairman of CSM in the Netherlands, on the issue of decision making. He remarked that in Holland decisions were made by consensus. Having known Carrie for many years, I pointed out that most of the big decisions at CSM had been made by him. With a wicked smile he replied that he allowed everyone to discuss things long enough that they reached a consensus that he should make the final choice.

The notion of democracy is also a dangerous one. It assumes that everyone is equally well informed and equally capable of making the necessary trade-offs in reaching a final decision, which is seldom the case. It is the leader's responsibility to identify everyone's point of view, test their data and reasoning and then make a decision that is in the best interests of the firm. But when the decision is ultimately made, it is particularly important to explain the logic of the choice so that everyone sees it as fair, to thank those who disagreed for their input and to ask them to support it.

Defined this way, informed autocracy is what business decision-making is all about. But this should not be confused with blind autocracy, where headstrong leaders make decisions without gathering input from those with relevant data and experience. This makes for poor decisions and weak alignment.

In designing a decision process, it helps to put in a "contingency" step that identifies what the company will do if the decision turns out to be wrong. This often makes the decision easier because it reduces the fear and uncertainty of choosing a particular path. It also weighs the downside risks of each of the choices and prepares the firm for change if the wrong choice is made.

Explicitly making the choice is also important. After a big decision meeting, I have found that it is not uncommon for half the executives to be convinced a decision went one way while the rest believe it went the other. People tend to hear what they want to hear, so they're likely to interpret an ambiguous message in their favour – often with disastrous results. To avoid this problem, the leader chairing the decision meeting should explicitly declare the decision made and go around the table to ask everyone what it means for them. This guarantees that everyone has understood both the decision and its personal implications. It also allows those who face particular challenges as a result of the decision to give expression to their fears and be thanked for their commitment to the choice.

There is some debate as to the order of the steps in a decision process. I prefer to flesh out the criteria fully before moving on to the options, since these act to remind everyone of the company's goals and help to identify what information is required in each option. However, whatever order is followed, members of the group will often want to revisit earlier conclusions. For instance, when someone realizes their option is likely to be eliminated by one of the criteria, they tend to want to revisit the criteria again. This behaviour can be quite irritating but it helps to flesh out hidden agendas and get everyone on the same page. Ultimately, if it helps to make and execute better decisions, the investment is worthwhile.

There are numerous frameworks for making decisions, often using mnemonics to help people remember the steps involved (e.g. DECIDE).[12] Whatever the framework, the principles embodied are very much the same, so wasting time on deciding how to decide makes little sense. Just pick one! The power is in establishing a common language and a clear process to follow. I have found that the most effective way to encourage executive teams to adopt a decision process is to help them to design it for themselves. I ask them to purposely design a really bad one – the "decision process from hell". This creates a lot of energy and allows everyone to declare their worst fears and most unpleasant experiences. Once this horror process is shaped, it is a simple matter of reversing it to identify the ideal.

Testing

Part of the skill of making better choices is having better information. Research and analysis is helpful, but only goes so far; there is no good substitute for a real live test, and the bigger the risk of doing something, the more it makes sense to test it first. Don't take risks, manage them!

Testing new products in the marketplace is standard practice in the fast-paced consumer goods sector. Companies try out new product ideas in a few test markets that are thought to represent the market as a whole. Capital One has taken the concept of testing to new levels in credit cards by running more than 50,000 tests a year for new credit card products. It is looking for small but important effects in large samples of data, so it runs large-scale tests with thousands of consumers.[13]

In the same way that many companies test new products, they should also test new business models. Progressive does its homework first and then tries out new models in a few regions of the USA, comparing the results with geographies where it has changed nothing to ensure their validity.[14] Best Buy, a frequent innovator in consumer electronics retailing, does the same thing in a few test stores.[15]

Testing new business models often meets with resistance, both external and internal, and this must be taken into account when setting success measures. Resistance biases results down, but over-enthusiasm can have the opposite effect. It is easy to commit too much to new ideas that are failing, especially if egos get tied up in the results. Tests require clear measures of success and failure. An independent review also helps when it comes to deciding whether to pull the plug.

Failures are inevitable. If you are right every time, you are not testing enough ideas. But managing the cost of failure is important. Fail early, fail cheap! Test the crucial assumptions on which the idea depends as early and cheaply as possible before investing too much.

Firms must be prepared to admit failure, learn from it and avoid blame games. Progressive tried homeowners insurance but stopped it when it didn't meet expectations. It also stopped its pay-as-you-go insurance, a radical new business model. In both instances, it eventually found a new business model that exploited the opportunity these concepts were designed to capture.[16]

It is also important to budget for failure. Shareholders are very critical of unpleasant surprises, and apt to punish the stocks of companies that generate them. In high technology firms, budgeting for failure is common; it is called R&D. Most of what gets developed in a lab fails but it provides learning which leads to the successes. Drug companies are expert at managing this. But in low technology businesses such as retailing, market analysts don't expect firms to have a significant R&D budget, and yet innovation is critical to long-term health. This is why Best Buy's CEO Brad Anderson was so committed to trying new concepts when times were good, because the shareholders wouldn't let him when times were bad.[17] In this respect, the markets prevent innovation at the very time when it is needed most and drive firms into extinction.

Sharing and Declaring

Once the strategic choice has been made it is time for implementation, but this is hard if no one knows what the strategy is. Some companies believe strategy is the preserve of the senior management team and that communicating it widely represents a security threat – the *secret strategy syndrome*. This might make sense in some instances – a major acquisition, for instance – but generally it is better to communicate strategic intent because this leads to better action planning and more committed execution.

Just telling people what to do robs them of esteem and encourages the bloody minded to work to a minimum; "I will do exactly what I am told and no more." Communicating the strategy and declaring the logic behind it encourages understanding and shows respect; this motivates people to act and helps them to do a better job. Soliciting feedback and listening carefully is even better. If there is a flaw in the logic, workers will almost certainly spot it and may even offer a way to design around it if they are encouraged to do so. This is the sort of behaviour that smarter firms encourage.

Strategy Execution and Change

Once the new strategy is shared and declared and support built for action, expectations are high. Implementation must begin in earnest or people will get frustrated and demotivated **waiting for change**. The goal is to build an action plan that identifies exactly what needs to be done, and to get everyone synchronized in taking action to execute it.

Old-Co, New-Co and Change-Co

Strategy implementation requires the right structure: an appropriate set of assets and a formal architecture to organize these assets to deliver the desired value. Putting this in place is a complex task by itself, but it is made all the more complex by the fact that most companies already have a whole host of legacy assets and a complex architecture in place to execute their old strategies. Let's call this Old-Co. The challenge is to change all this to meet the demands of the new strategy, to get to New-Co. In between is the gap we must cross.

Crossing the gap is no easy task. The first problem is inertia; structure is notoriously difficult to change. We address how to overcome some of the causes of structural inertia in **Part Two: Smart Structure.**

The second problem is that shutting down to make the changes is typically not an option; we have to keep the current business running. We must live in the house while it is being refurbished and put up with all the discomfort and inefficiency this creates. Moreover, our customers must not notice; they cannot be inconvenienced because they have other options.

This begs the question of who will do the refurbishment and how. Who is going to design New-Co? Who is going to build it? Renovations require specialized assets, experienced executives, clear roles and responsibilities for critical tasks, efficient processes to do the work, well trained people to execute, measurement and reward systems to track progress and motivate and information systems to hold everything together; in short, we need a strategy and a structure to cross the gap. We need Change-Co.

Making the Change

In an ideal world we might build New-Co quite separately from Old-Co and run both in parallel for a while until we are comfortable that New-Co works well enough to satisfy our customers. We would then shut down Old-Co and go live with New-Co, transferring seamlessly from the customer's point of view. We simply build a new house and knock the old one down once the new one is ready. Having taken on many house refurbishment projects in the last 30 years, I am sure, in retrospect, this would have been quicker and cheaper.

The Old-Co, New-Co parallel processing logic is often used in introducing new IT systems. General Electric uses it when transferring the location of manufacturing plants: its "pitcher–catcher" change process. The pitcher team, Old-Co, continues to run the old plant and the catcher team, New-Co, runs the new. Meanwhile a whole bunch of GE engineers and project managers design and build the new plant, installing and testing equipment, working with both the pitcher and the catcher teams to get the new plant going. They are Change-Co. The old plant is not closed down until the new plant is running at least as efficiently as the old. This works very effectively but it is dependent on both sides being motivated to make a successful transition. If the pitcher team is out of a job once the work is over, then the motivation disappears. Turkeys don't vote for Xmas! But this means GE needs slack in its organization to make the change. Once the old plant is closed, the pitcher team and the change managers must be reassigned to another task.

Muddling Through

Not all firms approach change management with the same discipline or commitment of resources. The **muddling through** technique doesn't require a well-defined New-Co design, so the gap is not clear. Instead, the top team publishes a new organization chart and managers are expected to figure everything else out for themselves. Executives take up their roles in New-Co in the vague hope that they will continue to fulfil their responsibilities in Old-Co until others have assumed them. Many balls are dropped in the process. No extra resources are added to make the change, so progress is slow. While running their new businesses and keeping an eye on the old, New-Co executives are expected to run Change-Co, making big changes to their processes, people development systems, measurement and reward systems and information systems to support the new strategy. Not surprisingly, very little changes. The result is a lengthy and painful period of change which is very visible to customers and seldom supports the new strategy well.

Outsourcing Change

Other firms add resources by **outsourcing change**, subcontracting Change-Co work to change experts for the duration of the project. The logic here is that once the change is over, everyone can get back to business-as-usual. Often, the spirit in which this is done is far from ideal. Top management want to "whip a reluctant organization into making the changes" and "provide a bit of discipline" to the approach. Good project management to cross the gap is essential, so if the company doesn't have these skills in-house, hiring outsiders makes sense. But treating reluctance in the management team with discipline may not be the cure. Of course, the problem may simply be personal inertia, but it is equally possible that managers simply don't have the time. When this is the case, more focus on the change process may divert attention from the business and undermine competitiveness. Companies must understand the root cause of the apparent inertia.

Often managers are actually punished for devoting time to change, so it is no surprise that they resist it. On average, executives spend a large percentage of their time on cross-functional change initiatives at the expense of their normal functional responsibilities. But the problem is they only get rewarded for their day jobs. By neglecting them to contribute to change programmes, they are actually being punished for change. Companies need to adjust their reward systems to motivate executives to sign up for change.

Another important reason why managers resist change is that they believe the changes are a bad idea. It is not personal inertia that is driving their behaviour but fundamental disagreement with the new direction. It may be that their views were not considered during the strategy formulation process and would have materially affected the outcome if they had been. In this instance, the company would do well to listen carefully rather than proceed. However, if their views were considered but the decision went the other way – a simple disagreement – then the managers must either sign up for the change or get out. The danger of using outsider change experts to drive the changes is that they don't understand the strategy and structure of the firm well enough to tell the difference.

Building Capacity for Change

In a fast-changing competitive environment, change is required regularly, so it makes sense to consider building in-house capability, developing a "change asset". This could include people with change skills and change processes such as GE's pitcher–catcher system. To maintain financial discipline and allocate resources effectively, the cost of maintaining this capacity must be covered by the benefits of the change programmes that draw upon them.

The change asset may be a central pool of resources in the strategy and change department or it may be distributed throughout the organization by training line executives in the skills of change. GE has its pool of six sigma black belts. Danaher, on the other hand, has developed a whole range of training programmes to support change, and experienced executives teach their colleagues in other divisions how to apply them in practical action learning programmes. This approach distributes the asset throughout the organization.

In support of these approaches, companies must make sure they measure the changes and reward the change makers. Those who are full-time change makers get rewarded for the changes they make while line managers get two sources of income: one from making changes and the other from delivering good results in their line job.

The ability to build new processes, recruit new people and develop new skills are all important elements of putting a new structure in place, but two of the most important in executing a new strategy are the measurement and reward systems. For this reason, we will pay particular attention to the **strategic scorecard** and aligning rewards.

Strategic Scorecard

Firms need good strategic metrics and milestones to test assumptions and track progress, or the company is **flying blind**. Many firms track metrics that don't make much sense strategically because they are not related to advantage. To climb to the next step, firms must create a strategic scorecard.[18]

A strategic scorecard measures the competitive advantage a firm has achieved and the drivers of that advantage. These are compared with the goals the company has set itself and the milestones on the way.

We discussed the range of metrics a company might consider in its scorecard in **Chapter 1.3: What is Strategy?** The objective is to make sure that everyone in the organization knows what they need to do to help build competitive advantage and has metrics that show they are on track and making progress.

The process of building a strategic scorecard normally begins at the top of the organization and cascades down to front line supervisors. The CEO agrees on targets with the Board of Directors and then works with the top executive team to convert these into more specific targets for each member of the team. In turn, they discuss their target with their reports and agree to more specific targets for the next level down in the hierarchy.

The goal at each level is to identify variables over which individual executives can have a material effect, estimate how much effect is required and by when and identify what they need to do to deliver this. This makes the measures more meaningful and motivational.

In firms of moderate strategic intelligence, the process is largely a matter of communication of broad objectives, checking for understanding and then development of more detailed measures for the next layer down. In firms aspiring to higher strategic intelligence, it is more of a two-way dialogue. Strategic ideas pass up through the organization, compelling changes in broader objectives at higher levels in the hierarchy.

We return to the process of changing a strategic scorecard when we discuss the inertia that formal processes create in **Chapter 2.3: Formal Architecture – Navigating the Architecture Labyrinth**.

Aligning Rewards

A strategic scorecard helps to drive behaviour that delivers strategic success; meaningful metrics motivate! They point to what is important and provide everyone in the firm with fast feedback on the contribution they are making. But while people are motivated by results, they are even more motivated by income. Peter Lewis, chief executive of Progressive Insurance, once said, "If you want to improve something, start measuring it! Then attach rewards to positive measurements, or penalties to negative ones, and you'll get results."[19]

Rewards that are not aligned with strategy can have unintended consequences with sometimes disastrous results. Energis, the number 3 UK telecommunications provider, developed a strategy to exploit its new, high-quality fibre-optic network. The goal was to capture sophisticated, high-margin customers with demanding technical needs. Such relationships take years of hard work to develop. The sales force was paid a commission on sales and found it easier to chase price-sensitive customers with commodity products to hit the revenue targets. As a result, Energis eventually went bankrupt.[20] When people are paid to do one thing and the strategy calls for them to do another, the reward system invariably wins. To make strategy happen, it is important that rewards are aligned with strategic objectives or the firm will fail to deliver.

Rigorous Revision Cycle

When all the work is done and the strategy is working well, it is too easy to relax and simply repeat past behaviour! But the competitive environment moves on, and soon the strategy is out of synch with reality. The longer the firm stays on its current path, the farther it drifts from a winning strategy, the bigger the problems get and the more difficult they become to solve. Meanwhile, the skills required to make the changes dissipate. Firms making major strategic changes every five years have largely forgotten how to do so.

It is like learning all over again with the pain and incompetence that entails. To retain and enhance their expertise, firms must revisit their strategy regularly, driving a rigorous revision cycle. This means going through the whole formulation and implementation process on a regular basis.

Revisiting work already done is not easy. The firm must first *think again*; update the data and identify what has changed; test the original logic; revisit the assumptions. This helps to keep the model in everyone's minds rather than allowing it to drift into the subconscious where it becomes tough to challenge; explicit rather than implicit; a continuing reminder of what the firm is trying to do.

Thinking again is hard work. The human brain burns a lot more energy when it is trying to solve a new problem, but once solved, it goes onto autopilot and offers the same solution, conserving energy for big surprises. The corporate brain amplifies this behaviour. It is difficult to see alternative solutions to old problems when the current solution is working well. Only a major new threat is liable to awaken it.

But firms must force themselves to rethink what they are doing on a regular basis. They should look to inject fresh viewpoints into the process and to use creativity tools and techniques to help see old problems in a new light. The goal must be to deliberately break the model that has formed in the collective mind and find new ways to put it back together.

Many firms claim to review their strategy regularly. Some schedule a strategy review annually as part of the planning cycle. But in an increasingly competitive world, is an annual thinking session enough? And do they *really* rigorously review their strategy? Many annual planning processes are devoid of any critical strategic thought. Instead, they are opportunities for managers to showcase their businesses and their management teams in lengthy presentations – death by PowerPoint – carefully excluding critical issues that might trigger awkward questions from the top. Others are glorified budgeting exercises.

IBM has long had an annual review process, but top management now meets on a monthly basis to force reflection on the strategy and ask difficult questions about what they may be missing. The top echelons attend, along with a number drawn from the senior management from around the world.[21] The invitees change periodically to provide fresh perspective and expose the next generation to the challenges involved. A monthly meeting of this kind dedicated purely to strategy is unusual, and shows the commitment of IBM's leadership. But shouldn't the top management team of every business spend 5% of its time critically reflecting on strategy?

But thinking again is not enough. The firm must *act again*, modifying the current strategy; testing new ideas; communicating the changes; modifying the metrics; updating the reward systems. Firms that wish to remain strategically competent must maintain the ability to make strategic changes; if the capacity to act declines, then Strategic IQ declines with it. The need to act regularly increases the burden on management enormously. Thinking takes less than 5% of the time; acting takes the rest. This effort discourages many firms from thinking about it in the first place. But firms must have the courage to act, adapting their strategy on a regular basis to keep their strategic change skills well honed and adjust to changes in the marketplace.

Prepared for Change

At the top level of moderate strategic competence, firms must invest in dealing with unforeseen circumstances that drive them off track. Ironically, many of these circumstances are predictable surprises[22] that could have been anticipated with contingency planning. But firms setting out to plan for such contingencies find that it is not so easy. When they start to outline the many ways real-world events might unfold, they quickly face a dizzying number of possible outcomes. In the face of such complexity, some management teams simply give up and agree to deal with eventualities as they arise. Ideally, firms need to find a middle ground, to keep the organization on edge and ready to react to change without bogging it down in overwhelming detail.

Scenario planning can be a smart way of finding that middle ground.[23] The objective is not to predict the future but to identify the largest trends and uncertainties faced by the business and construct a small number of scenarios, internally consistent pictures of future worlds, against which management teams can test their strategies. Another approach is to identify the key assumptions behind the strategy – those assumptions which, if proven wrong, would require a strategic change. These might be a technological advance, a major competitor move or the emergence of a new distribution channel. Companies must determine what they would do if the assumption didn't turn out as expected.

When he fired half his planning team and pared General Electric's planning process down to a five-page report, Jack Welch took an even simpler approach to preparing his businesses for change. He asked each to identify the biggest competitive threat they faced and set out what they would do about it.[24] Rather than focus only on threats, it also makes sense to ask "What is the biggest opportunity you face, and how can you make it more likely?"

War games and simulations are an excellent way to get management teams ready for change. The purpose of such exercises is not to prepare the team for every eventuality but to help it to learn to deal with any eventuality. Risk management exercises are a good example of this. Many consumer product companies train their senior managers to deal with events such as the poisoning of a customer or a fatal accident involving their products. Such training is also common practice in the airline industry, where the crash of a passenger jet can threaten the future of the enterprise. Pharmaceutical companies also use such exercises to help managers make the tough choices that are integral to drug development.

Challenges of Maintaining Competence

It is hard to maintain strategic competence. Circuit City once had a great strategy in the consumer electronics retailing sector but it slid into denial, incompetence and finally extinction.[25] What causes firms to back-slide in this manner?

The first danger sign is complacency. The strategy is going well; sales are growing fast and profits growing faster; it is hard to contemplate change. Companies get **fat and happy**. Complacency shows up in strategic reviews. New threats are dismissed too lightly; the old logic is not tested; assumptions are not revisited; lazy thinking prevails. And as thinking becomes less frequent, the logic is lost, the assumptions are forgotten and the firm becomes increasingly blind. Strategic thinking doesn't take much time, so guard the 5% time allowance jealously or it will be crowded out by everyday challenges.

Perpetual deferral is another warning signal. Human beings have a huge capacity to procrastinate even though we know it is bad for us. As groups we can be worse. And for companies, it is an even bigger danger because what is bad for the company may be good for the top management team. They may move on before the crisis hits and leave it for the next generation to deal with while bathing in the glory of the short-term profit boost that deferral provides.

But the biggest challenge for competent companies is the **stop–start mind-set** – treating strategy as something that is so expensive that it should only be done infrequently; short but intense periods of disruptive change, typically triggered by the appointment of a new CEO, followed by long periods of relatively mindless (from a strategic perspective) execution and tactical adjustment – the five-year planning cycle. For firms of this mind-set, the key question is *when* to change. Too early is expensive, but leaving change until too late may be fatal. Waiting for the crisis is dicing with death. Some firms recover, like IBM;[26] others, like Kmart and Circuit City, struggle for years and finally go bankrupt.

Summary

To develop moderate Strategic IQ (Figure 22) firms must learn to review their external environment with a strategic eye and identify what it takes to be a long-term winner. They must also shrewdly assess their own strategic strengths and limitations to see which opportunities they are best able to exploit. They must develop skills in building strategic options and making timely and well-informed choices, and converting these choices into a sound strategic business model that will guide their everyday actions. This must be embraced throughout the organization and translated into a programme of strategic change that drives everyone to steer the organization onto its

Figure 22: Building Moderate Strategic Intelligence

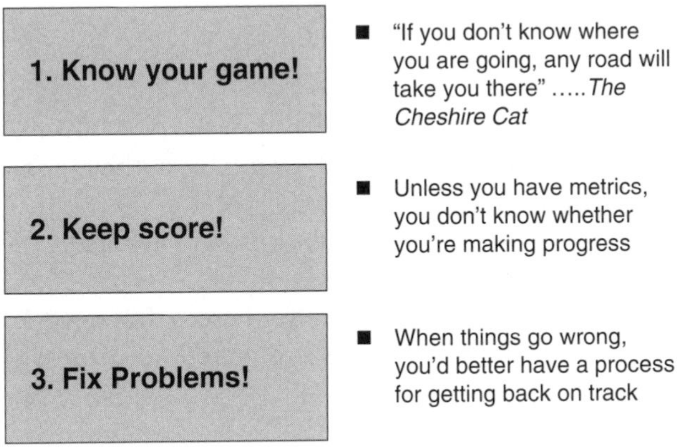

1. Know your game!	■ "If you don't know where you are going, any road will take you there" .....*The Cheshire Cat*
2. Keep score!	■ Unless you have metrics, you don't know whether you're making progress
3. Fix Problems!	■ When things go wrong, you'd better have a process for getting back on track

new path. Once on that path, to avoid flying blind, firms need a strategic scorecard that measures progress and signals the need for change. Aligning reward systems to the strategy adds further to strategic success, but to maintain capacity for change, these firms must review their strategy rigorously on a regular basis, going through the whole process again and again, refining their strategic thinking and action skills. The more they do it, the better they will get. And to reach the top end of the moderate strategic intelligence scale, they must learn to seek out predictable surprises and prepare for them, while developing the ability to deal with the unpredictable.

And who in the organization must demonstrate strategic competence? Obviously it is critical in the top management team, but every manager must be well trained in strategy and change. It is not the preserve of senior executives; it is a core part of every manager's job to ensure that they understand the firm's strategy and their part in it and how to adjust that strategy when required to do so; this is as fundamental to management as team leadership skills or project management. And companies aspiring to high Strategic IQ must ensure that those leading front-line teams think and act like strategists, executing well today while learning what changes to make tomorrow.

But strategic competence provides no guarantee of long-term success. It is too easy to become complacent and slide gently backwards down the IQ scale into incompetence, denial and blindness. Competent firms often fall into a mind-set that argues for periods of intense strategic change followed by years of executing the same model. But this begs the question of *when* to change. For strategically smart firms, this question is irrelevant – they are always changing. For them, the question is *how*. We address this in **Chapter 1.5: High Strategic Intelligence.**

Notes

1. For an up-to-date view on global trends and their implications for business, visit www.globaltrends.com.
2. See Taleb's (2007) discussion of "Black Swan" events.
3. Bazerman and Watkins (2004).
4. For a detailed discussion of the Five Forces framework to analyse industry structure, see Porter (1980) *Competitive Strategy,* Chapter 1, pp. 3–33.
5. Wells and Raabe (2006).

25

6. Fung and Magretta (1998); Fung, Fung and Wind (2008).
7. For a framework for competitor analysis, see Porter (1980) *Competitive Strategy,* Chapter 3, pp. 47–74.
8. Ghemawat and Nueno (2003).
9. Blenko, Mankins and Rogers (2010).
10. Wells and Haglock (2005) *"The Rise of Kmart".*
11. Blenko, Mankins and Rogers (2010) describe the positive impact on numerous companies of improved decision-making in their book *Decide and Deliver.*
12. DECIDE: the mnemonic is particularly easy to remember but the description of the steps stretches the English language so far that it is tough to remember what they are!
13. Wells and Anand (2008).
14. Wells, Lutova and Sender (2008).
15. Wells (2005) *"Best Buy Co., Inc."*
16. Wells, Lutova and Sender (2008).
17. Wells (2005) *"Best Buy Co., Inc."*
18. Kaplan and Norton (2000).
19. Wells, Lutova and Sender (2008).
20. Wells (2003).
21. Harreld, O'Reilly and Tushman (2007).
22. Bazerman and Watkins (2004).
23. Schwartz (1991); Van der Heijden (1996).
24. Bartlett (1999).
25. Wells (2005) *"Circuit City Store, Inc."*
26. Austin and Nolan (2000).

1.5

HIGH STRATEGIC INTELLIGENCE

Moderately smart firms recognize and solve strategic problems; really smart companies create them. They are never satisfied, always changing.

What makes us powerful as a species is not our ability to solve problems. Chimpanzees are good at that. So are crows and dolphins. Our strength is in our ability to think and communicate in the abstract, to go beyond the here-and-now and imagine alternative futures. At our best, we are innately curious, always looking to improve what we are currently doing while delighting ourselves with completely new ideas.

How do we harness this behaviour to drive strategic change? How do we deal with all the problems the behaviour creates? Where does the management capacity come from? How can we afford it? This chapter aims to answer these questions.

A Mind-Set of Change

Many senior executives see strategic change as very expensive, involving a lot of top management time, something that should only be contemplated periodically and delayed until absolutely necessary. But framing the problem in this way becomes a self-fulfilling prophecy. Delay makes the eventual change more expensive because more needs to be done. Meanwhile, resources are wasted on tactical fixes which could have been invested in charting and pursuing a new strategic direction. Expensive mistakes are made that could have been avoided with a little strategic forethought. Meanwhile, the ability of the organization to make changes is declining through lack of practice.

A firm trying to make the call on when to change is in danger of waiting too long, with fatal consequences. Once the critical point is passed where the size of change required exceeds the capacity of the firm to execute it, it is only a matter of time before the firm fails.

But in high Strategic IQ firms, the question of when to change is not relevant. They are always changing. The concept of Old-Co and New-Co no longer makes sense. There is only Change-Co.

Creating Problems – Systematically Dissatisfied

Problem creators are never satisfied, always looking for ways to improve their current strategy and build greater competitive advantage. Wal-Mart and Kmart both entered the US discount retail business in 1962, and it was Kmart that initially had a clearer model of success.[1] Within a decade, it had rolled out its stores nationwide and was 20 times bigger than Wal-Mart. But while Kmart continued with the same model, Wal-Mart was improving by leaps and bounds, continually learning from the competition and generating new ideas, often from its store employees on the front line.[2] Although Wal-Mart had got off to a slower start, it had become an innovation machine while Kmart was a blind execution machine.

Companies committed to learning are, like Wal-Mart, systematically dissatisfied. They refuse to accept an upper limit on the performance of their current business model and are forever seeking improvements. They continuously seek to raise revenue per customer by offering more value, cutting costs per customer, widening the gap between price and cost and pushing out the envelope to define new boundaries. They do not accept the notion that an improvement in quality necessarily means an increase in cost, and often push for both at the same time, using technology to help.[3]

The systematically dissatisfied are passionate benchmarkers, carefully studying the moves of their rivals. They copy what works and improve on it, while they avoid repeating mistakes. Sam Walton probably spent more time in Kmart stores than in Wal-Mart and would fly his plane over his competitor's parking lots to check out the level of traffic.[4] They appear paranoid about the competition because, in tough environments, as Intel chief executive Andy Grove famously wrote, "Only the paranoid survive."[5] They generate clear strategic metrics for measuring up to their direct competitors, and are always labouring to be at the front of the pack. But they recognize their competitors are also improving, so they set their targets based on where they expect their competitors to be tomorrow, not where they are today. They define competition broadly, looking to beat the "best in class" from other sectors. And they use internal benchmarking to promote healthy competition between operating units.[6]

The systematically dissatisfied take continuous improvement programmes such as Six Sigma[7] and Total Quality Management[8] very seriously. Danaher is a case in point.[9] One of the most successful, fast-growing conglomerates in the USA as of 2011, Danaher has delivered stock returns of 15–25% for 25 years. At the core of this success is the Danaher Business System which integrates *kaizan* (or continuous improvement) into everything the company does. Danaher is careful to recruit people that are accountable, driven to deliver results and passionate about continuous improvement in themselves, their teams and the company. It insists on rigorous strategic plans, owned by those who execute them, and converted into specific metrics that are posted on their doors for everyone to see. Every month, plans are revisited; everything from long-term strategy to short-term results is discussed and the question always asked is: "how can we improve?" It has developed a comprehensive suite of over 50 training modules for improving processes that are delivered by its own managers on the job as action learning. It is a continuous improvement machine.

Creating Problems – Creative Destruction

Breaking the Model, Self-Cannibalizing

At the same time as they push their current strategy to new limits, smart firms seek out new ways to compete before their rivals do. They find new models to serve their current markets, and new markets in which to apply their current assets. They have the courage to "destroy" themselves, cannibalizing their current business to allow the growth of new business models. Wal-Mart did this when it launched the superstore category in the 1980s.[10] Best Buy, despite being the USA leader in consumer electronics retailing in 2003, similarly redefined how it would compete and introduced its customer centricity model, driving decision-making down to the store level.[11]

Shaping the Environment to the Firm's Advantage

Problem creators don't just accept the current competitive environment – they shape it to their advantage. In 1990, Progressive, one of the USA's top four auto insurance providers, changed its successful old operating model and introduced Immediate Response, a new way of dealing with road accident claims that put adjusters on the road 24/7 to provide a better service to customers.[12] Instead of waiting weeks for an adjuster to arrive, a customer in a road accident could now expect them within minutes, and they were ready to settle claims on the spot. To deliver this kind of service Progressive had to maintain a large fleet of vehicles on the road at all times, link them to computers at head office and convince its adjusters they must now work shifts. This raised fixed costs considerably, a dangerous thing to do in a volatile world, but the cost of claims fell dramatically, more than covering the extra fixed costs. This was because Immediate Response helped reduce two of the biggest costs in the auto insurance business: fraudulent claims and lawyers. Getting to the scene fast and settling quickly eliminated a lot of unnecessary costs.

The new business model was more profitable for Progressive, but it also improved the industry structure. Major competitors copied, but the hundreds of undercapitalized new start-ups that plague the industry could not afford to do so. These new entrants have kept prices so low that the industry has made underwriting losses for about 25 of the last 30 years. But the need for major infrastructure to serve the market raised barriers to entry and improved average profitability for incumbents. Progressive had therefore shaped the industry to its advantage as well as improving its competitiveness. And Progressive did not stop with Immediate Response. It subsequently introduced innovation after strategic innovation.

JCDecaux is another example of a company that shaped the environment to its advantage.[13] Based in France, the company is one of the world's biggest outdoor advertisers. In the early days of the company, the founder Jean-Claude Decaux faced a major problem because the French authorities banned outside advertising on major roads outside cities. Since this was the core of his business, his livelihood was at stake. While passing through Paris at the time, he noticed that someone had illegally fly-posted a bus shelter. He commended the fly-posters on their efforts; an excellent place to advertise, a captive audience of high-income city dwellers waiting for a bus as well as passing vehicles. He only wished that it was legal, but then thought "why not?"

He took pictures of the bus stop and circulated thousands of copies to municipalities across France, promising to build and maintain the bus shelters in return for the exclusive advertising rights for twenty or thirty years. To reinforce his point, he built a sample bus shelter, loaded it on the back of a truck and drove it around France. At last, the mayor of Lyon agreed and the street furniture segment of the outdoor advertising market was born. This was in 1964. Despite many imitators, JCDecaux is still the world's largest outdoor furniture advertiser and is constantly innovating to stay ahead, with everything from automatic toilets in San Francisco to phone boxes in London and bicycles in Paris.

Breaking Out – Creativity

Generating new business models requires more than analytical skills. It requires breaking out of current thinking, seeing beyond the way the current organization has framed its world. As the Nobel Laureate Physiologist Albert Szent-Gyori once said, "Discovery consists of looking at the same thing as everyone else and thinking of something different." Jean-Claude Decaux is a classic example; he saw something that was illegal and wondered how to legalize it.

All human beings are innately creative, yet we are practised at suppressing our own creativity and equally prone to suppress creativity in others. When challenged, we generate plenty of ideas, but our brains are wired to compare these ideas with our past experiences and rapidly eliminate those that don't make sense to us while choosing solutions that are more familiar. Hence, before we have had a chance to reflect on our extraordinary new ideas, our brains already have rejected them. We critique the ideas of others in a similar way, sending negative signals both verbally and physically without really thinking them through.

To escape from this mental prison, we must suspend our self-judgment. Creativity tools and techniques permit us to do this,[14] increasing our creative output materially. We will discuss how in **Part Three: Smart Minds**.

The Problems with Creating Problems

The process of creating problems can itself create problems. A relentless drive for improvement can be demoralizing, almost overwhelming, for people. Firms that are never satisfied must be careful to identify short-term goals and to celebrate achieving them. The continuous striving to improve is part of human nature but it is easily overwhelmed by a sense of insecurity and fear. It is important to provide a firm and secure base for people from which to strive, and to reward them emotionally and financially for making progress along the way. The objective for a company is to live in a state of positive dissatisfaction, forever striking a balance between celebrating success and further raising the bar. We discuss this in more depth in **Part Three: Smart Minds**.

A sense of direction is also an important issue for the dissatisfied and creative. Never being satisfied and not knowing where you want to go is my definition of depression. To be positively motivated to put in all the extra work, people need to feel good about where they are headed. Likewise, generating lots of creative wild ideas is a recipe for chaos and confusion if there is no guiding hand. People must know where they are headed in the long term and it must be an attractive place to be. To deliver greater sustainability, it must also drive the firm towards increasing competitive advantage. Companies must have a **vision** that creates purpose and guides strategic choices about what to do and what not to do.

Now, how are firms aspiring to become strategically smarter going to handle the extra work that all these new problems generate? Creating more problems is dangerous if a firm has no extra capacity to deal with them; everything quickly grinds to a halt. Where does the firm find the capacity? The answer is to tap into its own people, **distributing strategic intelligence**.

And how do they afford the cost? Strategic change takes time and money. How can it be funded?

We now take a closer look at vision, distributed intelligence and funding strategic innovation.

Smart Vision

It has now become more fashionable to have a vision because it is considered motivational, but anyone who has read a few vision statements knows that they can range from pipedreams and platitudes to mind-numbing growth and profit targets. Smart firms must be more disciplined. They must be committed to a vision that forces thinking well into the future, motivates people to accept constant change and directs the firm towards greater competitiveness.

Aspirational

A smart vision is aspirational. It sets a goal far ahead of where the enterprise now stands. Daring to dream the impossible drives creativity and encourages the search for new opportunities rather than simple extensions of what the firm is currently doing. For example, Wal-Mart was always striving to beat Kmart even when it was one-tenth the size. But once it closed the gap on Kmart, Wal-Mart founder Sam Walton declared a new vision: to build a $130 billion business.[15] With such a stretch target, Wal-Mart's discount format would not be enough. It was forced to find new retail formats to grow to its current $400 billion sales level, more than ten times Kmart's sales.

Inspirational

Change is hard work, and employees have got to feel that it is all worthwhile.

An inspirational vision helps to create a sense of purpose. As human beings we need purpose to motivate us to act (see **Chapter 3.5: Harnessing Insatiable Human Needs**). A motivating vision paints a picture of the future that everyone would be happy and proud to reach. It promises that everybody in the firm will be better off, members of the winning team, but it also calls for a contribution to the greater good, to help humanity. For instance, Progressive Corporation, one of the USA's largest auto insurance companies, aims "to take the trauma out of road accidents".[16] This is much more inspiring than merely making more profits out of writing insurance policies. An inspiring vision is a licence to change, to make short-term adjustments consistent with the vision. If people understand the long-term path, the pain of change is more bearable. A sense of purpose makes it easier for employees to right themselves and move forward when they hit bumps in the road.

Grounded in Advantage

Inspirational and aspirational are not enough. A smart vision drives firms towards building greater competitive advantage and superior profitability. Firms that do not always strive to do this are leaving themselves vulnerable to attack and will eventually succumb. Progressive aims to take the trauma out of road accidents, but in profitable ways! It is always seeking to do a better job than the competition. Driving a company in any other direction is no recipe for long-term success.

Articulating a Vision

Articulating a vision is no trivial task. It cannot be done effectively by whisking top managers away for a sun-drenched visioning weekend. Top-down vision statements seldom inspire buy-in. Developing an authentic vision involves finding what is really meaningful to employees throughout the organization. What will resonate with them and drive the business forward? The role of the leader is to identify the natural resonant frequencies of the firm and select one that's also in its best long-term economic interests. Walking the floor and listening is critical, though modern information technology can help. IBM deployed online collaboration software, called Buzz, to gather feedback from several hundred thousand employees in shaping its vision.[17] Once the desired resonant frequency is identified, the objective, as with an organ pipe, is to start the organization reverberating in small ways with constant pressure until it builds up to a boom.

Capacity for Change – Distributed Intelligence

Generating a lot of new opportunities for strategic change worries some senior executives. The initial fear is that they may have to think of them, but the thought of executing them is enough to create panic. Thinking is easy; acting takes a lot more time and effort. Strategic change is very demanding of top executive time. Overcoming these fears requires breaking free of another common senior executive mind-set: the command-and-control perspective that all strategic change must be driven from the top. Smart firms distribute responsibility for strategic change throughout the organization. The role of senior management is no longer to command but to shape a context that engages everyone effectively in the strategic change agenda.

There are many arguments for involving front-line teams in developing and adapting strategy. Often, the need for change is first visible on the front line, much closer to the customers and competitors than the boardroom. Therefore it is important that front-line eyes are open to what may be a strategic problem, so that they can keep senior management informed. Also, the front line are invariably tasked with executing any changes and they are more motivated to do a better job if they understand why they are being asked to change. Finally, since it takes a lot of time for the signals of change to pass up the hierarchy and the instructions for change to come back down again, and there is ample opportunity for misunderstandings on the way, why not short circuit this process and let the front line do some of it for themselves? If authority is delegated to the front line for smaller changes, it frees top management up to deal with bigger issues. In the process, strategic intelligence is distributed throughout the organization.

Whole Foods Markets, the USA's biggest organic grocery chain, has done this in its stores.[18] One key to Whole Foods' success is offering merchandise local customers want that is highly differentiated from anything else on offer in the area. This delivers high margins but means that each store must adapt rapidly to local changes in customer needs and competitor moves. Rather than try to manage this from the centre, Whole Foods puts the power of choice into the hands of the store staff, allowing them to choose what they stock, how they display it and even, in some instances, where they buy it. Each department within a store operates as its own profit centre, running its own business. Data are widely shared to help departments to learn from each other, and members of staff visit other stores to transfer know-how that is not captured in the information system. In this way, Whole Foods shares the burden of responding to the competitive environment throughout its system. This is only possible with a very different structure than normally deployed by large supermarkets. We will return to Whole Foods when we discuss structures to support smart strategy in **Part Two: Smart Structure**.

Capital One generates and tests more than 50,000 new credit card product ideas a year – each requiring trade-offs between marketing, risk management and operations. These decisions are made not in the executive suites but by commercial teams on the front line.[19] The rules are clear on what decision rights these teams have and their actions are tracked carefully, but they are empowered to make decisions on which customer and product groups to serve. Senior management spends its time on other strategic issues. When Capital One is considering a move into auto loans or retail banking, this is made at the top. Delegating smaller strategic choices to commercial teams frees up leaders to look for bigger options and new models.

Capital One specifies most of the way new ideas must be executed, but this doesn't always need to be the case. When ideas are generated on the front line, front-line employees can be encouraged to organize themselves and design new processes to implement them. They can work out what skills they require and commit to training. They can identify metrics that make sense and suggest rewards for achieving these metrics. All of these issues are up for discussion with senior management, but most of the work is done on the front line. This is the profile of a self-adjusting, High Structural IQ firm, which we will discuss in more detail in **Part Two: Smart Structure**.

Funding Strategic Innovation

Thinking and Acting at the Same Time

All this strategic change costs a lot of money. How do firms that are always changing afford it? The first issue is they get much better at it the more they practice, so the costs come down and the effectiveness goes up.

As described in **Chapter 1.4: Moderate Strategic Intelligence**, strategic change is a complex, expensive and time-consuming process. But the good news with complex processes is that they offer lots of opportunities for reengineering. When managed effectively, the more often they are repeated, the lower the cost, the better the outcome and the faster they are achieved. Since the learning curve is steep in knowledge-intensive activities, the gains are significant.

A firm only attempting a major strategic change once every five years will always find itself at the top of the learning curve, beginning all over again. Since most executives change jobs more frequently than this every time they try their hand at strategy they are in a new position and doing it for the first time. This is designed-in incompetence.

Companies that go through the process of strategic change more frequently will invest more in early years but will soon be delivering more and better change at lower cost. As the firm gets better and faster, eventually the process becomes a continuous cycle of strategic thinking and action to the point where the two blur and the firm just manages strategically, thinking and acting at the same time.[20] The firm has then reached the highest level of strategic intelligence.

Danaher reviews its business unit strategies every month as part of its "policy deployment review". (The literal translation from the Japanese *Hoshin Kanri* – guiding light – provides more insight on what these reviews are about.) Financial results, operating performance metrics, big change initiatives and strategic objectives are all part of the same conversation. There is no separating formulation from implementation; thinking from action.

Creating an Innovation Machine

Each of Capital One's new ideas is run like an entrepreneurial business. Anyone can generate an idea, and if they think it is good enough, they seek out others to form a business team to test it. The roles and responsibilities of each member of the business team are pre-assigned. The processes they go through are specified. The people are recruited and trained with this activity in mind. And the way they are measured and rewarded drives them to seek out winning strategic directions. Capital One doesn't run a credit card business; it runs a strategic innovation machine designed to seek out more profitable credit card customers.

Much of the routine work at Capital One has been automated, but in ways that support rather than impede change. Information technology is a critical enabler of this. Just imagine the challenge a call centre operator at Capital One would face without technology support. A calling customer could be participating in any one of 50,000 tests. There is no chance of memorizing them all, and finding them in the manual would take forever. Instead, the operator is automatically presented with an on-screen script to read that has been selected to suit the customer's profile and anticipate their needs.

The role of top management at Capital One is not to generate new credit card ideas or select new, more attractive market segments, but to create the platform that encourages others to do so.

Building a strategic innovation machine is the same as creating any innovation pipeline. The first stage is the idea generator. The good news is that there is no limit to the number of ideas the members of a firm can generate when motivated to do so. If the process is opened up to outsiders,[21] then the supply expands dramatically.

But not all ideas are good ones, so everything must be passed through a first-stage filter to provide a rough test of potential. This takes resources, so it is important to invest sufficiently to deal with the idea flow. Those that get through the first stage are subjected to more rigorous tests which provide a clearer assessment of the opportunity. The most attractive are allowed through to the next stage, and to the next, depending on how many stages have been designed into the pipeline. Each stage gets more expensive, so a significant number of ideas must be weeded out at each stage. It is important not to let too many through because there is only a limited amount of resource available at each stage; backing too many ideas spreads resources too thinly, reducing the probability of success. Pharmaceutical companies are expert at this, but all smart firms need to be. Finally, those ideas that have ridden the gauntlet and appear out of the other end of the pipeline are actually launched in the marketplace (Figure 23).

Figure 23: Strategic Innovation Pipeline

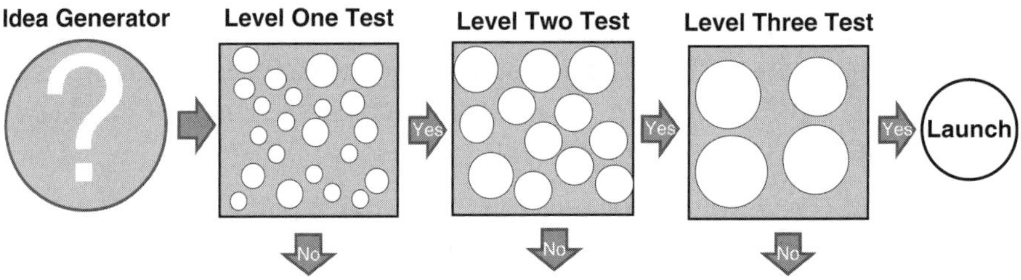

Capital One's pipeline is relatively simple. Anyone can generate an idea, and the first step in evaluating it is to bring a business team together to review it. If it passes a paper review it is tested in the marketplace. If it passes the market test it is launched. It is then retained in the market until performance drops off below a certain threshold whereupon it is withdrawn.

Self-Funding – Make Strategic Change "Free"

Funding strategic innovation is an important issue. It requires investing in lots of experiments, many of which end in failure. The goal should be for the winners to more than cover the costs of all the losers. The pipeline is then self-sustaining. This is not a foreign concept in the electronics or pharmaceutical sectors. It is called R&D. However, some firms make the mistake of funding R&D as a discretionary expense, when it is really an investment in the future. Cutting back funding today has serious consequences down the road. In retail or financial services, which invest less in new ideas, an innovation pipeline is a less familiar concept. But the principles are clear. The purpose of the strategic innovation pipeline is to identify ways of making the company more valuable and the objective is for the winners to more than cover the cost of those that didn't make it. If this discipline is followed, then strategic innovation is "free".

It is not always easy for leaders to invest in new ideas. Shareholders often view investments in creative self-destruction sceptically, especially if a firm is under profit pressure. In the face of an uncertain future, they will often vote for short-term profits rather than investments in new business models. This is why it is important to try new ideas when things are going well rather than wait until problems arise. If the firm is generating enough profits to cover the costs of strategic innovation for the future while still delighting shareholders today, then the future of the company is more secure.

Managing the Strategic Innovation Portfolio

Strategic initiatives have different risk–return profiles (Figure 24). Improving current competitive advantages normally provides returns at relatively low risk, but programmes to lower cost are more certain to provide good returns than those to increase differentiation. Firms seeking to break out and be more creative are taking on more risk, although the potential returns can be much higher. In this category, new business models to serve current customers are inherently less risky than using current assets to serve new markets, because understanding the customer is so important to business success.

Figure 24: Strategic Innovation Portfolio

Project Risk

	Low	High
High	Drivers	Delights
Low	Distractions	Disasters

Project Return

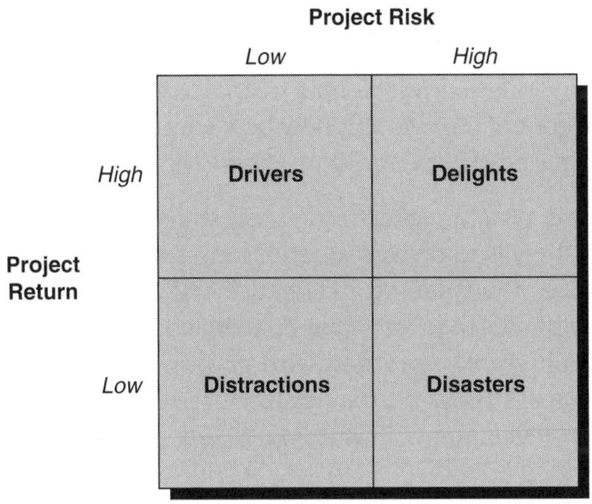

When the risks of projects are low, companies simply need to prioritize and plan when they are going to do them. Low-risk, high-return projects are key drivers of performance and help fund strategic innovation. They don't need an innovation pipeline to manage the process.

For high-risk, high-return projects, a portfolio approach is more appropriate and an innovation pipeline is useful to weed out all but the very best ideas.

Low-risk, low-return projects are often distractions. They are easy to do but a waste of resources. Firms should focus on higher return initiatives.

Finally, high-risk, low-return projects are disasters to be avoided at all times. For instance, launching new products that customers can easily copy and do more effectively makes no sense.

Driven to Strategic Success

If firms want their people to be fully committed to continuous strategic change, then they must pay for it. This means realigning rewards with each change of strategy. But this is easier said than done. Changing reward systems is a politically sensitive issue at the best of times, and so the idea of constantly changing rewards to match changing strategic objectives is quite daunting (see **Chapter 2.3: Formal Architecture**).

Smart firms look to reverse the logic. Instead of adjusting rewards to align people to the proposed strategic changes, they create rewards that drive the change in the first place.

If the reward system drives people to improve the strategy, then it is less likely to need frequent change. But how do such systems work? They reward people for increasing the net present value (NPV) of the firm.

Many reward systems tend to focus on short-term profits whereas the objective of strategy is to deliver superior long-term performance – to build NPV. NPV captures the trade-off between the short and the long term. For instance, it may be worth investing in building customer relationships today because it will be amply rewarded with good business for many years to come, but reward structures that only reward short-term sales do not encourage such investment. Rewarding based on NPV would help solve this problem.

The NPV of a firm is equal to the NPV of all current and potential future customers, so the goal must be to serve the accounts that score highest on this parameter. In this respect, it is not always the biggest customers that are the most attractive, because they are often very price sensitive and sometimes quite disloyal. Indeed, I came across a retailer recently that discovered, through its loyalty data, that its biggest customer generated a negative gross margin. Every time the store offered a loss-leader promotion, the customer would come in to stock up, but bought nothing else. Firms often find medium-sized, loyal customers are more attractive, and the question is how to serve them better to increase their NPV. If firms reward their people for improving NPV, then they will seek out more strategically attractive customers and product segments and serve them in ways that increase the value of the firm.

Allstate has designed its pricing structure to attract higher NPV customers – those that purchase more products and are more loyal.[22] Capital One also seeks out such customers.[23] The important issue here is that conventional strategy argues for making clear choices between market segments because some are more attractive than others. But attractiveness changes, so the strategy must also change. If employees are rewarded for seeking out the most strategically attractive segments, they drive the strategy in the right direction. Capital One moved rapidly away from sub-prime customers in the 2000 financial crisis to more attractive segments because of this focus on NPV. The subject of aligning rewards to strategic success is discussed further in **Chapter 2.3: Formal Architecture**.

Strategy as Learning

Smart companies are always learning from trial and error; few new business models emerge as flashes of inspiration, complete in every detail. Capital One is possibly one such example. Much of what it did was in the original business plan. But most companies start with a reasonable notion of what they are trying to achieve and they then begin looking for a suitable path, building on the idea and adapting it as they go.

Wal-Mart's original notion was that discounting branded merchandise was a better way to make money in retailing; but beyond that, in the early days, they had no idea what they were doing. They built stores in small towns, which turned out to be a good idea because the competition was low, but the original choice was made because the founder's wife didn't want to live in a large town, not because of some blinding strategic insight.[24] However, once the lesson was learnt, it became part of the business model.

Wal-Mart was also quick to build its own warehousing and distribution system. This also turned out to be a major source of advantage, but the decision was originally driven by the fact that distributors couldn't or wouldn't deliver to Wal-Mart's remote, small town locations on a reliable basis. Again, the lesson was learnt and integrated into the business model. Meanwhile, Wal-Mart watched Kmart very carefully, copying the things that worked and avoiding those that didn't, using its leading competitor as a low-cost source of research.

Wal-Mart was a purposeful learner. It wasn't a matter of "try lots of stuff and repeat what works". This is a very expensive search path. They were collecting data, looking for attractive positions in the marketplace. They were asking their customers what they wanted.[25] They were looking for ways of building on their internal strengths in warehousing and distribution. But, ultimately everything they tried was a test and they treated it as such, happy to roll out what worked and withdraw from what didn't.

Individual learning requires the ability to reflect honestly on perform-ance and seek feedback on how to improve. If we cannot admit our mistakes, then we cannot learn from them. But if the only opportunity for learning was from making mistakes, then it would be a sorry world. There are opportuni-ties to learn from every experience, whatever the outcome. In the case of successes, it is important to celebrate them, but then ask, "How could I have done even better?" For failures, the objective is to avoid repeating them.

Collective learning suffers from many of the same challenges as individ-ual learning. When companies make mistakes, instead of reflecting on the mistake honestly, they often revert to identifying a scapegoat to take the blame. But few mistakes are the result of one person's actions; there is always some degree of collective or institutional culpability. Companies must take time out and reflect on performance, good or bad, and identify how they can improve.

And yet, it is amazing how short-term tactical problems crowd out strategic thinking. I vividly recall waking up one day to realize I had spent the last six months fighting fires and not thinking strategically about the business I was running. As a confessed strategist, I found this profoundly worrying. It was then that I committed to the 5% rule: spend 5% of every day thinking strategy and the rest taking action. IBM has committed to the 5% rule.[26] Its top management team spends a day a month talking strategy. Danaher also revisits the strategy of all its businesses once a month.[27] This is expensive, but surely the most important task for leaders is to ensure that their companies are heading in the right direction? Many do not make the 5% commitment. Strategy only comes up when a major (and typically foresee-able) crisis hits or the annual planning cycle comes round. This is not enough.

In a fast-changing world, there is no option other than to learn quickly. Strategies only remain effective as long as the enemy allows them to. Reflecting to learn is the goal of After Action Reviews (AARs), practised by the US Army.[28] At all levels from the platoon up, troops conduct their AARs, addressing four basic questions: What did we set out to do? What actually happened? Why did it happen? What are we going to do next time? The troops are trained to undertake these reviews as part of gruelling battle training exercises in the Mojave Desert in California. These are massive simulations of real theatres of war. Every action is monitored on video cameras, every shot fired is tracked, so when it comes to the AAR process there is no place to hide. The goal for the troops is to learn how to learn together so that they can adapt rapidly to a fast-changing enemy in theatres such as Iraq and Afghanistan. The stakes are high; failing to learn is often fatal.

Perspectives on Leading Highly Intelligent Firms

The goal of intelligent firms is constantly to improve strategy to ensure long-term success. But if the leadership of the firm takes a short-term view, this leads to short-term behaviour at the expense of the long term.

CEO tenures have become shorter and shorter over the past two decades.[29] Firms which change their chief executive every five years should consider keeping their CEOs longer and changing faster. Firms must get out of the mind-set that a CEO's job is to develop a strategy, implement it and move on; this only leads to self-inflicted boom–bust cycles. A CEO's most important task is to build and maintain the capacity for continuous change, shaping the environment to the firm's advantage.

There is a common fallacy that bringing in outsiders and changing the CEO faster drives more change.[30] Most new CEOs start out with a bold new agenda, but they soon get worn down by the guardians of the past, especially if they don't know the organization well. The more cynical either revert to taking credit for what was happening anyway and move on, or they exploit their firm's asset base to give the appearance of progress.

It is tough to change big organizations in only a few years, so most claims of turnaround are overstated. But CEOs who stay longer have time to implement several rounds of major strategic change. They avoid playing games to boost short-term profits at the expense of long term competitiveness. They learn from their mistakes and gain a deep understanding of how to do it. *To create a smart organization, driving change is not about setting ever-changing agendas that confuse and demotivate. It is about encouraging behaviours throughout the organization that embrace strategic change and seek out ever-higher long-term performance.*

Summary

Moderate and high strategic intelligence are based upon the same foundations. Both require a clear strategy for success with metrics to measure progress. Both require the capacity to adjust strategy when things go wrong. However, superior strategic intelligence is reflected in a different attitude of mind when it comes to strategic change.

Moderately strategically intelligent companies execute their strategy until they see the need to change it. For them, the critical question is when to change. For firms of superior strategic intelligence, this question is not relevant; they are always changing. High IQ firms are never satisfied with their current model. Everyone in the organization is looking for strategic improvement. They're always looking to improve. They are driven on by lofty and inspiring goals to deliver higher performance, always seeking to improve their current model while setting aside time and resources to test radical new approaches. They generate many strategic options and develop superior decision-making processes for choosing between them. They seek to align their organizations continuously by focusing on measures correlated with strategic success and rewarding those who deliver it. And they operate on the edge, always prepared to change and learn from experience.

To move from moderate to high Strategic IQ, companies should drive their strategic review cycle harder by rigorously testing their current model to see if they can break it, identifying more opportunities for change and seeking out innovative new business models (Figure 25). At the same

Figure 25: Strategy as a Continuous Learning Process

- Strategy as a continuous process

- Driving the cycle of formulation and implementation harder and faster

- Going down the learning curve, getting better, faster, lower cost

- Merging thinking with action

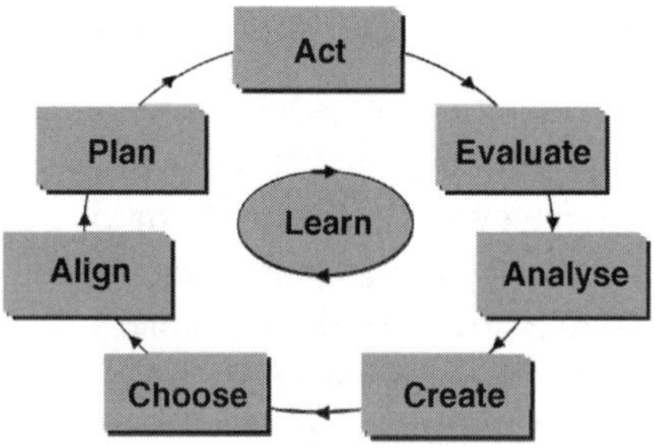

time, they should be refining their strategic change processes to take costs out and make them better, faster and smarter. Most critically, they should develop and integrate their people into the process, all the way down to the front line, to distribute strategic intelligence throughout the organization.

Notes

1. Wells and Haglock (2005) *"The Rise of Kmart"*.
2. Wells and Haglock (2006) *"The Rise of Wal-Mart"*.
3. Porter (1996) argues for an efficiency frontier at which firms must trade off differentiation and lower cost. This can be pushed out with technology.
4. Wells and Haglock (2006) *"The Rise of Wal-Mart"*.
5. Grove (1996).
6. Ghemawat and Stander (1992).
7. Pande, Neuman and Cavanagh (2000).
8. TQM explanation.
9. Anand, Collis and Hood (2008).
10. Wells and Haglock (2006) *"The Rise of Wal-Mart"*.
11. Wells (2005) *"Best Buy Co., Inc"*.
12. Wells, Lutova and Sender (2008).
13. Wells, Dessain and Stachowiak (2005).
14. Glassman (1991).
15. Ortega (1998).
16. Wells, Lutova and Sender (2008).
17. IBM CEO Samuel J. Palmisano wrote an open letter about the experience *Our Values at Work on being an IBMer*, http://www.ibm.com/ibm/values/us/, accessed October 30, 2011.
18. Wells (2005) *"Whole Foods Market, Inc."*
19. Wells and Anand (2008).
20. Paparone and Crupi (2002).
21. Chesborough (2006).
22. Wells (2008).
23. Wells and Anand (2008).
24. Wells and Haglock (2006) *"The Rise of Wal-Mart"*.
25. See Garvin's (2000) discussion of three types of organizational learning.
26. IBM 5% strategy.
27. Danaher case.

28. Wells, Hazlett and Mukhopadhyay (2006).
29. This is partially due to short-term pressures of the stock markets. The rise of shareholder activism has also contributed to shorter CEO tenures.
30. Bower (2007).

PART TWO

SMART STRUCTURE

2.1

THE NEED FOR SMART STRUCTURE

To execute a strategy effectively, a firm needs the right structure.[1] And if a firm wants to change its strategy, then it must be able to adjust its structure to match. But this is not easy. Executives commonly complain that it is not so much a shortage of new strategies that leaves them vulnerable to competitive attack, but inflexible structure. Thinking up new ideas is easy; turning them into action is much harder. Structure demonstrates a lot of inertia.

While some theorists argue that a firm must decide its strategy first and then develop a structure to support it, practitioners are more aware of the time, money and effort required to effect structural change.[2] Large organizations are enormously complex;[3] reorganizing a Fortune 500 company with a rigid legacy structure can cost many hundreds of millions of dollars and take several years. Hence, it would be foolhardy not to factor the costs and time required for structural change into any evaluation of strategic choices. In this respect, structure always drives strategy to some degree.

The Stop–Start Cycle of Change

Logically, firms should wait until it makes economic sense before they switch strategies. The time to act is when the rising economic penalty of continuing with the old strategy matches the cost of making the move. However, resistance to change is not logical. Firms often wait too long; indeed, a crisis is often required to drive action, and only then are people prepared to stop debating the alternatives and get on with it.

Waiting for a real crisis is dangerous. By then, it is often very difficult to recover. This is why many CEOs create a crisis, a burning platform, to drive major changes.[4] Once made, the firm settles down into its new routine. Large corporations repeat this pattern, normally every five years or so in synch with changes in CEO; short but intense periods of strategic change and reorganization interspersed with longer, quieter periods of execution when they ignore the changing environment, drifting slowly away from a winning strategic path.

This start-stop cycle means that the strategy-structure combination is never ideal; the firm is constantly behind and must pay a penalty for this. In slow-moving competitive environments, this may be relatively small, but the faster the rate of change, the higher the costs.

Smart Structure

The costs of each change can be reduced by reorganizing more frequently, but the idea of undertaking an annual major reorganization fills even the most fearless captains of commerce with dread.

But what if companies took a completely different approach to the problem?

What if they designed their structures to make them easier to change? This would reduce inertia and make it easier to adjust.

What if they invested in capacity to support continuous change? As long as there was a payback on these resources, this would reduce structural inertia to zero for "free".

What if the structure self-organized, changing automatically with strategy in an intelligent and self-organizing way rather than requiring the energy and undivided attention of the top management team? This would free up more time to focus on strategy.

What if the structure actually drove strategic change? We would then not only have reduced structural inertia to zero, but the structure would help reduce strategic inertia too.

Sceptics may intuitively conclude that such an intelligent structure doesn't come for free; it must require investing in significant organizational slack.[5] But the experience of strategically intelligent companies shows that a lot of intelligence can be "designed in" as long as a firm is conscious of how it might need to change. For example, as we have already highlighted, Capital One tests more than 50,000 new credit card product ideas in the marketplace each year, thousands of which are rapidly implemented. This would not be possible with a traditional, functionally organized credit card business, but it is executed with high precision by Capital One's self-organizing, team-based structure.[6]

Careful design can create very high levels of intelligent structure. Indeed, with component-based design[7] in structure and systems, the costs of making changes drop significantly. Such a shift in design thinking is analogous to the issue of quality in the 1970s, when it was argued that the additional costs of investing in quality were quickly repaid in overall system gains.[8] With the right design and mind-set, intelligent structure may be cost effective, making a continuous change model economically viable.

Part Two of *Strategic IQ* investigates the concept of smart structure. We examine what it is about organizational structures that make them difficult to change, and look for ways of making them more responsive to the competitive environment.

Smart Asset Management

To understand what causes structural inertia, we must not take too narrow a view – structure is not just an organization chart. We should look at all the structural elements that get in the way of change. One obvious limit on the ability of a firm to change is the assets in which it has invested. Once these commitments are made, most companies find it is difficult to throw everything away and start again.[9] Hence, the current asset base influences strategic choices and impedes change. In **Chapter 2.2: Smart Asset Management**, we begin by examining the wide range of assets firms invest in and the logic for such investments. We highlight the need for **nurturing** assets that are critical to long-term success. We also look at how assets can trap companies when the competitive environment changes. We identify two approaches to this problem. The first is to play **asset-lite**: don't invest in the assets in the first place, simply use someone else's. The second is to be **asset-flexible**: design in the capacity to deal with a range of possible changes the firm might face.

Formal Architecture – Navigating the Architecture Labyrinth

We now turn from assets to architecture, the way a firm's assets are organized to work together to create value. We use the term "architecture" rather than organization because the word organization often conjures up a picture of the firm's organization chart, and there is much more to organizing assets than this. Indeed, architecture is made up of a host of interrelated elements which can each create inertia. When combined, the capacity to resist change is quite formidable.

In order to reduce the size of this challenge, in **Chapter 2.3: Formal Architecture – Navigating the Architecture Labyrinth**, we review a number of the important elements of formal architecture individually. We look at how each creates value, why they suffer from inertia and how this might be overcome. Later, in **Chapter 2.5: Towards Smarter Structure**, we take a more integrated approach, but it is useful to defer this discussion until we have addressed the role of informal architecture in **Chapter 2.4: Informal Architecture – Leveraging Social Mechanics**.

In Chapter 2.3, we begin with the organization chart which maps out roles, responsibilities and reporting relationships (the three "Rs"). We discuss the logic of formal hierarchy and identify its limits. Instead of large, monolithic structures and a centralized command-and-control approach to strategic change, we argue for dividing firms into **strategic business components (SBCs)** and distributing strategic and structural intelligence to them – **object-oriented organizations**. We also investigate a logical extension of project management structures, the **opportunity-oriented organization**.

We then move on to business processes. While the three Rs focus on *who* is responsible for the work, processes describe *how* it should be done. We discuss the merits of formal processes, the inertia they can create and how to help overcome it. This requires reducing the level of process interdependencies with object-oriented organization and building appropriate capacity for process change.

Distributing more strategic and structural intelligence throughout the organization means recruiting the right people and developing the right skills. We therefore single out the processes involved in developing the human asset base for special attention, although this topic is addressed in more detail in **Part Three: Smart Minds**. Since we also want to motivate the right sort of change, we also focus on measurement and reward systems and argue that rewards must be carefully aligned with long-term strategic success.

The final elements of architecture discussed in Chapter 2.3 are information and communication systems. These tie everything else together. Indeed, effective communication is critical to coordinating the actions of many individuals in pursuit of a common goal. And it is equally important in developing the choices that drive these actions and motivating everyone to act. To be more responsive to change, firms must take care to do more than use communication systems simply to inform people of what is going on, or to issue instructions; in a world of continuous change where strategic decision making is distributed throughout the firm, communication is the learning vehicle that supports change, and executives must be trained to **communicate to learn.**[10]

We then turn to information systems. Information systems can help firms to be smarter; indeed, many of the examples of smart firms in this book rely on information systems for their superior intelligence. However, information systems can also be a formidable impediment to change. We argue that they must be **designed to be changed** with object-oriented architectures and agile programming methods.[11] And the front line must be encouraged to drive changes rather than have them imposed on them. We also caution firms which are in danger of losing control of their information architecture; never pass control of the central nervous system of a firm to outsiders.

Informal Architecture – Leveraging Social Mechanics

While changing the formal architecture is hard enough, much of what gets done in firms is through the informal architecture. How do we change something that is undocumented and largely invisible? We could, of course, ignore it, and many firms do on the grounds that it is hard to handle. But when the informal architecture works against the objectives of the firm it can undermine success, so it must be addressed. It also represents a huge opportunity if handled well because it forms without conscious effort, operates without formal support and can adapt very fast. It could be a powerful weapon for change.

Chapter 2.4: Informal Architecture – Leveraging Social Mechanics turns to neurology, evolutionary biology, anthropology and social psychology to try to understand the human behaviours that help shape informal architecture. The goal is to understand it and align it with the formal architecture to create a smarter, more adaptable structure.

Even though we believe we are in conscious control of our destiny, most of the time we are driven by our genes to behave in very predictable ways – social mechanics. These subconscious behaviours provide us with our ability to work cooperatively together, to form effective communities and network between them.[12] This makes us more powerful as a species. And we do not need formal systems or procedures to shape informal architecture because we are experts at it. We simply draw subconsciously on our genetically inherited capabilities.

Analogous to formal architecture, we form informal hierarchies, develop informal processes, recruit and mentor people, create social measures of success and find effective ways to communicate. This informal architecture can complement, substitute or even conflict with elements of formal architecture. The goal must be to use it as a complement and substitute to make the structure smarter, and to avoid energy-sapping conflicts.

But how do we go about harnessing informal architecture if we cannot consciously see it? First we must reflect on what we know is there and open our eyes to it. Then we need to decide how best to shape it to our advantage.

Let's take the example of processes. One approach is to try and document informal processes and then redesign them to be more efficient. However, making the informal formal is a challenging task, and no sooner have new processes been implemented than they are modified and improved by those executing them, making them informal once more. Instead of going through all this rigmarole, it seems to make more sense to simply motivate the informal architecture to improve itself.

But is there any way we can help, perhaps by turbo-charging the informal architecture to give it more capacity, make it more effective? Social networking technology (SNT) promises to do this, massively expanding the capacity for social exchange. In the process it promises to reshape firms, institutions and society as a whole in many ways. Firms ignore it at their peril because their employees will use it anyway. And those firms that fail to recognize its power and harness it in the service of the firm may find that their employees are using it against them.

Towards Smarter Structure

Having navigated the formal architecture labyrinth and learnt how to leverage the informal architecture, in **Chapter 2.5: Towards Smarter Structure** we reflect on the different levels of Structural IQ demonstrated by firms (Figure 26). There are those at the bottom end of the spectrum that fail to develop an internally consistent formal structure – the elements are in conflict and the structure is at war with itself. The most common problem here is expecting employees to do one thing but paying them to do the opposite. Then there are firms that have developed a consistent formal structure but unfortunately it is not aligned with the strategy. In such cases, the structure often wins, driving the strategy in quite unexpected ways.

Figure 26: Climbing the Structural IQ Ladder

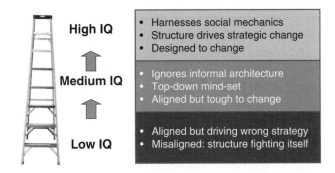

Moderately structurally intelligent firms manage to get alignment between strategy and structure, but they take a top-down approach to structural change and find it is terribly unwieldy. Smarter firms enlist their people to help, distributing structural intelligence throughout the organization. The smartest seek to fully leverage social mechanics and shape their formal organization to do so.

Finally, we pull things together, identifying the key steps in adjusting the formal architecture to drive higher Structural IQ, leveraging the informal architecture while we do so.

We argue that the place to start is with the reward systems. Firms which want rapid response to strategic change should reward everyone for strategic success. Rewards are sufficiently powerful in shaping behaviour that this will drive alignment regardless of what the formal architecture demands. If the current formal architecture gets in the way, people will just reshape the informal architecture to get the job done.

Of course, the misalignment between the resulting informal and formal processes from this approach causes waste and creates tension, so firms must motivate the front line to eliminate these problems by creating new processes more aligned to the strategic agenda. For this, they need "processes-to-improve-processes" that empower them to do so.

In a world where processes are highly interrelated, solving a problem in one part of the total system causes more problems elsewhere. To reduce these effects, we recommend reducing the level of interrelatedness by reshaping the organizations into semi-independent SBCs using object-oriented design techniques. Each component should be motivated to self-improve and adjust fast to changes in its local strategic environment.

To coordinate the efforts of SBCs, firms should look for a combination of rule-based, market and social coordinating mechanisms to keep their components aligned. When market mechanisms are used, top management's role shifts from one of command-and-control to becoming shapers and regulators of markets. When social mechanisms are used, they become social engineers.

To drive such an approach, a new breed of manager must be hired and trained to run SBCs and front-line teams strategically. They must seek out new business opportunities, make decisions that are in the best interests of the firm, lead continuous change and develop their people.

Measurement and reward systems must provide SBCs and top management with a clear view of what the SBCs must do to drive performance, and the SBCs should share in the rewards of that performance. All of this requires flexible information systems that can be shaped to the needs of individual SBCs while providing top management with a clear view of what the SBCs are doing, so that it can fulfil its fiduciary responsibilities to the shareholders.

Such a structure positions a firm to take full advantage of social mechanics. If each SBC is designed to be within the limits of social mechanics to operate, then it will naturally form into a social mechanics component (SMC). The informal and formal architecture are now mapped onto each other and fully aligned. By shaping the conditions, enforcing the rules and encouraging the behaviours that make an SMC strong, leaders can maximize the benefits of social mechanics within their SBCs.

SNT promises to make this even more effective, increasing the size of a viable SBC and increasing its geographic scope. Moreover, SNT helps to document informal exchanges, providing an audit trail that allows top management to fulfil its fiduciary responsibility to the shareholders.

And all the while, firms looking to avoid structural inertia should be looking for business models that minimize commitment to assets and make those they must commit to more flexible and more variable in cost.

Notes

1. For early discussions of the relationship between organization and environment, and strategy and structure, see Chandler (1962), Thompson (1967), Lawrence and Lorsch (1967), Galbraith (1973; 1977) and Miles and Snow (1978). For more recent work, see Nadler and Tushman (1997).
2. Anyone who doubts large organizations are hard to change should read Rossbeth Moss Kanter's discussion of the leadership challenges involved. See Kanter (1982) and Kanter, Stein and Jick (1992).
3. For an excellent collection of early theories of organizational design, see Pugh (1971). The complexity of formal architecture is well illustrated by Galbraith (1973; 1977) and Mintzberg (1979). Hall (1972) balances formal with informal architecture. Morgan (1986) describes organizations from eight very different perspectives.
4. See Kotter (1996) on leading change.
5. DeMarco (2001); Nohria and Gulati (1996).
6. Wells and Anand (2008).
7. For a discussion of the flexibility provided by component-based design of industry structure, see Baldwin and Clark (2000). Fairtlough (1994) discusses the benefits of component-based structures within the firm. Brown (2000) describes its application in large software systems. Taylor (1995; 1998) focuses on business process design.
8. Cosby (1979).
9. The persistence of strategic choices is discussed by Ghemawat (1991). The resource-based view of strategy specifically addresses the firm's assets and how they can provide competitive advantage, see Hamel and Prahalad (1989); Montgomery and Collis (1998).
10. Argyris and Schön (1978); Argyris (1990).
11. Cockburn (2002); Taylor (1995).
12. Clippinger (1999).

2.2

SMART ASSET MANAGEMENT

Introduction

Businesses buy and build assets to secure a future return, investing today to generate profits tomorrow. This raises two fundamental issues. What happens if firms don't invest sufficiently in their asset base? Even though their short-term performance may look excellent, their long-term sustainability is at risk. This is "stealing from the balance sheet". If they continue with this behaviour, they will reach a point where they can no longer afford to repair their damaged asset base and then they will fail. Companies committed to smart asset management identify the assets critical to long-term success and nurture them whatever the short-term challenges.

The second issue created by up-front investments is the risk it entails. Investments are based upon future predictions. What if these turn out to be wrong? Once the money is spent, it is often very hard to get any of it back. The company is caught in an asset trap. Economic logic, financial reporting and human emotions trap companies in different ways, but the result is the same – inertia. We discuss how firms can minimize up-front investments, playing an asset-lite game. And when the investments are truly necessary, we examine how they can make them more flexible; robust in the face of change.

The Nature of Assets

The term "asset" conjures up pictures of factories and equipment, but we use the term assets here more broadly to include both tangible and intangible assets – indeed anything a firm has rights over today, resources

Figure 27: Classes of Assets

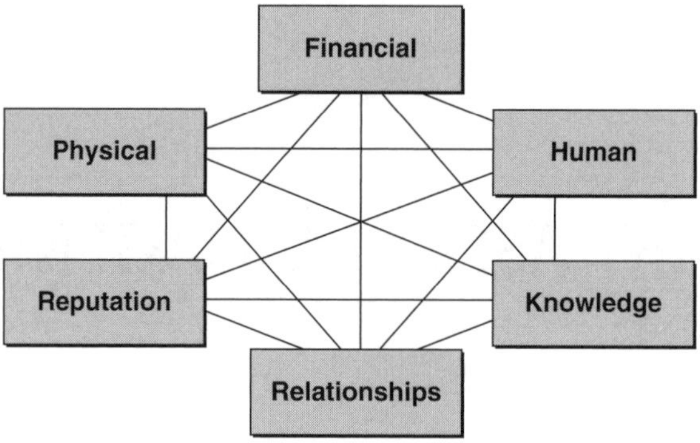

that it can draw on to create value tomorrow (Figure 27).[1] This obviously includes physical assets such as plant and equipment, but "reputation" assets such as brand are also vitally important in building and sustaining competitive advantage. Reputation for quality, integrity and being a good employer are very valuable. Financial assets include cash, working capital and debt capacity. Knowledge assets encompass patents and process know-how. And human assets, popularly described in annual reports as a firm's most important asset class, can often be so.

All these asset classes have similar economic characteristics. They involve up-front cash expenditures that promise to yield cash income in the future, and if the discounted value of the projected future cash income exceeds the up-front cash expense, then the investment is deemed worthwhile. Firms make such investments every day.

Accounting for Assets

While the economic characteristics of assets are similar, the accounting treatments differ markedly, and this can affect firm behaviour.

The cost of building intangible assets, such as brand awareness, customer relationships or intellectual property, is normally written off in the year in which the investment was made. This means that heavy investments for the future reduce current profitability. Ironically, the faster a firm expects to grow, the lower its reported profits. It also means that when profits are disappointing, there is a temptation to cut such investments to below the long-term sustainable level to improve reported returns. Even in industries such as pharmaceuticals, where continued R&D investment is critical to long-term business health, evidence suggests that the level of investment is highly correlated with short-term profits.[2] This makes no economic sense. Firms should be nurturing such assets to protect their long term health.

For tangible asset classes such as plant and equipment, the up-front expenditure is capitalized in the firm's balance sheet and depreciated over the life of the asset. The depreciation charge is designed to align the cost of the asset with the revenues it generates to provide managers and shareholders with a "fair" view of the profit generated in any given year. The original cost of the asset minus all depreciation to date appears in the balance sheet as an estimate of its remaining value.

When changes in the competitive environment reduce the future cash-generating ability of an asset, this impairment should result in a write-down of the value of the asset in the balance sheet (and vice versa). When an asset is taken out of service, the remaining value should be written off. Both actions result in a one-off charge against profits which may be substantial. Companies are often reluctant to do this because they fear shareholder reactions. They would rather conceal the change in value. Given the subjectivity of valuing assets; most accounting standards do not expect firms to make adjustments to their value unless it is material – for instance as part of a major restructuring.[3] The result is that the book value of the assets in most balance sheets has very little to do with economic reality. Firms can continue to operate undervalued assets at an accounting profit when they are really making an economic loss. This works until the assets need to be replaced and the true situation is then revealed. Equally, firms can fail to mark down asset values, creating the semblance of a future value stream that will be hard to deliver. In either case, managers are slow to react to changes in economic reality, creating inertia.

We first look at the problems created by not nurturing assets and prescribe ways to discourage such behaviour. We then move on to asset traps – investments that are rendered sub-optimal or even obsolete by changes in the competitive environment. We discuss ways of playing **asset-lite** – getting someone else to make the investments and take the risk – and **asset-flexible** – designing assets to flex to potential changes. We then apply the principles of asset nurture, asset-lite and asset-flexible to different classes of assets. Finally, we declare war on fixed costs; a stream of fixed costs represents a liability that must be funded by an uncertain stream of revenues. The more that costs can be tied closely to revenues, the better. Finally, we examine ways of turning asset traps into opportunities.

Nurturing Strategic Assets

Assets are stores of value that can also be sources of competitive advantage. For example, firms can build a manufacturing cost edge by investing in superior scale plants, the latest technology or superior know-how in operating them. When this cost edge is critical to the firm's competitive advantage, then it is important to nurture it. Simply making one up-front investment is not enough. Competitors have a nasty habit of catching up. Management must continuously upgrade the facility, strive to find new ways of operating it more efficiently and maintain it to the highest standards.

But this is not always what managers are rewarded for. The easiest way to increase plant profitability is to cut back on maintenance. If this is rewarded with bonuses and promotion, then such behaviour is encouraged. In the short run, there is no incentive to invest in the future, and if the person making the short-term decisions is not around to suffer the long-term consequences, then we have created a moral hazard − there is a huge temptation to steal from the balance sheet and overstate earnings.

Nucor's key source of competitive advantage is its ability to operate steel mini-mills more cost effectively than anyone else. It pays its people handsomely for achieving this, and every plant manager strives for greater productivity. One year, the manager of the most productive plant turned up for what he expected to be a great performance review only to find that he was fired. Top management had figured out that he was taking short-cuts with maintenance, stealing from the company's asset base and endangering long-term advantage. Not all firms are quite so disciplined in dealing with executives who deliver the right results, but not in the right way.

Firms must not allow assets that are critical to long-term success to be dissipated for the sake of short-term profits. To do so as a matter of policy is a dereliction of duty. Allowing it to happen unwittingly, or through the surreptitious actions of others, is little better. Leaders should identify their critical strategic assets, those on which they rely for long-term advantage, and put measures in place to ensure they are properly nurtured. This is not easy, especially in a downturn, but a short-term cut-back will leave a gap in the future profit stream for many years to come and may even throw away competitive advantage. The firm's asset base, on which the whole community depends, must be protected.

Trapped by Past Decisions

Economic Asset Traps

Asset traps exist because much of the expense of buying or building assets is specific to the firm, and so once the commitment is made it is a sunk cost. Second-hand factories sell for cents on the dollar, often for the value of the building and real estate; equipment is sold for scrap value and the cost of installation is lost forever. Once the investment is made, there is no going back without accepting significant penalties.

Being trapped with obsolete assets is a common problem when a new, more cost-effective technology comes along. If the costs of switching to the new technology deliver a positive net present value (NPV), then it makes sense to switch, but if the NPV is negative, then economic logic demands that the company continue to operate the less efficient assets until competitors using the new technology force it out of business. This may be fine for shareholders – they can invest in companies with the new technology – but it is not very attractive for the management or workforce and doesn't fulfil a responsibility to build sustainable returns, even though it is the economically logical thing to do. The firm is in a genuine economic asset trap.

How does a firm get out of such an economic trap? Does it give up and run the assets into the ground for the benefit of shareholders? Certainly not! The choice of what to do is management's responsibility, not the investors, so don't give them the choice of industrial *hari kari*. Simply remember that they are free to make investments wherever they like. So the only way the company can justify investing in the new technology is that it can make better returns than anyone else. If this is the case, then shareholders who want to retain a stake in the industry will stick with the firm. For the company, this means it must stay on top of the technology cycle and remain the best at exploiting technological innovation. This has clear implications for nurturing intangible, knowledge-driven assets.

A commitment to an old asset class can trap a firm into making more investments in the same class even though there are better solutions available – a case of logical incrementalism or throwing good money after bad! On an incremental basis, an extra unit of the old class is cheaper, perhaps because it can share costs with assets already purchased. For example, once an airline has made a commitment to one type of aircraft, it is hard to buy another because the cost of operating the fleet with multiple types is much higher.

How do firms avoid getting caught on the treadmill of logical incrementalism? There is no easy answer, but step back and take a look at the big picture. A series of individual decisions can often be justified on this basis, but if they had been considered together, the new asset class may well have proved the more logical path. The key in such situations is to take a long-term view, to look several steps ahead to see whether a switch to a new asset class is justified.

Financial Reporting Asset Traps

We have already touched on the effects of accounting for assets on a firm's behaviour. At the one extreme, companies are slow to divest positions they should really get out of for fear of market reaction to the write-offs. At the other extreme, management underinvests in the future because of the negative impact on short-term profits.

The fear of write-offs is mitigated by the fact that they are mostly non-cash items, and Chief Financial Officers have made an industry of reporting them "below-the-line" as "exceptional items". In fact, some financial reports feature a regular "exceptional items" section year after year. For good measure, they often include a number of cash expenses labelled as "restructuring charges" which helps to boost above-the-line profits. Hopefully, such reports trigger thoughts in some minds that these items are actually an on-going cost of doing business!

The fear of adverse shareholder reaction is a real one. Shareholders take exception to surprises, especially self-inflicted ones. Admitting mistakes can be painful for the top management team, so it is not surprising that it sometimes tries to hide them. But in today's networked world, the truth eventually comes out and any evidence of attempts to conceal it does even more damage, completely undermining trust, which is very hard to re-establish. This is the challenge News Corp faced in 2011 as a result of a phone-tapping scandal.[4] Honesty, however painful, is the best policy.

Maintaining open and frank communication with shareholders helps to avoid surprises, but many companies are loathe to reveal too much about future intentions because this means telling competitors what they are planning. Shareholders are left to take management decisions on trust, and unless the management team has built up a track record of delivering the results it has promised, this is often hard.[5] Best Buy was fortunate that it had such a record when deciding on the future of its Musicland acquisition. It acquired the 1,300-outlet retailer for $685 million in 2001 when revenues were $1.9 billion and operating profits $58 million, but performance deteriorated rapidly. By 2003, revenues had fallen to $1.7 billion and operating losses were $234 million, and Best Buy decided to get out. In June 2003, it gave Musicland away. On the news, Best Buy stock rose 5% to an all time high, representing an increase in value of $700 million. Clearly, the shareholders considered this a sound, long-term move for the company.

Underinvesting in the future in the face of a short-term profit squeeze is also a constant danger. It is not that the markets do not understand the logic of investing today for profits tomorrow. The astronomical price–earnings multiples enjoyed by fast-growth firms are testament to this. In October 2011, in markets generally depressed by political paralysis in both Europe and the USA, Amazon was trading at a price–earnings ratio of more than 100,[6] indicating just how much investors believed the company was investing in the future. However, CEO Jeff Bezos was often being criticized in the press for too much attention to long-term growth rather than profitability.

Emotional Asset Traps

Our discussion on economic and financial reporting traps was based on logical behaviour from managers, but the reality is they are human. Individuals often hate to change and collectively they can be even worse. Firms become emotionally attached to the way they do things and the thought of change triggers negative emotional reactions. We will discuss how to deal with these issues in **Part Three: Smart Minds**.

Playing Asset-Lite – Smart Fashion

One way of avoiding asset traps is to avoid investing in assets in the first place. Playing asset-lite means subcontracting as much activity as is strategically prudent to others while retaining strategically critical stages of value-added and the all-important integration within the firm. This works best when it is very difficult for the subcontractors to get together to do the work for themselves and dis-intermediate the integrator; for instance, when they can only participate in the market because of the firm's ability to integrate their work. Li & Fung is an excellent example of this.[7]

Li & Fung is a major competitor in the fashion garment sector, but few would realize it. Indeed, between 2005 and 2010, the company became the world's leading player in the sector, displacing Gap.[8] In 2010, Li & Fung supplied about $22 billion of fashion goods, up from $12 billion in 2005. Gap, once the world's leading fashion retailer, sold less than $15 billion, down from $16 billion in 2005. Inditex, owner of the popular Zara fashion chain, sold nearly $17 billion, up from $11 billion in 2005. While Inditex has clearly passed Gap, it is no match for Li & Fung.

Winning in fashion clothes retailing requires stocking only the hottest selling lines to maximize sales and avoid costly end-of-season mark-downs. Ideally, retailers need a supply chain that provides an instant refill capability rather than waiting many months for supplies. Li & Fung provides just this. Small retail chains describe broadly what they want, and Li & Fung will come up with a range of alternative designs within days and deliver the product within weeks. Few can match this response time, so retailers are prepared to pay Li & Fung a price premium for the service. This allows Li & Fung to extract some of the profit from successful fashion retailing without having to own retailers to do it.

Li & Fung does not manufacture garments itself but subcontracts to over 15,000 manufacturers in its supply system. It achieves the speed by splitting batches of product across several manufacturers so that they can produce in parallel. Everything must look as if it came from the same factory, so highly sophisticated quality control, information and logistics systems are required to achieve this. And every time a new batch is ordered, Li & Fung identifies the optimal configuration of plants, based on current costs and capacity availability to produce it – a unique pipeline. Batches ordered only weeks apart are produced by completely different manufacturers, making it virtually impossible for small retailers to go direct to the manufacturers and disintermediate Li & Fung. Moreover, because factories get 30–70% of their business from Li & Fung, they offer very competitive prices. In this way, Li & Fung shares in the manufacturing profits without owning any manufacturing. This is truly asset-lite.

As a matter of policy, Li & Fung provides each factory with a large part of its output in order to gain control over what the factory does. However, it is careful not to commit to 100% of any factory's output. This allows factories to learn from working with other customers, but there are other good reasons. Agreeing to take all of a factory's output is not much different from owning it, because you have to cover all the costs of keeping it going, even when it is idle. Allowing the factory to supply third parties increases utilization, reducing overall costs, so economic value is created by smoothing demand. And, best of all, the customer taking the lion's share of the output has huge negotiating power. If a powerful customer purchased 100% of a supplier's capacity and forced prices down below full cost, that supplier would eventually fail. But by buying 30 to 70%, a company can negotiate very low rates, below full cost, and force the supplier to charge higher prices to smaller customers which just happen to be their competitors. This is a great way of getting competitors to pay for your manufacturing.

Wal-Mart uses similarly aggressive purchasing to drive down its purchasing costs. In an interesting turn of events, in 2010, Wal-Mart hired Li & Fung to provide some of its needs. It remains to be seen whether Wal-Mart is able to turn the tables on Li & Fung.

Manufacturers are often prepared to provide their largest customers with preferential rates because they have created an asset trap of their own making. Once the plant is built, they need to fill it. Many food and beverage metal can manufacturers found this out to their detriment. They built a plant near to a customer to minimize the cost of transporting finished cans, but once the plant was built, the price pressure from the customer was more than sufficient to offset any savings. Crown Cork and Seal (CCS), on the other hand, was always careful to avoid building plants in locations where it did not have many customers to choose from. This helped CCS to generate superior profits for decades.[9]

It is remarkable how many firms fall into asset traps of this kind. Sometimes firms simply don't think ahead when they make such investments,[10] but often these predictable surprises[11] are ignored because the management team is heavily rewarded for short-term profits or fast growth. For instance, the electronics manufacturing outsourcing industry grew very rapidly in the late 1990s as firms acquired old plants from established manufacturers and agreed to operate them as an outsourcer under contract for a number of years. However, the plants were fundamentally uncompetitive, so when the contracts came up for renewal, the outsourcers were faced with restructuring them radically or even closing them. Many of the outsourcers had not allowed for this in their original investment proposals, and as a result suffered massive losses.

Some businesses would rather own their assets because they feel it gives them greater control. In cases where proprietary skills or intellectual property are involved this is quite understandable; why give away your advantage to competitors? But in many other instances, subcontracting has its benefits, especially if it is structured to provide high control without ownership. Victor Fung, chairman of Li & Fung, once warned me of the danger of confusing ownership with control. He observed that many firms own assets but have precious little control over them, whereas his goal was to own no assets but be able to exert strong control. *It is control that firms should seek rather than ownership.*

The underlying principle of asset-lite is to pass on the risks of committing to assets to third parties, making all costs as variable as possible, and use negotiating power to minimize the premium paid for such flexibility. This type of business model is very scalable since expansion costs are also borne by suppliers. For example, between 2005 and 2010, Li & Fung expanded its factory network by more than 1,000 factories a year – all without capital investment.

Playing Asset-Flexible

It is not always possible or strategically desirable for firms to depend on the assets of others. When a firm feels it necessary to invest heavily in its own assets, it is useful to build in flexibility. Samsung, the global leader in semiconductor memory chips, does this when it makes multi-billion dollar investments in silicon fabrication plants.[12] It designs the plants to produce older-generation chips as well as new, so it can continue to supply markets that others have abandoned. As the supply tightens, those customers unwilling to switch to the new generation pay a significant premium for continued supply.

Samsung also designs its chips with a common core and an easily customizable periphery that can be adapted to future customer needs. This allows Samsung to supply higher-margin speciality markets. Designed-in flexibility cannot respond to every change, but by anticipating different ways markets might evolve, Samsung exploits "predictable surprises".

Samsung also strives to get to market well ahead of competition with the next generation of chip, because prices remain high until others catch up. This also puts it first on the learning curve to bring costs down. As a result, Samsung achieves lower costs through scale and learning and superior price realization because of its flexible plant design and speed to market. This flexibility comes at a price – Samsung invests more in its plants – but the flexibility more than pays for itself in lower costs and higher price realization.

Another illustration of the financial benefits of flexible assets is the switches used in large telecommunication networks. Much of the functionality of these switches is determined by their software – hence the name "soft switches" – and this can easily be modified to meet different communication protocols and network configurations. While the costs of designing such telecom switches are higher, this must be weighed against the benefits of economies of scale in hardware production and the flexibility the switches provide to customers.

The challenge of designing in flexibility is in knowing precisely what flexibility might be needed. This requires superior market intelligence. Samsung goes to great lengths to understand what its customers are looking for in the next generation of memory chips. It also seeks to influence their views to expand the potential of its design choices. The company works not only with memory chip customers but with its customers' customers, the consumer electronics companies. Indeed, Samsung often has a more informed view of the future evolution of consumer electronics than some chip purchasers, much helped by its own consumer electronics business which is increasingly leading edge. Ultimately, though, market forecasts are no more than educated guesses. The challenge is to make more educated guesses than competitors and build in flexibility to adjust where uncertainty is at its greatest.

Working Capital Lite

The benefits of being "asset-lite" can also apply to other asset classes. Working capital is one example. Working capital is expensive to hold and to maintain, and logistics experts have expended much effort over the last 25 years to reduce working capital in supply chains. Wal-Mart[13] has long been passionate about increasing inventory turnover, managing to double it between 1975 and 2005 while its big competitors Kmart and Target hardly changed. New demand-driven business models have been developed to minimize inventory, including PC producer Dell's[14] make-to-order processes and Zara's[15] fast refill system. These make firms more responsive to changes in the marketplace.

During times of rapid growth, high working capital requirements create heavy cash demands, which can take companies by surprise. I learnt this to my cost in 2003 when I funded a friend's fruit packing business with a US$50,000 investment. The business was very successful, reaching US$5 million in sales in its first year. Margins were only 5% but working capital requirements were 25% of sales, so the business required another US$1 million in investment! Success can be very expensive.

Negative working capital is often seen as more attractive, but this has its dangers too. Negative working capital arises when customers pay in advance before a product or service is delivered, such as the auto insurance or package holiday travel businesses. It is also possible in retail businesses if the products sell so fast that the retailer gets the money from the customers before they have to pay suppliers. The faster such businesses grow, the more cash they bring in and the more tempting it is to spend it to support more growth. The ready supply of cash also attracts a lot of new entrants. But when the growth slows, the source of new cash dries up. And when sales decline, extra cash is required to keep the business going. Few investors are willing to fund a shrinking business, so the risk of bankruptcy in a downturn is high. This is why there are so many company failures in auto insurance and package holidays. It is not uncommon in the USA for rating firms to declare a significant percentage of the hundreds of competitors in property and casualty insurance financially impaired.[16]

To become working capital lite, the ideal level of working capital is zero. A business operating a zero working capital model need not be concerned by changes in the rate of growth when assessing working capital needs. The asset base is then designed to be less affected by change.

Financial Assets

A company's most liquid financial asset is cash, but firms also have a debt capacity that reflects the capital market's opinion of how much financial leverage they can support on their balance sheets. As such, unused debt capacity is a financial asset. Many businesses choose to use their debt capacity to the full; indeed, with private equity deals, the leverage some firms accept is well beyond what would be considered rational. Rather than taking a long-term view, such firms are gambling that they will be able to sell the company to new investors before a crisis hits.

Firms that have used their full debt capacity have very little flexibility to invest in change unless they are prepared to go to the capital markets for more equity, and it is precisely when firms are under pressure and need to change fast that the support from capital markets withers. My rule of thumb is that *money is typically available only when you don't need it*. Most CEOs are only too well aware of how much their flexibility to change is reduced when they are under profit pressure. Indeed in 2006, Brad Anderson, the CEO of Best Buy, claimed that he was driving the company to reinvent itself despite its market-leading strategy precisely because it was not currently under pressure to do so.[17]

If capital markets were truly efficient, it would make sense for firms to rely on them to provide sources of funds to invest. Hopefully, the global financial crisis of 2008 has finally put an end to this notion. Many well-run firms faced extinction because the capital markets dried up. But this is not a new phenomenon; there have been many financial crises, and no doubt we will see many more. Firms wishing to respond intelligently to changes in the competitive environment would be wise to reduce risk by holding financial assets in reserve. This is why Capital One diversified into retail banking; it needed the low-cost deposits to fund its credit card business rather than rely on the vagaries of the financial markets.[18]

Firms are sometimes guilty of stealing financial assets from their balance sheets to inflate short-term profits at the expense of long-term performance. CFOs have a great deal of discretion over how profit is defined, so they can hide profits in the balance sheet in good years and scrape them back out again to boost profits in bad years. This is called *earnings smoothing*. Many firms actively "manage" their earnings in this way rather than simply report them because markets discount volatile earnings.[19] In one survey, over three-quarters of the CFOs surveyed said they would sacrifice long-term value to smooth earnings.[20] Richard Fairbank, CEO of Capital One, has complained that the markets systematically undervalue the company's stock because it refuses to do this.[21]

Capital One is a passionate believer in "horizontal accounting". Everything is considered to be a project involving investments today for returns tomorrow. The company's reported financial results are simply a vertical slice of all these projects for a particular period of time, and this slice will be heavily affected by the mix and maturity of projects at that time. Some are mature, spinning off cash; others are still in investment mode. The company sees no logic in changing the rate of investment in a given period to manipulate earnings. Such adjustments simply make the firm less valuable and the markets should take this into account. Unfortunately, the markets aren't this insightful and often don't see through this earnings manipulation.[22]

Earnings smoothing raises questions of integrity, but it only starts to do really long-term damage when underlying profits are declining and the balance sheet is being scraped to create the illusion of growth. Companies often fool not only the shareholders but themselves when they misrepresent performance in this way, and fail to react to the underlying problem in a timely manner.[23] Eventually, earnings collapse and painful change is required that might have been avoided with more responsible reporting.

Human Assets

It is almost a matter of routine that leaders proclaim in annual reports that the company's employees are its most important assets. Far fewer firms actually behave as if this were true or manage their human asset base strategically. It is a rare instance that a firm can actually identify the net present value of its people or measure the payback they get from investing in them.[24] But few firms would deny that talented people can make a huge difference to performance and that training can make them much more productive.

Maintaining a healthy pipeline is an important issue for firms committed to developing and nurturing their human assets base. I once had a lunch-time conversation with a major UK industrialist on the biggest mistake we had ever made. He claimed that his was cutting back on recruiting during a major economic downturn. This created a gap in the management ranks that was still a problem 15 years later.

Despite the payback that investing in human assets can deliver, not all firms bother to do this. Some companies simply recruit people with several years of experience at a firm known for its superior selection and training, exploit them for several years until they become demoralized and then replace them with a fresh batch. This works well until potential recruits find out what the firm really offers in the long term.

Sometimes the failure to develop people is not a matter of policy but individual members of the firm taking advantage of the system. In many professional service firms, managers build a successful track record by exploiting members of their teams, forcing dull, routine work on them, working them to exhaustion and doing little to develop them. This is stealing from the company's human asset base. Others invest in training their people, providing them with challenging tasks, coaching them to help them deliver their best and leaving them more valuable at the end of a project than when they started. Firms committed to developing high quality human assets must reward such behaviour and punish those who exploit the asset base.

Investing in people has its risks. Recruiting and training employees requires significant resources, while firing the weak is slow and expensive, and retaining the strong is hard as they get cherry-picked by the competition. Moreover, workers often resist change. So human assets create traps for companies.

One way to reduce the costs of human asset management is to go asset-lite; try to minimize the headcount within the firm. Hiring subcontractors to cover peak-load requirements is one solution. Many seasonal businesses such as retailing, farming and the hospitality trade would not survive if they didn't use this asset-lite approach.

Firms should also resist headcount increases wherever possible and constantly drive for productivity in the current human asset base. In practice, there are normally huge opportunities for productivity gains, especially in the management structure. As with so many things, the 80:20 rule applies in executive work[25] – 20% of the work creates 80% of the value. Firms need to exert constant pressure to identify activities that can be eliminated. They should also press to find ways to execute valuable activities in much less time. In this respect, paying high performers to be more productive is always more attractive than adding headcount.

But some people are always required, so the goal must be to make human assets more flexible. Hiring the right people helps because some people are much more adaptable to change and curious to learn than others. Pay for performance is beneficial because it drives more output per head and makes pay more variable – costs fall in a downturn. Finally, creating an environment that makes people more open to change and learning helps to create greater intelligence throughout the firm. This is discussed in more detail in **Part Three: Smart Minds**.

Knowledge Assets

Knowledge assets are wide-ranging. The more tangible knowledge assets are the intellectual property rights bestowed by patents, but most firms have extensive proprietary knowledge that is not protected in this way. It may be knowledge of a particular production process that delivers lower costs than the competition. It may be skills in managing a logistics pipeline. It may be knowledge of the marketplace and customer needs. Some firms have better knowledge of competitors and their likely moves and countermoves. In the pharmaceutical industry, it may be experience of the regulatory process for approving drugs. All these examples constitute knowledge assets just so long as they deliver a positive net present value for the firm.

When a firm is critically dependent on knowledge assets for competitive advantage, it is important that it nurtures them. High technology firms must invest steadfastly in R&D to keep their innovation pipelines full or they face an uncertain future. And yet, there is always the temptation to invest in the good years and cut back in leaner times, as the correlation between profitability and R&D in the pharmaceutical industry attests. Treating the cost of building and maintaining strategic assets as a discretionary expense is a game of Russian roulette – it can have fatal consequences.

There are two challenges of investing in knowledge assets: deciding what the appropriate budget should be and managing the expenditure wisely. The size of the budget is always a matter of judgment, but since the objective is competitive advantage, it is worth taking a look at what the competitors are spending. Comparing budgets as a percentage of sales doesn't help much – it is absolute spend that matters, not percentages. But it is also important to look at what each dollar buys. Cisco of the USA competes in world markets for telecommunications equipment with Huawei of China. Huawei has grown impressively with relatively modest research budgets, $2.6 billion in 2010, 9% of its $29 billion in sales.[26] The same year, Cisco spent 13% of its $40 billion sales on R&D, $5.3 billion, more than twice as much Huawei in absolute terms.[27] But Huawei funded a team of 51,000 engineers at a cost of $50,000 per engineer, while Cisco employed 20,000 at a cost of $265,000. Now, these numbers may not be comparable; Cisco engineers may be five times as productive as Chinese engineers (although they were probably both taught by graduates from MIT and Stanford). Huawei's nearly 18,000 granted patents might not be as valuable as Cisco's 8,000. But it is possible that the recent stall in Cisco's growth may have something to do with competition rather than slowing customer demand!

Knowledge assets typically take a lot of time and money to build, but their value can change very quickly with shifts in the competitive environment. A patent on technology is only valuable until a better technology comes along. And developing process know-how can create traps. As firms go down the learning curve, they become very effective at what they are doing and increasingly loathe to change, because it requires going through the pain of starting all over again. The need for process change is addressed in more detail in **Chapter 2.3: Formal Architecture – Navigating the Architecture Labyrinth.**

When old knowledge becomes obsolete, the challenge is to find new knowledge. Many companies focus on building their own knowledge base and ignore third parties – the not-invented-here syndrome (NIH). There is no doubt that home-grown initiatives have advantages – they fit better into the firm's way of doing things while the ideas of others require integration and often create conflict. But self-aggrandizement is a bigger driver of NIH; idea generators within the firm must prove they have all the best ideas to justify their existence.

Smart firms must suppress NIH behaviours and seek out knowledge elsewhere, dedicating a proportion of their research and development budgets to finding out what others are up to. Nucor was a strong advocate of such an approach.[28] Though it was consistently first to market with new mini-mill steel-making technologies, it only employed one person in R&D with the role of investigating what suppliers could offer and what rivals were doing. Procter & Gamble, much lauded for its high level of innovation since 2000, achieved this by refocusing its product development efforts on outside sources, building a network of developers for new product ideas capable of delivering 50% of its ideas from the outside within five years.[29]

Relationship Assets

Relationships can be valuable assets in business and a source of competitive advantage. Loyal customers keep coming back, providing a company with a stream of future profits. They are also more likely to be forgiving when things go wrong and allow time to fix problems rather than switching to a competitor. Supplier relationships can provide preferential access to raw materials when supplies are tight, or quicker access to new technologies. But these relationships must be nurtured to maintain trust – give-and-take, a constant flow of small favours back and forth to keep them alive and well.

Relationships also have their downsides and can turn into liabilities. For many years, Allstate's exclusive agents were a big advantage in selling car insurance because they provided a cost-effective route to market.[30] However, with the advent of online sales, direct selling became an increasingly important sales channel, yet Allstate was slow to capitalize on the

Internet for fear of upsetting its existing channel. Hewlett-Packard and Compaq faced the same problem in selling computers against Dell's direct distribution model.

When building relationships, it is important to think ahead, identify where they might lead and consider whether they might create dependence and inflexibility. Many small manufacturers celebrate when they manage to get their products accepted by Wal-Mart because of the huge sales opportunity this can represent. They are less delighted when they find they are dependent on Wal-Mart for a large percentage of their sales and lose control over sales price in the marketplace.

Business relationships should be treated as joint ventures and approached with all the discipline that JVs require. They normally begin as a courtship between two parties that are attracted by the fact that they each have something the other needs. The combination creates value, and it is important that this value is explicitly measured and shared fairly. If one party begins to feel that it is being short-changed, resentment builds fast and sours the relationship. Shifts in payoffs over time may require a rebalancing of the surplus to keep the JV healthy. Finally, when it no longer makes sense to continue together, it is very useful to have clear rules of disengagement – a pre-nuptial – that determine how the relationship will end. With this sort of framework in place at the outset, ironically JVs are much more likely to last longer and be more fruitful.[31]

With forethought, the right contractual relationships with suppliers and customers can make costs more variable and reduce risk. For instance, in the aluminium industry, a large part of the cost of smelting is the cost of electricity. Since the price of aluminium is quite volatile, producers are exposed to high risk. To manage this, companies such as Alusaf in South Africa have structured contracts for electricity prices tied to the price of aluminium.[32] This passes some of the risk of smelting aluminium to electricity suppliers in periods of low metal prices but provides them with an upside when aluminium prices are high. It also means that the power generator can keep generating even when demand for aluminium is weak rather than lose a large part of its base generating load when the smelting plant has to close. Both sides benefit from the relationship.

Reputation Assets

Many aspects of a firm's reputation are assets that create shareholder value. Brands are the most obvious example. Brand loyalty creates a valuable relationship with customers that can increase size and frequency of purchase, and reduce the likelihood of switching to competitors. This translates directly into a higher customer net present value. While the value of a brand doesn't show up in historical accounts, various institutions estimate brand value. According to BrandZ's annual study of the world's top 100 brands, Apple topped the list in 2011 with a valuation of $153 billion, about half of Apple Inc.'s market capitalization. In total, BrandZ valued the top 100 brands at $2.4 trillion.[33]

While the exact figures are open to debate, few would dispute the value of strong brands. They create formidable barriers to entry. It is hard to imagine a firm introducing a new cola into the North American market to compete against Coca-Cola. Just to match Coca-Cola's annual advertising would require investments of hundreds of millions of dollars per year, and to overcome the cumulative effects would cost many billions. This is reflected in BrandZ's $74 billion value of the Coca-Cola brand in 2011.[34]

But brands are not the only type of reputation assets. For instance, reputation for integrity is crucial in forging partnerships. Reputation for aggressive competition, such as that typified by Procter & Gamble and Microsoft, can inhibit potential rivals, giving companies a freer rein to make more profits.

Building reputation assets takes a long time, requires great commitment to consistency of action and is often very costly. And yet, reputation assets can be quite fragile; it takes many years to build trust and only one momentary transgression to undermine it. Sometimes it is not the company's fault, but the way it responds is still critical to reputation. Johnson and Johnson set the gold standard nearly 30 years ago when, in 1982, someone laced its painkiller, Tylenol, with cyanide, killing a number of people in the Chicago area. Putting consumer safety first, the company withdrew the product from the shelves at a cost of over $100 million, and later relaunched it at considerable expense in a tamper-proof bottle.[35]

But sometimes the fault does lie with the company. Take, for instance, the insurance company that was advised to cut costs by delaying payments to customers. This undoubtedly helps to improve short-term profits but the long-term potential damage to the brand is huge. Supplying a product that does not live up to the brand promise is stealing from the balance sheet as well as misleading customers. Strong reputation assets must be fiercely guarded, carefully nurtured and protected in times of crisis.

Brands can be a valuable asset but they can also reduce flexibility. The Disney brand stands for family values and this limits the scope of the activities it can compete in. I found it somewhat of a surprise that the first film Michael Eisner backed shortly after taking over as CEO of Disney in 1982 was R-rated *Down and Out in Beverly Hills*. The reaction at the time was muted, but Eisner subsequently ran into a number of problems with content that some customers deemed inappropriate.[36] They also had difficulty responding to more aggressive children's fare from MTV's Nickleodeon and Warner's Cartoon Network. A strong brand is an asset, but it also creates constraints.

Firms can strengthen their reputations by partnering with highly regarded companies. Co-branding is one example. Betty Crocker uses Hershey's chocolate syrup in its brownie mix. JetBlue serves Starbucks coffee. Others look to exploit their strong brand reputation by licensing it to many markets. Virgin Group has done this in records, books, bridal wear, cars, airlines, holidays, games, cola, drinks, healthcare, flowers, spacecraft, mobile phones and energy.

Reputation can be an asset or a liability in unexpected ways. For instance, some firms invest significantly in social responsibility programmes but they avoid publicizing the fact, fearing that by drawing attention to themselves they could become more vulnerable to attack. Instead, they prefer to "fly below the radar" and play "reputation-light". Research would suggest that this is not necessarily a bad idea. The biggest polluters have less to fear from action groups than big brands because attacking high-profile brand names attracts more publicity.[37]

Declaring War on Fixed Costs

Assets provide a stream of positive cash flows into the future and, as long as the net present value of this stream is greater than the cost of the asset, it is worth the investment.

In contrast, fixed cash costs represent an on-going liability into the future that must be paid whether the cash is available or not. This is a clear risk. If revenues fall and costs remain the same, the firm is in danger of extinction. Companies should try to make all costs vary with revenues to avoid exposure in downturns. This is what aluminium producer Alusaf did by linking the price it paid for its electricity to the price it received for its metal.[38] It is often preferable to share the downside risk in return for a share of the upside potential than to bear the full downside risks alone. The electricity generator also enjoys a more stable base-load because Alusaf is less likely to shut down its smelter facilities when metal prices fall.

Turning Asset Traps into Opportunities

Firms may accumulate an extensive set of legacy assets only to find that their current strategic focus requires a new set. While it may make sense to rebuild their asset base, it is also worthwhile investigating whether other businesses might benefit from their old resources. In this respect, structure drives strategy. A brand, for instance, might be used to support different businesses (admirably demonstrated by Virgin Group); a distribution channel might be used for other product types; customer relationships expanded to add additional products and services. In this way, the risk of entering new businesses is reduced and valuable assets put to good use.

In 2011, the luxury charm bracelet producer Pandora was looking to diversify its base in this way. The company had built a strong brand and distribution system on the back of a huge surge in demand for its charm bracelets. Pandora more than doubled in size between 2008 and 2010 to become the third largest jewelry brand in the world, but the vast majority of its sales were still bracelets. This made the company vulnerable. Was the boom in sales a fashion craze or a fundamental shift in the jewelry market? The company issued profit warnings in the second half of 2011, taking much of the shine off its stock price, but it was not clear whether this was a logistics problem or a more fundamental strategic issue. Either way, Pandora was not standing idly by to find out. To diversify its risk and build on its brand reputation and distribution channels, Pandora was extending the brand name to other luxury goods categories including sunglasses and watches.[39]

Summary

To execute on a strategy effectively, firms need to invest in an appropriate set of assets. Some of these assets can provide an important source of competitive advantage and companies should make sure they nurture these to sustain long-term returns.

Assets require up-front investment in return for a stream of future cash flows. When circumstances change, this stream of cash flows may be severely impaired or even turn into a liability. But it is difficult to change the strategy once the money is spent; firms find themselves caught in asset traps. They can help to avoid this by adopting asset-lite business models that rely on third parties' assets; they can also alleviate the problem by identifying the ways in which their strategy might need to change, "predictable surprises", and investing in flexibility in their asset base in order to be prepared to change – buying real options on possible futures. Finally, they should also consider deploying their assets in different ways to exploit new business opportunities.

Notes

1. Montgomery and Collis (1998) describe many classes of assets as resources in the resource-based view of strategy.
2. Scherer (2001).
3. It is hard to calculate the net present value of the cash flows produced by an individual asset when it is used in conjunction with other assets. What share of the cash flows should be attributed to the asset in question? Financial firms are often expected to value their financial assets at market value, but since they are readily tradable, a market price is easy to estimate. Manufacturing firms only make such estimates when there is a material impairment of assets – for instance during a major restructuring.
4. "Behind the veil of ignorance; New allegations raise questions about News Corp's culture", *Financial Times*, 23 July 2011, accessed through Factiva on October 30, 2011.
5. Wells (2005).
6. Based on Amazon stock price of $234.78 on COB October 21, 2011. Source: NASDAQ.
7. For a brief description of Li & Fung, see Fung and Magretta (1998). For a complete history, see Feng (2007) and Fung, Fung and Wind (2008).
8. Wells and Raabe (2006).
9. Hammermesh, Gordan and Reed (1987).
10. Ghemawat (1991).
11. Bazerman and Watkins (2004).
12. Siegel and Chang (2005).
13. Wells and Haglock (2005); Wells and Haglock (2006).
14. Rivkin and Porter (1999).
15. Ghemawat and Nueno (2003).
16. Wells (2008); Wells, Lutova and Sender (2008).
17. See Wells (2005) for a description of Best Buy's many strategic changes.

18. Wells and Anand (2008).
19. Magrath and Weld (2002).
20. Graham, Harvey and Rajgopal (2005).
21. Wells and Anand (2008).
22. See Alexandra Fong's (2006) survey of the literature at http://eview.anu .edu.au/cross-sections/vol2/pdf/ch06.pdf. Retrieved October 31, 2011.
23. McNichols and Stubben (2008).
24. Wells and Anand (2008). Capital One measures everything, including the value of its people.
25. See Koch (1998) for an in-depth treatise on the 80:20 principle as applied to business. He also applies it more personally in Koch (2002; 2004).
26. Huawei (2011).
27. Cisco (2011).
28. Ghemawat and Stander (1992).
29. Chesborough (2006).
30. Wells (2008).
31. I make these prescriptions based on long and painful experiences trying to rectify JV relationships that had already soured.
32. Corts and Wells (2003).
33. Millward Brown Optimor (2011).
34. Millward Brown Optimor (2011).
35. These are my personal recollections of the event as reported in the press at the time.
36. Ruckstad, Collis and Levine (2001).
37. Eesley and Lenox (2005).
38. Corts and Wells (2003).
39. Whether Pandora's diversification efforts will be successful remains to be seen. Many luxury brands have added fashion accessories to their offering, including bag maker Coach and pen maker Mont Blanc, but found it difficult to build on their core offering.

2.3

FORMAL ARCHITECTURE – NAVIGATING THE ARCHITECTURE LABYRINTH

Introduction

The formal architecture of the firm consists of many interrelated elements which put the assets to work in a coordinated way.[1] We focus on a number that are critical in the strategic change process. The organization chart defines who is responsible for the work, mapping out **roles, responsibilities and reporting relationships** (the three Rs). **Business processes** describe how the work should be done. Because of the critical contribution of people to strategic success, we single out **human asset development** processes for special attention. Equally, **measurement and reward systems** play a critical role. Finally, since they hold everything else together, we highlight **communication and information systems** (Figure 28).

On its own, each of these elements of formal architecture can create inertia, but the degree of interrelatedness can make it impossible to change one element without changing many others. Indeed, large organizations can be like monolithic legacy IT systems; it is tough to make changes in one application without affecting many others. Small adjustments can explode into a complete redesign. Once undertaken, such efforts take time and effort, at considerable personal cost to managers and employees and often with little reward. It is no surprise that structure often falls out of step with strategy.

Figure 28: Elements of Formal Architecture

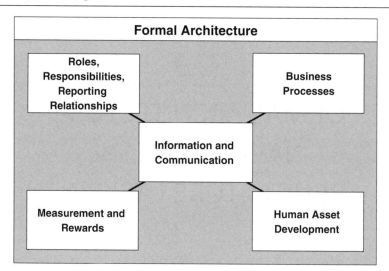

Given the linkages between the elements of formal architecture, it is difficult to decide where to start in unravelling its complexities. But we must start somewhere, so, in this chapter, we look at each of the elements in turn to understand how it creates value, why it also creates inertia and how this might be overcome. Later, in **Chapter 2.5: Towards Smarter Structure**, we take a more integrated approach but we defer this until we have discussed the role of informal social interactions in **Chapter 2.4: Informal Architecture**. Here, we begin with the three Rs.

Roles, Responsibilities and Reporting Relationships – The Three Rs

The Need for Hierarchy

The three Rs illustrate the formal hierarchy at work in the firm. Hierarchy is an efficient way of structuring the work of many people, but only up to a point. Most work in business is performed by teams, and teams operate more efficiently under a team leader. The good news is that we are genetically predisposed to operate this way; teamwork makes for a stronger species. This is why, properly motivated, teams are remarkably efficient units of operation; they are the fundamental units of value creation in businesses.

But as the size of the task grows, there is a limit to the number of people one team leader can coordinate – the span of control – and when this is reached, the work must be distributed across many teams. A manager is then needed to coordinate their activities, adding an extra layer to the hierarchy. In this way, as the size of the task grows, so does the number of layers in the hierarchy, and as each layer is added, the less efficient it becomes.

The span of control depends on the nature of the task and the experience of the people involved; the more uncertain and complex the task and the less experienced the people, the smaller the span that is possible. The smaller the span, the more layers required to organize a given number of people. Spans are typically in the 5–10 range. Some firms have a very small span and a huge number of layers. Indeed, one leading global bank I came across in 2011 found to its surprise that its average span of control was only 3.5. In this case, the low span was less to do with the nature of the task and more a result of creating opportunities for promotion. But whatever the reason for the number of layers, the more there are, the slower and less efficient the hierarchy becomes.

Adding layers means information moves more slowly and becomes more distorted as it moves up and down through the hierarchy. This reduces the quality and speed of response to change, and the top of the hierarchy loses touch with what is happening on the front line. Good information systems help, but they are only as good as the data that are input, and they only measure what they are designed to measure. To get a better view, there is no substitute for top management walking the floor and talking to customers. Danaher, one of the fastest growing and most successful conglomerates in the USA over the last 20 years, insists on top management doing this in its monthly business reviews.[2] It isn't a substitute for good information systems and fast and accurate communication channels, but it helps keep them honest and compensates for some of the problems that a multi-layer hierarchy creates.

The Limits to Hierarchy

But if hierarchy is an efficient way of organizing work, what is the optimal number of layers in a hierarchy? There seems to be a natural upper limit before problems set in. While the exact size is not clear, anyone familiar with growing a small firm through this limit is well aware of the challenges involved. In my discussions with companies making the transition, I notice common refrains. Leaders complain that they "cannot keep an eye on everyone any more" and express fears that they are "losing control". Firm members bemoan the fact that they "never see the boss any more" and "don't know everyone like they used to", and rankle at rising bureaucracy. There is generally unanimous agreement that "everything is slowing down" and "the fun has gone out of it".

The reason why small businesses appear to be so agile and effective without lots of formal bureaucracy is that they draw on the genetically inherited ability of human beings to work together cooperatively to achieve a common purpose. These social behaviours are quite predictable – social mechanics – and are programmed into our genes to make us stronger as a species.[3] And we like working together in this way – it triggers a positive emotional response that makes us happy. We will examine this informal architecture in much more detail in Chapter 2.4.

Once the group size exceeds the limit at which these skills work, more formal structures and processes are required. These are slow and expensive and can often undermine small firm profitability. It is not until the company has grown through this barrier and is big enough to capture scale economies to cover the extra costs of formal structure that profits start to improve again.

The natural size limit imposed by social mechanics is clearly of interest in business. These natural groups have been observed over millennia, and evolutionary anthropologists have estimated the upper limit on their size to be about 150 people.[4] But there is a big difference between a community performing a rich array of tasks to sustain a village and a group charged with running a steel mini-mill efficiently. Is the upper limit on group size affected by the sort of tasks involved?

Clues to the limits are visible in the language used by those experiencing the pain of going through the barrier. The hierarchy must allow the leader to be able to "see" everyone and exert a degree of informal control over them. Also, it is important that those in decision-making positions can see each other so that they can informally coordinate their work. My rule of thumb on the limit this imposes, based on personal experience and observation, is that things work well if there is **no more than one layer in the hierarchy between the leader and front-line supervisors**. This means that there is no fixed size limit; the maximum size of the group is determined by the span of control that is possible: the greater the span, the bigger the group. And the span is driven by the nature of the task. For creative, complex work where the span of control might only be 2–3, the "one-layer" rule argues for very small units of 15–40 people (one leader, 2–3 lieutenants, 4–9 front-line supervisors, 8–27 front-line workers). For example, IDEO, one of the world's leading creative agencies, has deliberately limited the size of its offices to about two dozen people to limit bureaucracy.[5] For more routine work that allows a broader span of 8–10, units of 500–1,000 people are possible. Nucor, the US's leading steel mini-mill operator, deliberately limited its manufacturing sites to 500 people to preserve its informal architecture.[6]

These size limits on natural hierarchy have important implications for designing smart structures. Firms with only a few layers of hierarchy don't need lots of formal processes and controls and they can respond really fast to change. But once the organization reaches a size where it is no longer transparent to the top what is going on, and where lieutenants and first line supervisors cannot coordinate their work informally through peer-to-peer communication, more formal structures are required which prove costly and slow. This causes problems in fast-moving environments requiring rapid response to change. Different architectures are required.

Object-Oriented Architecture

Most large firms have more than one layer between the CEO and first line supervisors. In an attempt to improve responsiveness and get the benefits of shallow hierarchy, some large firms embark on "delayering" exercises. But simply taking out layers without redesigning the work makes the hierarchy even less effective because middle managers must each now deal with much more work. As layers are removed, top management must delegate more strategic decision making to the front line, distributing the capacity for strategic response throughout the organization.

As we discussed in Chapter 1.5, delegating some strategic decision rights to front-line teams makes a lot of sense. They are often the first to see the need for strategic change, and they are typically expected to implement it, so why wait until everything has been reported up to the top and for instructions to pass down before taking action? It is surely quicker to give some decision rights to the front line. However, this requires a carefully designed structure. Some local actions must be coordinated with the centre and when local teams depend on each other, it is important that they don't get out of synch. However, if the interface with other teams is carefully defined – their inputs and outputs – then each team can make changes to improve local performance without affecting the work of others. These local changes might be externally focused like satisfying new customer needs and responding to competitors' moves, or they might be internal such as improving internal process efficiency. This is the essence of component-based design. The organization is divided into relatively independent components – called *objects* in the data processing field – such that most of the interdependencies occur within the component and the few that exist across components are well defined. This is an **object-oriented architecture**.[7]

Often, front-line teams work in close concert with other front-line teams to make strategic trade-offs – especially when functional teams are working together – so it is very difficult for them to act alone. Clustering them together to capture the major interdependencies under one management team makes sense. In this way, we can create a *strategic business component* (SBC) that runs its own business. And as long as we do not violate the "one-layer" rule we capture the benefits of low-cost, fast-response informal architecture.

As an example, we return to Whole Foods Markets (see **Chapter 1.5: High Strategic Intelligence**), the US's largest organic foods retail chain. Core to Whole Foods' smart strategy is tailoring its product offering to local customer needs and responding fast to local competition. The company has achieved this by delegating decision rights on product offering, merchandising and even some purchasing to the store level, but this requires an object-oriented structure.

Whole Foods breaks each of its stores down into departments, and each department is run by a team.[8] The teams choose what they are going to stock and how they arrange the merchandise, and are accountable for profits. But it is essential that these teams coordinate their activities to ensure store profitability. They share important resources such as the team on the cash register, shelf space, storage space, infrastructure costs, heating and lighting, so they must work closely together, but they don't need complex formal processes for dealing with this; the store manager and the department heads can sort it out amongst themselves. The store is thus a good choice for an SBC. Similarly, Nucor divides its mini-mill workforce into teams of 20–30 people, but their activity must be closely coordinated at the plant level. In this instance, the plant, seldom more than 500 people, is a good definition of an SBC.[9]

Centralization versus Decentralization – A False Dichotomy

The Whole Foods organization is, in a number of ways, a decentralized structure. In contrast, most large supermarkets make most of the merchandising decisions centrally and provide stores with planograms showing how the product range should be displayed on the shelf. The assumption is that consumer needs and purchasing behaviour do not vary much across stores. This standardized approach offers economies of scale but limits response to local consumer needs or competitor activities. Whole Foods trades off scale economies for greater responsiveness to local needs and competitor moves.

Each of the business models has its own merits. Indeed, debates often rage over whether a more centralized approach is better than a decentralized model, and many companies swing from one to another and back again. However, the competing claims for centralization versus decentralization are based on a false dichotomy. Most companies are a hybrid of both. Even in decentralized structures, there are clearly defined rules of the road and some functions remain centralized. Similarly, in centralized structures there is typically some capacity for adjusting to local needs. This is well illustrated by Li & Fung.[10]

At Li & Fung, some functions, such as finance and information technology, are very centralized. As Chairman Victor Fung often says, "there is only one way of invoicing at Li & Fung", and every line of credit must be approved by the chief financial officer. Everyone must also use the same information system. However, other functions are decentralized. Each of Li & Fung's major customers is served by a team which is free to tailor its approach to its customers' needs. The teams price to make a profit and they keep part of it. They operate as mini-businesses using the Li & Fung platform.

Historically, many firms in many industries have pursued versions of the SBC approach to increase responsiveness. In healthcare, Johnson and Johnson (J&J) created 188 separate operating companies, coordinating their activities through a process of dialogue between company heads, specialists and top management.[11] In instrumentation and electronics, Hewlett-Packard (HP) long operated many separate small divisions and split them when they exceeded 1,000 people. In engineering, Asea, Brown Boveri (ABB) limited its hierarchy to four levels, operated 5,000 profit centres of less than 50 people and kept its corporate staff to 120.[12]

The SBC approach does not simply mean wholesale delegation of responsibility for strategy and execution. Allowing SBCs to do what they like as long as they are profitable is fraught with hazards. It can lead to a lot of duplication of resources. (Many firms set up central service SBCs to try to avoid this.) It can also lead to competition between SBCs for customers or suppliers, which makes no sense for the firm as a whole. And top management also has a fiduciary responsibility to ensure that each SBC is making decisions in the best interests of the firm and executing them in a way which is consistent with the firm's values. But most important of all, not all strategic decisions are best handled on the front line.

Whole Foods store personnel decide on the local product offering, but it is the centre that decides where the next store will be. Frequently, SBCs must coordinate their efforts in the best overall interests of the firm, and it is the centre that must make sure this happens.

Coordination Across SBCs

How can companies achieve coordination across SBCs? There are three alternatives, frequently used in conjunction with each other. Top management can dictate the physical and information flows between SBCs in hierarchical, command-and-control fashion as they would normally do in a formal hierarchy. Alternatively, they can create market-based mechanisms to expose SBCs to market pressure and leave them to self-organize. In such a structure, the role of senior management changes from command-and-control to the design and regulation of efficient internal markets. SBCs are profit centres and negotiate market rates for inter-SBC transactions. Finally, they can encourage social mechanisms across SBCs to encourage coordination and facilitate change. In this model, top managers must build skills in social engineering. We will discuss this in more detail in **Chapter 2.4: Informal Architecture**.

The Death of Large Firms? Or a New Business Model?

If tasks can be broken down and executed by small teams within an internal market, then, in principle, the company doesn't have to own the components; it can outsource them as long as the outsourced components obey the internal market rules. By avoiding the commitment to invest in building components, a firm can more quickly shift between suppliers, making it more responsive to change. The firm's role shifts from ownership to integrating and managing the market. This is the model deployed by Li & Fung.

Historically, organizational hierarchies were more efficient than markets in coordinating the work of many workers.[13] The cost of contracting was too high and information availability too scarce to make self-employment an attractive option. The social contract between firms and employees was also different; people were willing to subordinate their interests to a firm and do what they were told.

Today, "information economics", the rapidly falling cost and increasing functionality enabled by information technology, particularly the Internet, is tipping the balance from hierarchies towards markets. It is now much easier to create markets of key resources and track individual performance. "Social economics" is increasingly favouring markets. People are now less willing to simply follow orders and place a greater premium on their independence. Finally, "logistics economics", the falling cost and increasing sophistication of logistics is enabling disaggregation of production, allowing the flow of products around the world to take advantage of the most cost-effective supplier for each stage of added value.

Thus we are seeing, if not a wholesale shift, then a new equilibrium point between markets and hierarchies. If firms insist on continuing to operate internally as hierarchies in circumstances that now favour markets, they may find that they are at a disadvantage to independent market operators. However, if they embrace the technology that can make markets work more efficiently internally than externally, they will flourish. Indeed, they could attract many outside players onto their platform and reach a tipping point where they are the de facto industry standard. They would then "own" the marketplace.

Opportunity-Oriented Architecture

Another architecture firms should consider in fast-moving environments is an **opportunity-oriented architecture**. Here, we move away from the notion of a fixed structure and reorganize around every new opportunity. This is an extension of project-based organizational forms in which resources are drawn from a central pool in an ad hoc way to meet the needs of each new task. This is a common structure in big project engineering businesses and professional service firms. However, the same principles have been applied to good effect in a number of ways. Perhaps the most obvious is product customization. Dell pioneered this approach in personal computers, making everything to order. Li & Fung is more unusual in that it creates a new global logistics pipeline for every batch of clothes it produces. Given the agonies some firms go through in engineering their supply chains, the idea of an ad hoc approach to supply chain management is counter-intuitive, but it has proven highly effective.[14] Capital One sets up a new business for every one of the 50,000 credit card ideas it tests each year. This is equally radical.[15] The approach these companies take is only possible because their business models have been designed from scratch to support it, and IT plays a critical role in making it happen.

A more detailed discussion of opportunity-oriented architecture is beyond the scope of this book, but for any firm that wants to toy with the idea, ask yourself the question, how would you set up a separate business for every customer you serve, every time you serve them? What extra customer value could you create by doing this, and how would you design a business model that ensured this extra value exceeded any extra costs involved?

Business Processes

The Benefits and Costs of Processes

Business processes define how the work of the organization gets done. A process consists of multiple steps, each performed by different machines or individuals with information technology in support. Well-designed processes make a firm faster, more efficient and more effective. Tasks are completed at lower cost, faster and better. And the more the process is refined and improved, the better it gets.

Business processes help us to be better at what we do, but, ironically, they can make it difficult for us to change. Part of the reason is that, as individuals, we resist being asked to do things differently. Once we have figured out how to do something, we don't want to go through the pain of learning all over again (see **Part Three: Smart Minds**). Unless it is worth our while, we are loath to do it, but we are seldom rewarded. Instead, during a process change we are normally penalized with extra workload, so it is small wonder that we don't welcome it. With business processes, the inertia is amplified by the fact that there are typically many people involved who must all change at the same time, so the resulting collective resistance is often overpowering. Unless there is a process owner who is really passionate about improvement and who has the power and resources to drive it, nothing much will happen.

Just to make it more difficult, process redesign normally requires modifications to information technology and this is a common source of structural inertia which we discuss in more detail later.

Overcoming Interrelatedness

The interrelatedness of many business processes also discourages reengineering initiatives, because changes to one process often mean that many have to be modified. The scope of the task then balloons to the point where only the fearless are prepared to attempt it. Major process reengineering exercises are much loved by consultants, but they are very expensive and highly disruptive.

However, the degree of interrelatedness depends on the type of process. Some processes are relatively **local**, where most of the steps are under the control of one manager. For example, producing a set of accounts or manufacturing a batch of products is quite local. These are easier to change because the manager "owns" the process and stands to benefit from any process improvements. **Dispersed** processes cross many functions and lines of responsibility and link with many other processes. Strategic planning and product innovation fall into this category. Dispersed processes are tougher to change and the benefits that accrue to each of the many departments involved are relatively small compared to the disruption suffered. Changing such processes requires a strong process owner with the resources and power to persuade all the departments to act.

One way of dealing with the interdependence issue is to reduce the number of dispersed processes and increase the number of local processes by adopting the object-oriented organization structure we have already discussed. Such a structure makes it easier for SBCs to improve their current processes and adapt to changes in the competitive environment without interfering with the actions of other SBCs.

Within an SBC, it also makes sense for the SBC manager to apply the same design principles to encourage front-line teams to improve themselves. This approach has been successfully followed by Nucor.[16] Each of its mini-mills is effectively run as an SBC, and the workforce at each mill is divided into small work teams that are responsible for different stages of production. The inputs and outputs of each team are specified by the nature of the manufacturing process. However, the productivity within each stage is determined by how effectively the teams work. Nucor pays team bonuses for productivity, which creates social pressure for everyone on a team to work effectively together. With such an incentive structure, the teams are always looking for ways to improve productivity, making Nucor one of the most productive steel producers in the world. The constant search for improvement also means that the teams are familiar with managing change. Indeed, they have become innovation machines. When presented with new technology to drive productivity, they quickly adapt to it and look to identify how to improve it. In this way, process improvement capacity is distributed throughout the organization without costly and lengthy bureaucratic business process reengineering exercises.

The Payback on Business Process Reengineering

The good news about business processes is that while they are hard to change, the payback on improvements can be considerable. Some sub-tasks can be refined, some automated, others eliminated and the process flow continuously rebalanced. This is Frederick Winslow Taylor's philosophy of scientific management[17] which drove industrial manufacturing efficiency gains in the early 20th century, applied now to all business processes. The rapid rise of the business process reengineering industry in the 1990s is testament to the rapid payback possible from improving complex processes, even when the environment is not changing. With discipline, this capacity can provide a payback from tactical improvements in stable times while maintaining capacity for major strategic changes when the environment demands it.

Lack of capacity for change often means firms resort to using outsiders to do the work. But delegating responsibility for improving processes to outsiders is a poor choice. In a world of continuous improvement, development is never completed, so giving control to outsiders is making them the owner. To build competitive advantage in strategically important processes such as product innovation, firms need to build strong internal owner/developers. Using outsiders for advice can help, but using a cadre of internal change agents such as GE's black belt six-sigma consultants keeps the knowledge proprietary. Danaher, one of the US's most successful conglomerates, goes one stage further. Managers with the appropriate expertise act as a faculty in helping other businesses by running on-the-job action learning programmes for them. Danaher offers more than 50 internal programmes on subjects as diverse as JIT Accounting and Lean Supply Chains.[18] Incredibly, Danaher has applied process flow techniques to the same plants many times and always managed to find dramatic improvements in productivity.[19]

Focusing Resources for Change

The low hanging fruit for developing change capacity is in SBCs. This is because they do the work; well-incentivized executives will find the greatest opportunity for boosting the productivity of their current business model. But there is another factor that makes SBCs the place to start. The earliest signs of the need for change are seen most often on the front line, so for an early response it is important to build change capacity there. Moreover, those who lead the SBCs are the natural owners of many local processes, so they have the incentive to change them and the authority to make it happen.

To support change, SBCs and front-line teams need to be trained. But it is not clear that they need complex business process reengineering tools to make changes. Much can be accomplished informally as Nucor teams demonstrate. They are always discovering new ways to beat their productivity targets, and they don't need business process mapping to do it.[20] However, "processes to improve processes" such as TQM, Six Sigma, After Action Reviews (AARs)[21] and GE's Work Out can help. Combined with an expert coach, they can be very effective as Danaher has shown.

Human Asset Development

We single out the processes involved in developing the human asset base for special attention because people are critical to good strategy execution. Moreover, for the capacity for strategic change to be distributed throughout the organization, people must be developed to take on this responsibility. Finally, when strategy changes, people must often change; the ability to hire and develop new skills and redeploy old skills in the labour market rapidly helps to improve strategic response.

In some respects, people are more flexible than other assets because we can be trained to do new things. And unlike plant and equipment, hiring people does not involve a major long-term commitment; in principle, it is relatively easy to hire and fire them. But hiring and firing people takes time, often more than it should, and incurs financial, emotional and social costs that cannot be ignored. Nevertheless, firms must confront the fact that if they want to adapt fast, they will always be hiring and firing people.

Becoming a Preferred Employer

Instead of seeing hiring and firing people as one-off events and behaving as if their people are lifetime employees, firms would do well to change their mind-set. Most new recruits leave within five years; indeed, the business models of many professional service firms depend on it. In such circumstances, firms should see themselves not as lifetime employers but providers of major value-adding steps in the careers of those who choose to join. New recruits get excellent training, great work experience and a brand name that opens doors to many other job opportunities when it comes time for them to leave. The company attracts the best talent, extracts a lot of value out of them for several years and then encourages all but the very best to move on, helping them to do so. The few that remain, having passed the test, move up to the ranks of senior management. With this process, the emotional and social guilt of parting is avoided as well as the economic costs of termination, and new talent is attracted to take advantage of the career advantages on offer.

McKinsey & Company, the world's leading strategy consulting firm, follows this practice. New recruits joining McKinsey all hope to become partners but the business model doesn't allow for it. Most of them leave to take up management positions that they would not so quickly have achieved without their work experience at McKinsey. Moreover, many of these alumni become valuable sources of consulting assignments for their old alma-mater, so the net present value of a new recruit to McKinsey throughout their careers is very high. This is how McKinsey can afford to hire the best and give them the best training.

Training in Strategy and Change

In smart firms, everyone plays a part in responding to strategic change. Training in strategy and change is therefore essential. The most effective way of doing this is through an action learning process – being coached to develop a strategy and execute a change programme while actually doing it. Since high Strategic IQ firms are constantly reviewing their strategies, the opportunities for doing this are on-going; indeed, it is part of daily management. Danaher's approach to business reviews encourages this. The strategic plan is linked to long-, medium- and short-term goals and progress against these goals is measured on a monthly basis, always linking it back to the strategy. Moreover, the measures are cascaded all the way down to the front line and everyone has their performance metrics posted on their doors. Everyone is accountable for delivering strategic success in a very visible way.[22]

Human Inertia

Still, individuals and groups can be notoriously reluctant to change. People resist even minor disruptions, and passionate beliefs can last for centuries, well beyond the lifespan of most firms. **Part Three: Smart Minds** addresses these issues in detail. For now, we summarize by saying that firms should focus on two responses: they should seek out curious individuals with high practical intelligence – the right blend of analytical, creative, social and emotional IQ combined with the curiosity and courage to learn and the desire to help others to do so; and they should create a context within the firm that motivates everyone to demonstrate high practical intelligence and embrace change.

Measurement Systems – The Strategic Scorecard

What we measure drives behaviour; it signals what is important and motivates the curious and committed throughout the organization to improve. To align everyone in the organization around a strategy, firms need a strategic scorecard – meaningful metrics at all levels that drive behaviours correlated with strategic success.[23] We discussed the measures we might expect on a strategic scorecard in **Chapter 1.3: What is Strategy?** Here we focus on the development process.

Developing a strategic scorecard requires passing strategic objectives down through the organization in ever-greater detail. The CEO agrees on broad strategic objectives with the board, and expands on them as they are passed down to direct reports. The direct reports follow the same process with their teams and the process is repeated until the front line is reached.

The way in which this cascade process is executed is critical to the level of strategic and Structural IQ that results. At one extreme, the *command-and-control approach*, team leaders merely tell subordinates what they must achieve. This is fast but it does not build commitment or understanding, and it creates an organization that responds slowly to change. Everything will depend on the leader spotting the need for change and issuing fresh instructions. Intelligence is not distributed throughout the organization.

At the other end of the spectrum, the *participative approach*, the team leader lays out what commitments have been made at the next level up, relates these to the overall objectives of the firm and explains the reasoning behind them. The leader then asks team members what the team's objectives mean for them as individuals. This ensures they understand the logic of what needs to be done and can relate it to the overall purpose of the firm. With this understanding, they are in a better position to identify meaningful metrics for themselves and for their teams and adjust them later if necessary while remaining consistent with the overall strategic goals. This builds in accountability and commitment to the metrics and more adaptability when things need to change. The participative approach takes longer but results in a smarter organization that, ironically, can change faster when it becomes necessary.

Too often, in developing a scorecard, firms follow the command-and-control approach and are disappointed with the results. They also fall into another trap – *metric proliferation*. In one company I discovered that some front-line supervisors had as many as 70 measures on their scorecard. This is probably ten times too many to get real focus. A few measures to ensure that the current business is operating properly (Business-as-Usual) and a few for making big changes (Make-a-Difference) is quite enough.

Reward Systems

Pay for Strategic Performance

What we measure drives behaviour, but pay-for-performance drives it much harder. As a species, we act to accumulate resources, and we are prepared to work hard to do so. Since smart structure aligns individual and group behaviour with the company's strategic objectives, rewards are a critical element of every firm's structure.

Rewards do not always drive satisfaction. In fact, they can be the source of much dissatisfaction, particularly when individuals are asked to do one thing and rewarded for doing the opposite. This is more common in the business world than one might expect. In a battle between a reward system that encourages one thing and a strategic imperative that requires another, the reward system will invariably win.

We saw this in **Chapter 1.3: What is Strategy?** with Energis, the UK's third largest telecommunications services provider. Its stated strategy was to provide high-margin, sophisticated services to large customers with complex telecommunications needs. But building relationships with such customers took many years, and it was easier for the sales force to sell high-volume, low-margin commodity services to hit their sales targets. And since they were commissioned on sales revenues rather than contribution margin, they were happy to do so. Top management did not intervene, and because the rapid sales growth was driving up the stock price and the value of their options, they had little incentive to do so. As a result, the enterprise drifted badly from its strategy and went bankrupt.[24]

Firms must take care to pay for behaviours that drive strategic success, but this is not easy. Pay-for-performance systems are fraught with unintended consequences. Firms can try to guess how employees will react to different incentive structures, but it makes more sense to ask them. It does no harm to share the firm's strategic objectives, discuss how they can best contribute to these objectives and ask them what sort of pay structure would encourage them to maximize their contribution.

Pay to Drive Strategic Change

If designing reward systems is difficult, changing them is a nightmare. Indeed, it is often the most politically charged process in structural change. No employee is going to support a reduction in their compensation, and everyone watches closely to ensure that they don't lose out relative to their peers. The tiniest details are scrutinized, exaggerated and criticized by everyone involved. Unless there are raises across the board, it is a time-consuming, gut-wrenching and emotional process for all involved.

Instead of changing reward systems every time the strategy changes, it makes more sense to turn the logic on its head and pay for strategic change. Capital One[25] and 24 Hour Fitness[26] have consistently out-performed their peers using this technique. A smart strategy delivers superior sustainable performance, not a quick financial hit, and these firms focus on the net present value (NPV) of future cash flows of the firm, not short-term profits. If everyone is paid for driving NPV, they will be constantly looking out for new ways of creating long-term value, and are less likely to trade long-term profits for short-term gains. The NPV of a company is the sum of the NPV of each of its current customers and potential future customers. Firms which focus their employees on building valuable relationships with current customers and seeking out more valuable relationships are not playing a traditional market segmentation game. They are encouraging their people to adjust the firm's strategy as circumstances change, adapting product lines and customer segments' focus to changing circumstances.

Credit card provider Capital One pays employees to seek out high net present value customers, and it runs 50,000 market tests a year to find them. At the earliest indication that the attractiveness of a market segment is on the decline, the company automatically moves on to more attractive areas as a result of the collective effort of its thousands of employees all looking for new opportunities. This has helped support industry-best returns over the wild swings of the economic cycle.

Health Club owner 24 Hour Fitness rewards its club managers each month for customer retention rate. They are paid for each customer who does not drop their membership. Retention is another measure closely related to customer net present value. As a result, local club owners are constantly adjusting their local strategies to retain customers. 24 Hour Fitness has now surpassed Bally Total Fitness as the leading health club operator in the USA, and Bally has collapsed.[27]

Communication

Communicating to Learn

Information and communications systems hold all the elements of formal architecture together. Given their ad hoc nature, communication systems are particularly important in supporting strategic change.

To coordinate the work of many people, communication is essential. In a command-and-control structure, instructions must be issued and feedback obtained to assess the impact the instructions have had. The purpose of communication in these instances is to coordinate and control a strategy that has already been decided.

In smart firms, the strategy is constantly changing and strategic decision rights are distributed throughout the firm. This creates a constant flow of insights and ideas from SBC to SBC and between SBCs and top management, so communication becomes even more important. But now the communication is two-way rather than one-way, and the objective is as much to learn as to inform. In such an environment, managers **communicate to learn**.[28] They balance advocacy with enquiry; everyone states their opinion and explains the logic and reasoning behind it and encourages others to test it. Learning occurs on both sides and the structure becomes more and more intelligent.

Communicating to Inspire

Persuasive communication motivates people and aligns them around a common purpose. With a shared purpose, human beings act with a sense of mission and work cooperatively together to achieve goals. They deliver more output over a longer period of time and feel better for it. They are also willing to adapt and make changes in the short run if they believe that it is in the long-term good. If they lack purpose, people quickly become dispirited, unproductive and even dysfunctional. A sense of purpose is a facilitator of alignment and change. We will discuss this in more detail in **Chapter 3.5: Harnessing Insatiable Human Needs**.

Communication helps establish a sense of common purpose and shape the values of the firm. Shared purpose emanates from an inspiring vision and shared values that guide everyone on the path to making the vision real. Merely presenting employees with senior management's views seldom has impact. The goal is to understand what inspires people, and what values they truly hold dear. Senior management's role is to create a platform for debate and test ideas that are likely to resonate. The goal is to get everyone to talk to each other about what matters to them, so peer-to-peer communication is required. Many firms use a whole series of departmental and cross-functional meetings and workshops for this, but some have turned to the Internet for help. In 2003 IBM was undergoing an identity crisis and felt the need to redefine its mission and values for the first time in 100 years. Using an online platform, IBM "jammed" with more than 300,000 employees on-line to agree on new values. "Given the realities of a smart, global, independent-minded, 21st-century workforce like ours, I don't believe something as vital and personal as values could be dictated from the top", wrote CEO Samuel J. Palmisano on IBM's website.[29]

Information Systems

While communication systems facilitate change, information systems often do just the opposite. Everyone knows a horror story about information technology (IT). Senior executives speak fearfully of massive cost overruns and late delivery; one recent study indicated that nearly 20% of major IT projects cost 300% of the original budget. And when it finally arrives, no one is completely satisfied. The reluctance to tackle big systems changes is a major source of inertia. This is particularly evident in firms that have outsourced their IT. Bills of $1 billion per year are not uncommon, and the cost of the most minor changes runs to tens of millions of dollars. But the problem is just as bad with in-house IT.

The sources of the problem are many fold. Often, the problem is poor design built out of historical accident; CIOs inherit multiple legacy systems that have been patched together over time. Each system is a challenge in itself because it has not been built to be maintained or improved, but multiple mergers and acquisitions compound the problem as organizations with different systems come together. It is not uncommon for large corporations to have hundreds of independent systems and multiple versions of customer records and product files, all of which must be accessed in different ways. The USA's number two personal auto insurer, Allstate,[30] operated a claims system that was actually 95 systems cobbled together before it began reengineering the business of claims.

Designed to Change

Changing or even maintaining such complex legacy systems is difficult. To make information systems easier to develop, maintain and modify, they must be designed around an object-oriented architecture made up of relatively independent components.[31] As long as each component communicates with other components in a well-defined way, then how a component works internally has no bearing on how the whole system operates. This allows engineers to maintain and improve each component independently. New objects can be added or old objects adapted relatively quickly and easily to take advantage of new market opportunities without having to change the whole system. Old legacy systems can be "evolved" towards such an object-oriented architecture by "wrapping" current applications in a layer of middleware through which they communicate with other applications. Over time, the wrapped applications can be replaced. This is painful, slow and costly, but may be less costly and risky than blowing up the organization and starting again. This approach also establishes a capability for continuous, intelligent improvement and change, the key to long-term success.

Managers also often get the information they deserve; information systems are hampered by poor specification because managers do not invest enough time in identifying the information they really need. Asked what data they require and how they would like them structured to facilitate their work, most executives would be at a loss to answer. But by working with a knowledge engineer who understands the firm's strategy, senior executives can quickly identify what is critical to them. Provided with examples of how the information can be structured, they can determine what is most useful. A quick prototype will provide fast feedback for the manager and the knowledge engineer that the needs are being met. In this way, through a series of rapid iterations, executives can help to design the knowledge system they need. This is the agile, rapid prototyping approach to systems development that is made possible by an object-oriented architecture built on a relational database structure.

Agile development methods help avoid imposing new systems on organizations. People naturally resist change, and when it is imposed on them they become very vocal about it. They must be convinced that it is worth their while to learn a new approach. If the system is designed by the user to make their life easier, then there is no problem with adoption. Indeed, the measure of a good system is that it spreads virally as soon as a few users are asked to test it; other people hear about it and demand to have it too.

IT for Advantage

IT can be a huge source of competitive advantage. It is a secret weapon to lower cost and increase differentiation at the same time.[32] It can make possible completely new business models such as Li & Fung's platform in the fashion industry, which helps create a unique supply chain for every customer order. Firms that benefit most from information systems use them to support new business models and create platforms that support rapid change rather than creating impediments to it.

When information systems are core to a firm's competitive advantage, it is dangerous to rely on outside vendors to build and maintain them. Capital One cancelled its contract with EDS, paying nearly $50 million in penalties, to get back control of IT when it chose a path of information-based strategy.[33] For a start-up, this was an extraordinary move. But Capital One could not afford to rely on "industry best practice"; it needed to build a competitive advantage that would not quickly find its way to competitors. And Capital One committed to object-oriented programming in the 1990s when it was more theory than practice. The company even had to train its own people to do it because there were too few programmers in the marketplace versed in the nascent technology. Such was their commitment to building competitive advantage through more agile, proprietary IT.

Summary

A firm's formal architecture is comprised of many interrelated elements that facilitate work. Each element can create inertia, but they are so interrelated that it is difficult to change one without changing them all. In this way, formal architecture is a major source of structural inertia.

In this chapter we reviewed a number of the important elements of formal architecture. We examined how each one creates value and why it suffers from inertia, and we described how to overcome this. We began with the organization chart which maps out the formal hierarchy. A hierarchy is an efficient way of organizing work, but as the task grows so does the hierarchy; efficiency then declines and inertia grows. Instead of large, monolithic structures and a centralized command-and-control approach to strategic change, we argued for an **object-oriented organization**; breaking up the organization into small, semi-independent businesses – SBCs – and allowing them to design their own work and respond to local strategic changes. In this way, strategic and structural intelligence is distributed throughout the organization. We also postulated that project-based adhocracy – an **opportunity-oriented organization** – is a structure worthy of serious consideration in fast-moving environments.

We then moved on to business processes. These make firms more efficient but also create inertia, especially since many processes are interrelated. We recommended reducing the level of process interdependencies (object-oriented organization) to make processes easier to change, rewarding process change rather than punishing it and investing in process change capacity, since this provides a good return on investment when the environment is not changing and provides resources to support change when the environment demands it.

Next we examined the firm's human assets. Distributing more strategic and structural intelligence throughout the organization means recruiting the right people and teaching them the right skills. Change often also means firing those whose skill-sets are out-dated. Firms that become preferred employers have little to fear from this.

We argued that measurements and rewards must be carefully aligned with long-term strategic success. And we advocated that firms should reward strategic change rather than chasing their changing strategy with painful adjustment to their reward system.

We then highlighted the importance of communication in driving change. We concluded that to distribute strategic intelligence throughout the firm, senior executives must communicate to learn rather than merely to inform. They must also communicate to inspire and encourage peer-to-peer communication to build and sustain a common purpose that will clear the way for change.

We turned finally to information systems. Information systems can help firms to be smarter; more able to react intelligently to change. Indeed, many of the examples of smart firms in this book rely on information systems for their superior intelligence. However, they can also be a formidable impediment to change. We argued that they must be designed to be changed with object-oriented architectures and agile programming methods. We also cautioned firms in danger of losing control of their information architecture never to pass control of their central nervous system to outsiders.

Notes

1. Mintzberg (1979).
2. Anand, Collis and Hood (2008).
3. Clippinger (1999; 2007).
4. Robin Dunbar's research (Dunbar, 1992) on primate brain size suggested the limit on a human social group was 148. This was rounded up to the "Dunbar Number" of 150. For an accessible evolutionary anthropology view of the history of the human species, see Dunbar (2004).
5. IDEO (2011).
6. Ghemawat and Stander (1992).
7. See Taylor (1998) for a description of object-oriented design. See Veryard (2001) for a bold attempt at applying it to businesses. Fairtlough (1994) describes how he applied the principles in practice and discusses the limits on clan size.
8. See Wells (2005) *"Whole Foods Market, Inc."*
9. Ghemawat and Stander (1992).
10. Fung, Fung and Wind (2008).
11. Meyerson (1996).

12. Zich (1997).
13. Williamson (1975).
14. Fung, Fung and Wind (2008).
15. Wells and Anand (2008).
16. Ghemawat and Stander (1992).
17. See Taylor (1911). The scientific management school of 100 years ago demonstrated the potential for manufacturing process improvements. It was quantified by the Rand Corporation in the 1950s as the learning curve effect. Rand based its research on the costs of aircraft production during World War II.

    In the 1970s, the Boston Consulting Group extended the learning curve concept to all costs incurred by the firm and called it the *experience curve.*

    The benefits of better process design were "rediscovered" in the 1990s, when an army of Business Process Reengineering (BPR) consultants emerged, promising fast payback on their services. This was in response to an influential article in the *Harvard Business Review* by Michael Hammer (1990) who argued that managers should use information technology to radically redesign their work, not simply automate existing processes. Hammer argued for a revolution (see Hammer and Champy, 1993) and this was enthusiastically endorsed by the consultants. I recall while I was at PepsiCo in the mid-1990s that several major consulting firms promised process cost savings of 20% or more on BPR exercises, and some were prepared to underwrite this promise by making part of their fees performance related.

    However, within a decade, BPR fell into disrepute because of the large layoffs that typically followed, the huge consulting fees and the major disruption caused. Nevertheless, it has re-emerged as business process management (BPM), which argues for a more incremental, continuous improvement approach. (See Vom Brocke and Rosemann (2010) for a comprehensive review of the field.) Whatever the label, the principles of BPR/BPM are now embraced by the majority of major firms throughout the world, which is a testament to the savings it can make.
18. Anand, Collis and Hood (2008).
19. Anand, Collis and Hood (2008).
20. Ghemawat and Stander (1992).
21. See Wells, Hazlett and Mukhopadhyay (2006) for a description of how the US Army uses After Action Reviews to train its troops.
22. Anand, Collis and Hood (2008).

23. Kaplan and Norton (2000); Kaplan (2010).
24. Wells (2003).
25. Wells and Anand (2008).
26. Wells and Raabe (2005) *"24 Hour Fitness."*
27. Wells and Raabe (2005) *"Bally Total Fitness."*
28. See Argyris (1990; 2004).
29. IBM CEO Samuel J. Palmisano wrote an open letter about the experience *Our Values at Work on being an IBMer,* http://www.ibm.com/ibm/values/us/, accessed October 30, 2011.
30. Wells (2008).
31. Brown (2000).
32. Michael E. Porter argues that there is a trade-off between lowering cost and increasing differentiation (see Porter, 2008), but technological innovation often allows both advantages to be increased at the same time.
33. Wells and Anand (2008).

2.4

INFORMAL ARCHITECTURE – LEVERAGING SOCIAL MECHANICS

Introduction

In Chapter 2.3 we discussed the complexity of formal architecture and how it stifles change. But much of what gets done in firms is done informally.[1] A firm's informal architecture – the unwritten rules, the power brokers, the rumour mill – can be an executive's friend or worst enemy. In this chapter we investigate the role of informal architecture, how it might contribute to inertia and how it can facilitate intelligent change.

Some people see the informal architecture as a handicap, a "political evil". From this perspective, individuals pursue their own agendas and manipulate the system at the expense of the firm. Sadly, if employees are not motivated to make the firm successful, then this can often be the case. But there is a counter view – that the informal channels and arrangements that spring up are often signs of "social good"; individuals working together to make the firm successful despite the formal architecture which often gets in the way. Human beings are inherently creative and skilled at self-organizing. They use social networks to achieve a common purpose, and this skill can be deployed in the service of the firm.

Informal architecture can contribute significantly to strategic change. It develops at no cost, operates without formal support and can adjust at lightning speed. But it can also represent a formidable source of resistance.

We must understand it well to be able to harness its strengths. To this end, we now turn to neuroscience, evolutionary biology, sociology and anthropology to help understand why we act the way we do.

Social Mechanics and the Evolution of the Brain

Most of us believe that the power of choice gives us some control of our destiny. In truth, very little of what we do is under our conscious control. The way we select a mate, trust a stranger, choose a friend, defend a kinsman or detect cheating is programmed deep within our minds. We act unconsciously at the behest of a set of genetically inherited social skills that make man a smarter, more adaptive social machine than any other species. The skills are quite predictable – a form of social mechanics.[2] However, we do have the power to reflect on who we are and what we do. We can learn to change. We can improve on the inherited behaviours that still make sense, and suppress those that are no longer relevant to our success or which might even get in the way.

Small Group Coordination Skills

As our brains evolved, we developed social coordination skills that made us stronger as a species. The earliest social development of the brain added small group, social coordination skills for groups of 5–20, usually family units. Group membership afforded greater protection from predators, more capacity to compete for food and the ability to bring down bigger game. Exclusion from the group could mean death. Group coordination skills are evident in many lesser mammals to varying degrees. They are clearly visible in the behaviour of the wolf pack, an extended family group working together to increase their chances of survival and, of course, to pass on their genes.

The wolf pack is led by the alpha male, working closely with its mate. The alpha male uses raw physical power and simple emotions like fear and intimidation to control pack members. Members defer to the leader with symbolic shows of submission to avoid too much costly and deadly fighting which would weaken the pack. We see the same when dogs fight; the loser rolls over in submission rather than fighting to the death. Coordination is through body movements, eye movements and rudimentary language. These mechanisms are quite effective for managing small groups. The behaviours, though crude from a human perspective, sometimes surface in small business teams, especially in a crisis. Under pressure, we revert to more primitive instincts.

Large Group Coordination Skills

Over time, small group coordination skills evolved to handle much larger groups. We added specialized roles, coordination skills and sophisticated emotional controls. Today, the human brain has evolved to the point where it can handle complex social coordination across groups of approximately 150 co-located people without much conscious effort.[3] This is the limit of social mechanics. We can think of this as the natural building block of society – a **social mechanics component** or **comm-unit.**[4]

In such a unit, a simple hierarchy of an alpha leading the group and everyone else following is insufficient. The alpha is helped by many lieutenants; "fixers", effective at marshalling resources to get things done; "connectors" who bring the right people together; "visionaries" who generate and circulate ideas; "gatekeepers" who determine who is a member of the group and who is excluded; "truth tellers" who keep everybody honest; "enforcers" who make sure members obey the rules. These roles create a natural hierarchy in the group, extending the scope of the alpha to influence behaviour amongst a larger group of individuals.

Members derive their identity from the role they play within the social group. High performance in any one of these roles creates a good reputation amongst all group members. A good reputation in the group is highly valued – more important than wealth.

In large groups, raw power, fear and intimidation are too crude to be major instruments of social control. Instead, a much broader set of social emotions is employed to control behaviour. These include sympathy, embarrassment, shame, guilt, pride, jealousy, envy, gratitude, admiration, indignation and contempt. Humans express these emotions through gesture, speech and facial expression.

Emotions are contagious; they spread quickly from one person to another. Sometimes one emotion triggers a different emotion as a response (e.g. anger triggers fear). All this happens subconsciously via rapid signals to the amygdala deep in our brains. In this way, we control others and are controlled by them without consciously realizing it. And all the time, we seek emotional satisfaction, seeking out the agreeable and avoiding the disagreeable, fulfilling our genetically inherited need to be valued members of the community.

Large Group Coordination Behaviours

Humans naturally demonstrate a number of behaviours that facilitate large group coordination and thereby make the group more viable.

Reciprocity. We are natural traders; we barter goods and services, as anyone who has observed a young child in the school playground will attest. We trade collectables, food, favours; anything of value to others in return for something that is more valuable to us. This is important in making a group stronger because it allows specialization of tasks.

Trust. Trading goes much better when we trust each other. One of the most important coordination mechanisms in large social groups is trust.[5] If I trust you, I will do something for you today in expectation that you will return the favour at some later date. This is barter, but with a time delay or "promise" and increases the number of opportunities for trading significantly – it makes the market more efficient. In modern society, we have replaced barter and promises with money and loans, but these too are merely promises. When the intrinsic value of the money or the loan is questioned, trust is undermined and transactions cease. This happened when the markets failed during the global financial crisis of 2008. In 2011, the danger of another loss of trust looms as the United States and Europe wrestle with enormous debt loads.

Trust is important in more than trading. We must trust other members of the group to fulfil their role in group survival and they must trust us to do our part. When we are asked by a group leader to do something, we must trust that they are not merely taking advantage of us for their own ends but are looking after the group's best interests. To support such behaviour, we derive chemical pleasure from trusting people; it triggers dopamine in the brain that gives a sense of well-being.[6] Hence, we like to be around people that we trust.

Humans are expert at detecting cheaters. There is a special region of the brain designed for this. Experimental work has shown that when this is damaged it is very difficult for the person to detect cheats.[7] When we sense cheating, we lose trust and feel uncomfortable. We do not like to be around people we do not trust.

Exchanging Gifts and Small Favours. Strangers start to build trust by exchanging gifts. Gift exchange is one of the most ancient and universal of human acts. The risks are small and the symbolism great. It is a means by which networks of reciprocity and trust are created. It is a signal of the willingness to work together cooperatively. Trust grows as more and more successful transactions between both parties are achieved. The equivalent in financial terms is a credit rating.

Exchanging favours is similar to exchanging gifts as a way of developing a productive trust relationship. While favour exchange may be hard to track, humans are intuitively very good at keeping score, and are acutely aware of who they think owes them a favour and who they owe favours in return. Moreover, most members of a group can readily identify those amongst their number who are "takers" – freeloaders who accept favours and do little in return – and "givers", those who give more than they receive. Those who take advantage are eventually isolated because no one wants to trade with them.

Making Introductions. Making introductions to others is an important group social behaviour. When a member of a group introduces an individual to another member of the group, they are vouching for the person, offering an implicit guarantee that they can be trusted and widening the trust network. This facilitates transactions between people who would otherwise be strangers, creating new relationships of trust and extending the effective size of the group.

Honesty and Integrity. Honesty and integrity promote trust. When people tell the truth and do what they say, it is easy to trust them. If they lie, we learn not to rely on their promises. We do not trust their intentions towards us.

Stealing from members of the community undermines how the community works and threatens to destabilize it, so logic demands that it cannot be tolerated. Human response to stealing is more emotional than logical, and the emotions are aimed not just at the thief. Those who steal are treated with contempt and banished, and those closest to them are made to feel guilt and shame. This creates social pressure to be honest within the group.

Fairness. Fairness also promotes trust. Where there is a high degree of interdependence, failure to share resources fairly leads to internal strife and undermines the strength of the community. We are programmed to react emotionally against unfairness and injustice. We respond with indignation and disgust. This has been shown to be a universal human response across many cultures.[8] It has also been observed in some apes. In experiments performed on brown capuchin monkeys, subjects refused to accept a reward for performing a task if they saw colleagues get a better one.[9]

Transparency. This is another important condition for effective group coordination. Obviously, it is easier to coordinate activity if everyone can see what everyone else is doing. But transparency also promotes trust. It reveals those who is underperforming and stops freeloaders. Those who hide cannot be trusted. The size of the group and how it is distributed place an upper limit on transparency. With 150 people in one location there are few places to hide, since "everyone knows everyone" and everyone can clearly see what others are doing. If groups grow beyond 150 people or operate in multiple locations, transparency becomes more of a problem. As transparency is impaired, trust begins to wane.

Accountability. Accountability is also important to group viability. Everyone must deliver on their role and faces punishment or even exclusion if they fail to do so. This demonstrates fairness and promotes trust. Enforcers play an important role in this regard.

Altruism. This is an even higher order of group behaviour. Altruism occurs when a member of the group does something for another member without expecting anything in return. Some would argue that the only reason a member of a group will do this is because they believe others will do the same for them – a form of altruistic reciprocity. However, altruistic reciprocity is an oxymoron. It does not explain why, in times of war, soldiers sacrifice their lives for the good of the group. This is true altruism. Research has shown that part of our brain lights up and gives us pleasure when we are being altruistic.[10]

The behaviours described above are hard-wired into the human brain. In the absence of any conscious effort to control them, and in the face of a common purpose, we will automatically self-organize to create highly effective groups to exploit these skills and respond to the challenge. Hence, small businesses that employ 150 people don't need lots of formal control mechanisms. If there is a clear common purpose, an informal organization will emerge that will deliver on that purpose with remarkable efficiency.

Firms aiming to benefit from these natural behaviours must heed the conditions under which they flourish and reward the behaviours that support them. Reciprocity and altruism are critical to group viability. Transparency, accountability, honesty and fairness all promote trust and make the group more effective. Anything that conflicts with these is likely to have the opposite effect.

Networking between Large Groups – Intergroup Social Mechanics

150 people may work naturally together as a comm-unit but what is to stop these groups from competing with each other and threatening their survival in the process? The massive societies we have created attest to the fact that the human species is collectively much smarter than this. How do human social mechanics components cooperate when it makes sense to do so?

Some lesser species have worked this out with some surprising results. Ants are normally very territorial. They attack each other's nests. But some species of ant have learned to detect ants from the same genetic pool and cooperate with these nests while attacking others. As a result, huge colonies of these rapacious creatures have emerged which are wiping out local ant species as well as flora and fauna. A colony more than 60 miles across was recently discovered in Melbourne, Australia.[11]

Structures created by human beings have grown well beyond the 150 person limits of group social mechanics, facilitated by inter-group social mechanics.

Humans demonstrate bridging behaviours, the willingness to transfer to other groups and create links between groups. The desire to reach out and discover new worlds and other groups is particularly evident in young people. They have been programmed this way as they reach breeding age, since the resultant genetic diversity serves the species well. There is always a risk of approaching a new group, but many cultures welcome in strangers, facilitating the absorption of a new gene pool. And new members maintain links with their families back in the original group, reducing the chances of inter-group conflict. Indeed, if there are enough links of this kind, it is difficult for the leaders of each group to incite their followers to rise up against each other. Coalitions, which are stronger than individual groups, form, and those not able to form such coalitions quickly perish. This is how early tribes and fiefdoms evolved into nations.

Some individuals move back and forth between groups with no apparent loyalty to either. They are "networkers". This behaviour creates an element of mistrust, so for self-preservation, good networkers must avoid being threatening and always show themselves to be useful to both groups. Their goal is to create a bridge of trust to both sides which requires superior social intelligence.

Networkers employ the usual social exchange mechanisms that take place within a group – exchanging favours, building relationships of trust, seeking out introductions – but with a much higher degree of intensity. Their reputation within all the groups they bridge comes not from position in the hierarchy but from the quality of their network and they guard this jealously. Indeed, it is not in their interests for groups to come together because the networker's personal value would be diminished. But for the groups themselves, when there is significant benefit from cooperation, it is in their interests to establish more bridging networkers to reduce this power and provide tighter coordination.

All human beings have the capacity to network, though some are naturally more predisposed to it than others. Traditional organizational roles like customer relationship managers are particularly dependent on such capabilities in order to create bridges between their own organization and their customers.

Everyone knows a good networker, but until recently few realized how much time they invest in building their networks. Social networking websites reveal the role of the networker and the scope of their networks. On the professional networking website LinkedIn, a small subset of members become networkers; they spend countless hours building tens of thousands of contacts to fulfil this role effectively. This behaviour is instinctive, even compulsive for some personalities.

Networkers within firms help bridge across both formal and informal boundaries. As firms build greater expertise in social networking, this is increasingly by design rather than by accident, as we will later discuss.

The Formation of Informal Architecture

Informal Hierarchy

Social mechanics help shape an informal architecture that has many analogues in the formal world.

Companies describe their formal hierarchy in an organization chart, but the less visible informal hierarchy more accurately describes the real leaders in the community, the ones people are prepared to follow.

People naturally respect leaders for their ability to lead, admire them for the way they conduct themselves and trust them to place the good of the community over their own self-interest. These are legitimate leaders and people are happy to follow them. Communities led legitimately are more adaptable and sustainable because people with a choice seek out more positive emotional and social environments where they are more willing to suggest changes and are more willing to change to remain part of them. Coercive leaders use reward and punishment to drive behaviour, relying on more primeval instincts. Where people have choice, they will avoid this or even rebel. Custodial leaders are there to maintain the status quo and are widely recognized within the community as unfit to lead.[12]

Firms must appoint legitimate leaders to formal positions in the hierarchy or there is a danger employees will ignore or reject them. And for those they fail to appoint, they must remember that though these natural leaders have no formal position, they wield great influence and cannot be ignored.

Informal Processes

Formal processes define how the work should be done in an organization. Few companies document all of their processes, and where documents exist, they seldom reflect reality because workers have already found faster and better ways of doing things. But without significant incentives to share the gains, the workforce will improve efficiency for its own benefit – for instance, to gain extra leisure time. However, if the firm provides the right incentives, social mechanics will carve new paths to make the firm smarter and more profitable. Formal training and processes-to-improve-processes may help, but well-motivated teams will figure it out for themselves and get a lot of social and emotional satisfaction in the process. At Nucor's steel mills, large team-based bonuses provide strong motivation to increase productivity, and the teams continue to find improvements without the need for complex, formal process-mapping exercises.[13]

Informal Human Asset Management

Informal architecture can also play a very effective role in developing the human asset base. Both Capital One[14] and Progressive Insurance[15] discovered that recruits introduced by current employees had a significantly greater chance of success. Some firms spurn this practice on the grounds that it encourages nepotism, but they fail to recognize how social networks operate. It would be very foolish for a valued member of a community to recommend someone who is not competent to do the job for two very important reasons. First, they would be undermining their own credibility. And second, they would be blamed by the person in question for setting them up for failure. Personal recommendations are a powerful screening device.

Informal networks are also more ruthless in weeding out the non-performers, as Nucor has demonstrated.[16] Nucor's team-based reward system creates strong social pressure for everyone to perform, and those who are not up to it simply leave.

Informal development systems can also be highly effective. Most successful executives can recall the major contribution a mentor and coach made to their career. Mentors not only help develop functional skills but also introduce new recruits to their social network. This helps "mentees" to establish themselves more quickly in the firm's informal architecture and begin trading social currency to get things done. Often the motivation for mentoring is selfish – you help me and I will help you – but many senior executives do it for the emotional satisfaction it gives them – altruistic reciprocity – in much the same way as parents develop their children with no particular reward in mind.

Informal Measures and Rewards

Social and emotional rewards are big motivators within the informal organization. Most formal reward systems focus primarily on economic incentives, but satisfying social and emotional needs can be much more powerful. There is nothing "soft" about social currency. Soldiers on the battlefield don't die for extra pay, they die for their colleagues. The social pressure for them to do otherwise is too great. For companies, the goal is to align internal social pressure with strategic success. This is what Nucor achieved by offering regular team bonuses linked to lower steel production costs. No one dares let the team down or they will never hear the end of it from their colleagues.[17]

Symbolic rewards are less expensive than financial rewards. Public recognition creates social esteem and costs very little, but it is a very strong motivator. Even publishing the performance rankings of business units can be quite effective. Those at the top of the list enjoy the fame, while those at the bottom feel the shame – what I call the "fame and shame game". And the shame can be very painful, even disruptive. It is often better to simply publish the top performers as a motivator because the problems created by singling out the poor performers are so great.

Informal Communication and Information Systems

Informal communication is a powerful force within all organizations, for both good and evil. Since effective communication plays a critical role in change processes, learning to tap into informal communication channels is very important.

Informal communication channels are lightning fast. This is because those "in-the-know" trade secrets; since secrets don't last long, they work hard to trade them before anyone else does to maintain their "in-the-know" status. Smart leaders forge links with these traders to provide an early warning system and broadcast messages rapidly.

Because the information is unattributed and off-the-record, there is no need to help people save face, no burden of proof and no danger of libel or slander laws. This means that the information is usually more accurate than the official version. There is always a danger of a malicious rumour, but there is a built-in self-regulating system that encourages traders to check their sources for veracity. Trading bad data can lead to loss of credibility and undermine the person's reputation in the network.

But informal communication networks have their problems. They tend to amplify relatively small signals, exaggerating reality; and in the absence of any real signal, they create and amplify noise. They can also be used by the unscrupulous to undermine others, especially given the anonymity they provide. The best way to avoid these problems is to make sure the network is filled with accurate information in the first place. Small and misleading signals must be replaced with stronger, more accurate ones that provide little space for noise. And those intent on spreading malicious lies have fewer opportunities if everyone in the organization has a clear view of the firm's objectives and the role they play in delivering them. It is the absence of information that creates the opportunity to play such damaging games.

The informal architecture also builds sophisticated databases of crucial practical information that are distributed throughout the collective mind. These contain a wide range of data fields including who-knows-who and who-knows-what, critical to getting things done; social esteem scores identifying those respected and admired and likely to wield influence versus those who are likely to be ignored or even reviled; reputation scores for who you can count on, who you can trust; the givers willing to help the community versus the takers who freeload. All this information is available to individuals well plugged into the social system. It is essential to getting things done.

Integrating Across Social Components – From Tribes to Nations

Most large organizations are divided into functions and departments, and these quickly form into social mechanics components, acting as a local community serving the larger organization. Since formal cross-functional mechanisms seldom promote trust, reciprocity, personal accountability and transparency, they often break down, creating functional silos.[18] The organization is divided into competing "tribes", each with its own identity and sense of purpose. Although there is strong coordination and cooperative effort within each function, the ability to operate effectively across functions is far from ideal.

Many business processes have been developed over the years to try to achieve greater alignment across formal organizational boundaries and eliminate the functional silo problem, but despite all these efforts, functional silos remain. Clearly our instincts are much stronger than the bureaucratic processes that we have put in place to try and overcome them. However, with the right processes and motivation, tribes will align with a larger common purpose to form a nation.

Intelligent firms exploit the power of informal networking to achieve cross-organizational coordination and cooperation. Common examples include communal coffee areas, company canteens, Friday afternoon beer bashes, team-building exercises and other social events. These are gentle ways of encouraging social exchange and are not always very effective. Indeed, they often result in colleagues socializing with people they know well instead of forging new relationships.

Halliburton[19] took a more systematic approach; it developed socio-grams[20] that mapped interactions amongst community members in order to try to shape more effective informal networks. They discovered that some individuals, when transferred to a different organizational unit, retained strong links with their old colleagues. This prompted Halliburton to transfer some managers between geographic locations to improve cross-unit coop-eration. The result was a marked improvement in performance. Using similar techniques, a major financial institution has recently discovered the reasons why its backroom and front-room operations were not working effectively together; the vast majority of exchanges between the two were channelled through just one bridging networker. They are now working to build bigger bridges.

Bringing tribal leaders together on a regular basis and encouraging them to help each other and shape overall strategy begins to establish relation-ships of trust and reciprocity, creating a tribe-of-tribes. J&J started doing this in 1993 with structured dialogues aimed at democratizing the way the company made strategic choices.[21] The legitimacy of the national leadership of the tribe-of-tribes is paramount. They must visit the tribes, showing respect, reinforcing a collective vision and common purpose, emphasizing the benefits of working together, demonstrating competence and integrity and building understanding. Danaher's monthly policy deployment reviews fulfil this purpose.[22] These visits also allow members of each tribe to meet with the national leadership and exchange views. This keeps the tribal leaders honest because they know their members have direct access to the top.

Regular multi-tribe meetings, cross-tribal task forces and informal, inter-tribe visits all create greater opportunities for communication and building of trust. Transfer of people between tribes also helps since transferees typically maintain networks in their old tribes and help to build understanding between the two – a sort of inter-tribal marriage. In this way, nations are born and held together. No amount of formal bureaucracy will have the same effect.

The challenge for firms is, therefore, not to avoid tribalism but to embrace it in ways that avoid dysfunctional silo behaviour. The goal is to nurture tribes that act as strategic business objects, driving the firm's local strategic agenda while working together as "one nation" for the overall good of the firm.

Aligning the Informal and Formal Organization

Instead of relying on a few of the features of social mechanics to refine our current structures, why not take a more radical approach and work to fully align formal and informal architectures? Restructure the organization into a number of strategic business components (SBCs), each of which is within the size limits defined by social mechanics. This will encourage social mechanics components to form that will self-organize. Systematically identify and invest in bridgers to tie the SBCs together and combine these into a super SBC, a tribe-of-tribes, which is itself a small community operating within the size limits of a social mechanics component. This allows firms to exploit the full feature set inherited by the human species and create more efficient, more adaptive, lower-cost organizations.

Some firms have exploited such a structure to good effect. Wal-Mart, in its early years, was a case in point.[23] Unlike many large retailers, Wal-Mart resisted creating a regional structure and instead co-located its regional vice-presidents at Bentonville with the buyers and corporate staff. The regional VPs were required to fly out to visit their stores every Monday morning and come back by the end of the week with an idea that more than covered the costs of the flight. They were called upon to share their ideas with their colleagues every Saturday morning in the company meeting. The social pressure guaranteed that few would not have a good idea! And by Saturday afternoon, the phones would be ringing as the stores called to find out what they needed to try the following week. This created a rapid learning loop. The Saturday morning meeting provided transparency and accountability for all members of the top management team (the super SBC), and huge social pressure to perform. And the regional VPs, key members of that team, bridged with the stores and distribution centres, each of which was an SBC.

Social mechanics was not the only coordinating mechanism at Wal-Mart. Indeed, the company had some of the most sophisticated information systems in the world. But the objective of the information systems was to provide store managers with data to run their stores better while allowing corporate to keep an eye on them, not to try to run their businesses for them. Good information is essential to provide transparency and accountability. But when it came to making changes, the formal processes and systems only reflected what the company already knew. The informal structure was the platform for learning rapidly what needed to change and for making the changes fast. In this way, Wal-Mart aligned its formal and informal architectures, making full use of social mechanics.

The results of this structure were plain to see. Wal-Mart started in discount retailing in 1962, the same year as Kmart, and within ten years, Kmart, with its superior resources, was the industry leader with ten times the sales of Wal-Mart. Indeed, Wal-Mart's early efforts were nothing short of terrible. But Wal-Mart learned and Kmart had no such learning mechanisms in place. Within another 15 years, Wal-Mart was the same size as Kmart, was growing much faster and was much more profitable. Kmart struggled for years to recover but eventually declared bankruptcy in 2002.

Turbocharging Informal Architecture – The Promise of Social Networking Technology (SNT)

The link between informal architecture and business success has long been recognized, but it is difficult to leverage it in a systematic way because of its very nature. Informal architecture is never written down or recorded anywhere. The social mechanics on which it depends are sub-conscious, instinctive and automatic. We are expert at it even though we don't know what we are doing. However, SNT has become a powerful tool to help us "see" the invisible.

Early tools included sociographs that attempted to map patterns of social exchange by using surrogates such as emails. Some firms have used such techniques to good effect, although issues of privacy arise in some jurisdictions. But social networking platforms such as Friendster, MySpace and now Facebook have taken social networking tools to a new level. They offer much more sophisticated ways to map social exchange and to measure social currency; they support many of the behaviours necessary for effective informal coordination and control that we have discussed, and provide the conditions of accountability and transparency that these require.

SNT promises to turbocharge informal architecture. It allows social components to operate effectively across geographies and time zones. It expands the size of natural social components beyond the 150–200 person level. And it provides an efficient platform to allow networkers to bridge across many more components.

The transparency provided by SNT also helps with the governance issues raised when firms rely on informal exchange. Top management has a fiduciary responsibility to shareholders to ensure that members of the firm are acting in its best interests and in ways that are consistent with the firm's values.

SNT promises to support new component-based structures for large organizations that help to overcome structural inertia. It also holds great promise for small organizations already benefiting from social mechanics.

Small firms below the maximum size of a social component do not need much in the way of formal systems and processes to operate. But as they grow, informal coordination and control breaks down and more formal structures are required. These are slow and expensive and often undermine profitability. It is only when economies of scale from being larger compensate for the extra costs of formal structure that financial performance is restored. This is why many industries have a few large players operating above the threshold and a plethora of small players serving niches that owe their survival to the superior economics and faster response of informal architecture. For small, growing organizations approaching the size barrier, SNT promises to delay the need to act by supporting larger social components. It also offers a way to avoid the barrier completely by building an object-oriented organization.

Progress in Applying SNT

Early social networking sites, such as Friendster,[24] MySpace and Facebook,[25] started out as communities for young people to seek each other out and exchange content, but Facebook in particular has migrated towards a platform that allows multiple communities to interact. Launched in 2004, by 2010 it boasted a remarkable 500 million active users. The top 30 profiles viewed on Facebook as of December 9, 2010 included many celebrities, with Michael Jackson and Lady Gaga in the lead, and many TV shows.[26] However, four brands were also featured: Coca-Cola, Starbucks, Oreo and Disney. Indeed, when combined, all of Disney's brands could claim 100 million Facebook fans.[27]

Facebook provides interesting insights on social order and enables individuals to actively manage the way they influence others. While numbers vary significantly, the average number of friends a Facebook member had in 2010 was about 200, similar to the limits of social mechanics. It seems we are all the central figures in our own social world, a social component of around 200 people, limited in numbers by our genetically inherited ability to socialize. This sets a limit on the direct informal influence we can have, but since our friends cross over into many other social components, the indirect influence is far greater. The more friends we have in diverse other groups, the more the influence we can wield, and we can now track this on Facebook. Facebook also makes it easier to maintain relationships with people across the globe. Gone are the days when those who moved around the world frequently had to make new sets of friends as they said goodbye to the old. Facebook allows us to keep in touch with people wherever they may be. It promises a whole new social order.

LinkedIn is marketed as a social network for professionals, but in reality the site is used extensively for recruiting.[28] Unlike sites such as Monster.com that list people actually looking for work, LinkedIn provides potential employers access to those who are gainfully employed, but might be open to another offer. This widens the target pool for recruiters and arguably improves quality. The professional networking features give "plausible deniability" to individuals on the site when their current employers find out they are on it.

Many new companies with innovative business models use some of the features of SNT, including eBay with its reputation scores, Amazon with its recommendations and eHarmony, a dating site which now accounts for 30% of all marriages in the USA.[29] Open source software and Wikipedia also rely on social exchange. Large, established firms are also embracing SNT, but few are using it yet to turbocharge their informal architecture.

The early impact of SNT in the corporate world was the power it gave small interest groups to attack them. A small group of students at a US university (The Rainforest Action Network) managed to stop forestry companies in South America, not by attacking the small logging companies themselves but by targeting Citigroup, the bank that was providing them lines of credit.[30] Large firms are increasingly keen to track the criticisms they are attracting in order to respond early before things get out of hand.

Activist attention is of particular concern to big brands because their high profile makes them more vulnerable.[31] Ironically, environmental activists are less likely to target the biggest polluters because they are not household names. Companies with big brands are also losing control of them. In the past, they could broadcast whatever information they liked about the brand with relative impunity, but social networking platforms give consumers a powerful way of talking back and getting together to protest. The number two USA discount hypermarket operator Target experienced a public backlash in September 2011 when it introduced a highly publicized clothing line designed by Missoni. The demand was so great that the website crashed and it ran out of product within hours. Many completed online orders were inexplicably cancelled the following day. A public relations debacle ensued as consumer outrage flooded Twitter and Facebook.[32]

The fear of consumer reprisals has given birth to a new science – online reputation management.[33] Major brands now provide their customers with ways to exchange views while the companies listen very carefully. Procter & Gamble has a successful site called Pampers Village for young mothers. It allows them to share problems and experiences and support each other at a time when such support is much appreciated; it also provides a useful platform for advertising P&G products.[34]

While large firms are increasingly willing to use social networking platforms to communicate with outside constituencies, fewer have considered SNT for internal communication or to turbocharge their informal architecture. This is a dangerous omission because employees don't have to wait for the firm to provide them with a platform to criticize; they can use Facebook. Facebook is no longer a source of entertainment for the young; an increasing number of their parents and grandparents are now on it. Firms ignore the threat of SNT at their peril. The London riots of 2011, which destroyed many businesses, were organized through social networking sites. Such sites also helped trigger the Arab Spring, which brought down the governments of Egypt, Tunisia and Libya in 2011 and still threatens Yemen and Syria.

Welcome to the networked world! Corporations must embrace SNT and use it to reach out to their main constituencies including customers, suppliers, employees, shareholders and regulators. And by using it to turbocharge their informal architecture, they increase their Structural IQ.

An important note of caution: many firms which apply SNT try to adopt an old command-and-control mind-set. They want to specify what exchanges can take place and limit the content that is allowed. Others argue that employees should be left free to generate their own social networks and do anything they like; the firm should simply supply them with a flexible platform to do so. The reality is a balance between the two. To work effectively, social networks need a good degree of freedom, but it is critical to feed them with valuable content which draws in users and drowns out amplified noise and malicious rumours. It makes no sense for firms to encourage social exchange that works against greater strategic and Structural IQ. Moreover, there are some regrettable social behaviours that should actively be discouraged.

What firms cannot afford to do is ignore SNT, because their employees will use platforms such as Facebook and Twitter anyway. And, left to their own devices, they may well use it to marshal the power of social mechanics against the firm.

Summary

Social exchange is the powerful force that binds societies together. Genetically inherited, it unconsciously shapes our behaviour and builds us into cohesive units that make us stronger as a species. We have the ability to think consciously about this force and turn it to our advantage. We also have the power in SNT to harness this force to create stronger social units to support more complex societal structures. We evolve from seeing the world as isolated units in competition to a network of networks made of inter-dependent components which both cooperate and compete at the same time.

Companies are vital components of a complex social system. They create the value, and without them society would not work. We all depend on them. The companies we create rely largely on social exchange for their success, although we try to fool ourselves that it is formal architecture that should take the credit. Those that embrace SNT to leverage the informal architecture in the service of the firm will enhance their capacity for change. Those who ignore it will find that their employees are using it anyway; it is freely available to them on Facebook and Twitter, and if they are unhappy, they will use it against the firm. And so will customers, suppliers, regulators and the general public. Welcome to a networked world!

Notes

1. See Cyert and March (1963) for a rigorous treatment of a behavioural theory of the firm.
2. Clippinger (1999; 2007).
3. Dunbar (1992).

4. I avoid the terms "commune" and "community" for the images they sometimes conjure up.
5. Covey (2006).
6. Lehrer (2011).
7. Young (2002).
8. In an experiment called the ultimatum game, one subject is given a sum of money and asked to offer part of it to another subject. If the second subject accepts the offer, both parties keep the money, but if the second party refuses the offer, neither can keep it. Logically, the second party should accept ANY offer because this is better than nothing. However, most reject the offer if they feel it is too low in order to punish the other party for being unfair. The threshold is normally about 30% of the total. The ultimatum game has been played in many cultures around the world, with remarkably consistent results. See Kagel and Roth (1995).
9. Brosnan and Waal (2003).
10. In an article published in *Proceedings of the National Academy of Science* on October 17, 2006, Jorge Moll *et al.* reported that both monetary rewards and charitable donations activated the mesolimbic reward pathway, a primitive part of the brain that lights up in response to food and sex. This suggests that altruism is hard-wired and gives pleasure. Charitable giving also activated the subgenual cortex/septal region, related to social attachment.
11. BBC News (2004).
12. Ansoff and McDonnel (1990).
13. Ghemawat and Stander (1992).
14. Wells and Anand (2008).
15. Wells, Lutova and Sender (2008).
16. Ghemawat and Stander (1992).
17. Ghemawat and Stander (1992).
18. For an excellent description of the problem of silos, read Gulati (2007).
19. Laseter and Cross (2006).
20. A sociogram is a "chart plotting the structure of interpersonal relations in a group situation". See http://www.merriam-webster.com/dictionary/sociogram. They are used to map and analyse social networks.
21. Meyerson (1996).
22. Anand, Collis and Hood (2008).
23. Wells and Haglock (2006).
24. Piskorski and Knoop (2006).
25. Piskorski, Eisenmann, Chen and Feinstein (2008); Piskorski (2011).

26. http://pagedata.insidefacebook.com/ Retrieved December 9, 2010.
27. http://mashable.com/2010/12/05/disney-100-million-facebook-fans/ Retrieved December 9, 2010.
28. Piskorski (2006; 2007).
29. Based on results from an 18-month study conducted by Harris Interactive and sponsored by eHarmony. See company *Business Wire* release "Study: 542 People Married Every Day in US, On Average, Through eHarmony; More Than 1 Million Non-Married People Said They Were In Monogamous Relationships With An eHarmony Match" August 16, 2010.
30. Baron, Barlow, Barlow and Yurday (2004).
31. Eesley and Lenox (2005).
32. D'Innocenzio (2011).
33. Gaines-Ross (2010).
34. www.pampers.com

2.5

TOWARDS SMARTER STRUCTURE

Introduction

Having discussed how structural elements of organizations create inertia, in this chapter we pull everything together to chart a course towards
higher Structural IQ.

Because firms demonstrate a wide range of structural intelligence, we
identify the different levels of Structural IQ and provide a step-by-step plan
to create a structurally smarter organization. To do this, companies must
embrace smarter asset management and smarter formal architecture. And
they must turbocharge the informal architecture.

Low Structural IQ

Low Structural IQ firms are mindlessly committed to assets they have
accumulated over many years, and any attempt at questioning them is met
with "this is the way we do things around here". They are trapped by the
notion that they have to own things to control them and must develop all
ideas for themselves – the "not-invented here" syndrome. When they
outsource, it is driven by cost cutting and conventional wisdom rather
than strategic logic and can often leave the firm vulnerable to hold-up by
suppliers.

The least structurally intelligent aren't aware of the need to align
elements of their structure. They don't recognize how interrelated the
elements of formal architecture are, so they are often inconsistent with
each other. The company is internally at war with itself. Individuals are
assigned accountability for things over which they have little control.

Processes duplicate work or drive activity that has no bearing on the firm's performance. People are expected to perform tasks for which they have no background or training. New people are recruited based on standard criteria with no thought as to what the job really requires. Employees are sent on "boondoggle" training programmes as a reward for good work rather than to develop relevant knowledge and skills.

Measurement systems serve to confuse rather than clarify, or drive steadfast focus on short-term profits at the expense of long-term success. Pay systems reward the number of direct reports rather than knowledge and skills or contribution to strategic success. There are no incentives to deliver results or, worse still, employees are rewarded to do the exact opposite of what is needed. Information systems produce reams of irrelevant data.

When such companies decide to make organizational changes, they approach it in piecemeal fashion without reference to strategy or the impact it has on the informal structure. Some force senior executives to reapply for their jobs, despite copious data on past performance, in a ritual display of fear-inducing public humiliation. Others reshuffle two or three layers of top management in a game of "musical chairs" for senior executives. When the music stops, the successful find themselves in new seats while the unsuccessful must leave the game. For everyone else, it is business as usual.

Low Structural IQ firms add new processes atop old ones in the hope of solving problems, but instead they create even more. They introduce new measurement systems in the guise of a balanced scorecard which impose dozens of priorities on bewildered employees. They make massive investments in new IT platforms that promise a custom, integrated approach but force everyone to change to the vendor's chosen standard solution. Conventional wisdom rules in each structural element and no attempt is made to understand how they work together. Frequently, this is because responsibility for each of the elements lies with different function heads, who seek functional excellence rather than integration for the overall good of the firm.

Companies with low structural intelligence ignore informal architecture or view it as a political evil. This becomes a self-fulfilling prophecy when frustrated and demotivated people use their innate ability to organize against the firm.

Some firms eventually realize the importance of structural internal consistency but they fail to make the structure consistent with the strategy.

This is a step in the right direction but is still low structural intelligence, and often leads to a different strategy being executed. We saw this with Energis; the strategic intent was to develop high-margin relationships with sophisticated telecommunications customers, but the reward system drove everyone to pursue low-margin commodity business.[1] Gap, the leading specialist apparel retailer in the US, has made multiple attempts over the last ten years to position itself in more fashionable segments, but it never works; it is structured to deliver basic merchandise.[2]

Moderate Structural IQ

Firms with moderate Structural IQ have taken steps to be more asset-lite. They focus their investments in activities that provide superior returns or proprietary advantage and subcontract where it makes strategic sense to do so. For example, Zara makes 20% of its own clothes in Spain, but even for this 20%, it subcontracts sewing to the many sewers in the Galicia region. It also uses third party truckers rather than owning its own fleet. This is because both sewing and trucking are low-profit, low-barrier-to-entry businesses where there are plenty of good suppliers.

Moderate Structural IQ firms align their structure with their intended strategy. Given the complexity of structure, this is a significant accomplishment. But firms of moderate Strategic IQ have designed a structure that is difficult to change, and they take a top-down approach which compounds the difficulties involved. They only attempt change when they consider it absolutely necessary and this creates significant inertia.

The logic of the command-and-control approach is beguiling, especially to engineers. First, map out the current structure – the initial state. Next, design the ideal future structure to support the strategy – the target state. Third, identify the big differences between where you are and where you want to be and prioritize the required changes. This all seems quite rational, but problems arise at the very first step. Mapping even relatively simple, small organizations is complex; most of the current formal architecture is only poorly documented and out of date, while the informal architecture defies description. There is so much to map that by the time it is completed, it is already time to change again. Consulting firms are always eager to help in such endeavours because the potential for fees is almost limitless. But the extra resources deployed seldom solve the real problem.[3]

Most top-down architectural change initiatives end up being relatively superficial, leaving employees – particularly those on the front
line – to pick up the pieces and try to make it work. The front line is
ignored in the process and the informal architecture treated with disdain
and even suspicion; but once the formal masquerade is over, firms rely on
the front line and informal architecture to come to the rescue and finish
the job. Imposing new structures on the front line in this way rarely
provides a strong incentive for change, and it may backfire if resentful
employees decide to sabotage top management efforts.

This is not to say that top management should not lay out a clear view of
what it believes to be in the best interests of the firm. The "commander's
intent" must be clear. But front-line personnel must be involved right from
the start, understand what needs to be done, believe in it and be rewarded
to deliver it. They can then safely be left to get on with the details for
themselves.

High Structural IQ

If your company is resting on a moderate rung on the Structural IQ
ladder, but has its sights on the summit, the roadmap below will lead to
greater heights. If your firm can master the methods for smarter asset
management, smarter formal architecture and smarter informal architecture, you will be two-thirds of the way towards grafting strategic intelligence
into the very DNA of your firm. (The final third is detailed in **Part Three:
Smart Minds.**) You are well on along the path to superior sustainable
profitability.

Smarter Asset Management

Firms with moderate Strategic IQ know what assets they need at their
disposal to make their strategy a success, but smart firms make a concerted
effort to stay "asset-lite", investing only in those assets which are crucial.
They outsource the remainder and aim to either "commoditize" or "control"
them. Commoditization means making sure that there are many vendors
providing these outsourcing services and that the cost of switching between
them is very low. Li & Fung built up a network of 15,000 manufacturers to
serve its needs and it can shift easily between them.[4]

If there are too few suppliers available, then smart firms look to encourage new players to enter, although they may need to invest themselves

until the supplier base is established. For example, Chilean pulp producer Arauco had to invest in trucking until it managed to persuade others to do so.[5] Control comes from making sure that each outsourcer is heavily reliant on the firm. To achieve this, Li & Fung purchases between 30% and 70% of each manufacturer's output – but never 100%.[6]

Li & Fung does not outsource everything. They invest in activities that are crucial to their competitive advantage. These include strong financial control systems, world-class modern logistics systems and leading-edge information technology. Li & Fung does not outsource these critical activities because they are truly strategic.

PepsiCo and Coca-Cola have historically played an asset-lite strategy. They outsourced the asset-intensive bottling and the complex logistics to dozens of regional bottlers and focused their own efforts on the relatively simple tasks of mixing the concentrate and marketing. The reason was simple: most of the profits are in the concentrate. Over time, they unwisely encouraged their bottlers to consolidate until they became a major threat to profits. In response, Pepsi and Coke have now acquired their bottling networks. But bottling is much less attractive than branded concentrate production. Will these megabrands refranchise bottling to small regional bottlers and become asset-lite once more or make a long-term commitment to the bottling business?

If it makes sense for a company to own assets, it must look for ways to build in flexibility to help avoid deadly asset traps. Planning ahead can help avert disaster. Managers must identify the ways in which the environment might change and design in flexibility to deal with these eventualities. And smart firms look for ways to shape demand to their advantage. Samsung takes this approach with its multi-billion dollar silicon fabrication plants.[7]

Finally, smart firms declare war on fixed costs, restructuring to make them as variable as possible. This might include pay-for-performance systems and contract arrangements that link the cost of inputs to market prices or firm profitability.

Smarter Formal Architecture

Reward Strategic Success. The elements of formal architecture represent the levers for change. But which lever should leaders pull first? Start with **reward systems**! Rewards drive strong behaviours and can be hugely dysfunctional when they are out of alignment with the firm's objectives. Smart companies reward strategic success at all levels within the organization. This drives employees to adapt their behaviours to the changing environment, modifying the informal architecture to stay ahead of the game even if this is in conflict with the current formal processes and systems.

Processes-to-Improve-Processes. However, operating in conflict with out-dated formal processes for very long is inefficient. It is better to align these processes with the new strategy. To achieve this, smart firms avoid top-down design approaches and employ continuous improvement programmes that encourage bottom-up initiatives. For example, General Electric's "Work-out" can be used to engage the front line in reshaping the architecture. This is one of many processes-to-improve-processes that help distribute structural intelligence throughout the firm, encouraging the organization to align itself with its strategy.

Object-Oriented Architecture. Nevertheless, it is still enormously challenging to reshape large and complex "monolithic" structures, because modifying a process in one part of the organization causes problems elsewhere. Smart firms break monolithic hierarchies down into strategic business components (SBCs) with fewer interdependencies, so that they can make local changes without affecting other SBCs – **object-oriented architecture.**

SBCs can now focus on local internal continuous improvement and strategic response to local changes in the competitive environment without affecting other SBCs. In effect, the SBCs become small business units. The smartest firms limit the size of their SBCs to take advantage of the more rapid and effective response to change that social mechanics allows. Each SBC then develops quite naturally into a social mechanics component. In this way, the formal structure is aligned with the informal.

While SBCs are designed to be relatively independent, some SBC-to-SBC and SBC-to-centre coordination is always required. This can be specified as a set of rules from corporate, specific market mechanisms or social coordination mechanisms. Most firms use a combination of all three.

When market mechanisms are used, SBCs can be made profit centres with full rights to set transfer prices, a model adopted by ABB. The market mechanisms can also be more constrained to achieve strategic alignment.

For example, Zara store managers are rewarded for store profitability, but they do not negotiate prices with corporate or set prices in the store; they decide which lines to stock and in what quantities. This encourages them to select fast-moving lines and not order too much of any one line to avoid costly mark-downs at the end of the season. This mechanism encourages store managers to behave exactly in line with Zara's fast fashion strategy.[8]

With market-based coordination, the SBCs are rewarded for performance in an internal marketplace designed by the firm. This market must be designed to be more efficient than the external market, with greater information transparency and trust. The role of top executives changes from being command-and-control to designing and regulating efficient markets. Moreover, the old functional hierarchy is inverted. The market-facing SBCs run businesses and the old corporate functions become service operations in support.

Firms can also use social coordination to align SBCs, encouraging bridgers to tie SBCs together or arranging informal get-togethers to share knowledge and skills. Whole Foods does this by sending teams from its stores to visit other stores (see below).

Building Expert Business Teams for SBCs. For SBCs to function effectively, SBC leaders must be recruited and trained to develop strategy, manage change and develop their people. Smart firms recruit and train managers to set strategic objectives, organize themselves to deliver results, adjust to change, strive for improvement, develop individual team members and flex to work well with other components.

IT Designed to Change. Finally, an SBC structure requires an object-oriented information architecture that must serve multiple purposes; it provides the right information for SBCs to do their job; it allows other SBCs to see what is going on so they can learn from each other and coordinate their activities; and it provides top management with the information it needs to fulfil its fiduciary responsibility to key constituencies such as shareholders and regulators.

Given the relative independence of SBCs, firms do not need to own all of them. Independent SBCs may be invited to play in the internal market as long as they obey the market rules laid down by top management. This provides an avenue for the firm to be more asset-lite. In the Li & Fung structure, in effect, each of the 15,000 manufacturers is an independent SBC, and Li & Fung owns none of them.[9]

Smarter Informal Architecture

Informal architecture is shaped by our genetically inherited ability to collaborate. We do it subconsciously and highly effectively, to which many small firms would attest. Large firms must recognize its importance and shape it to their advantage instead of allowing it to develop independently of the formal structure and potentially work against them.

Smart companies use the power of social mechanics to design more flexible formal structures. By limiting the size of SBCs to the number of people that can naturally form a social unit, firms harness the power and speed of social mechanics while avoiding lots of formal architecture. They make sure the conditions under which social mechanics flourish are maintained and the behaviours that create them encouraged. Reciprocity and altruism are critical to group viability. Transparency, accountability, honesty and fairness all promote trust and make the group more effective.

The exact size of an SBC is constrained by the one-layer rule – one layer of hierarchy between the leader and front-line supervisors. This means that the maximum group size is determined by the span of control that is possible and this is driven by the nature of the task. For complex uncertain tasks allowing only a narrow span of control, the limit may be a few dozen, as in the case of IDEO.[10] More uniform tasks allowing a greater span might support SBCs of 500 people; for example, Nucor's mini-mill sites.[11]

Smart firms use social mechanics to help bridge across SBCs, supplementing rule-based and market mechanisms. There are many ways to do this, including transfer of people across organizational boundaries, regular review meetings, beer parties and company picnics, but take care not to apply these social mechanisms randomly and hope they stick. Companies must identify where bridges are really needed and then build them. Sociograms – maps of internal communications – can help in this respect.

Informal architecture becomes much more effective when social mechanics are leveraged by social networking technology (SNT). SNT allows SBCs to work effectively across geographies and time zones; it expands the natural size limit; and it provides an efficient platform to allow networkers to bridge across many more components. SNT also helps with the governance issues raised when firms rely on informal exchanges because they can now be tracked.

Smart firms will thus invest in their own social platforms rather than leaving their employees to develop their own on Facebook.

Notes

1. Wells (2003).
2. Wells and Raabe (2006).
3. My personal experience suggests that, more often than not, they lead to the imposition of "industry best practices" for the formal architecture and an attempt to suppress the informal architecture completely.
4. Fung and Magretta (1998); Fung, Fung and Wind (2008).
5. Casadesus-Masanell, Tarzijan and Mitchell (2005).
6. Fung and Magretta (1998); Fung, Fung and Wind (2008).
7. Siegel and Chang (2005).
8. Ghemawat and Nueno (2003).
9. Fung and Magretta (1998); Fung, Fung and Wind (2008).
10. IDEO (2011).
11. Ghemawat and Stander (1992).

PART THREE

SMART MINDS

3.1

THE NEED FOR SMART MINDS

Introduction

The ability of an organization to change its strategy and structure in an intelligent and purposeful way is ultimately limited by the willingness and ability of its people to do the same; change must be embraced at all levels in the organization. Part Three of *Strategic IQ* addresses the search for smart minds: curious, adaptable individuals who are continuously looking to improve themselves and the groups they belong to. It argues that some people are more open to change than others, so personnel selection is very important, but it also argues that, in the right context, everyone can be made more open to change. The challenge for the firm is to create a context to make this possible.

As individuals, we often resist change; this unwillingness to adapt intelligently shows low personal IQ. Why do we endanger ourselves in this way, especially when we have the natural capacity to imagine new futures and demonstrate huge commitment to change? What drives people to behave more intelligently?

And if individuals resist change, as groups we often resist even harder, showing even lower IQ. And yet groups, when motivated to do so, can show much higher intelligence than the individuals that make them up. Again, what makes groups behave in smarter ways?

What is a Mind?

The answer lies in the way our brains have evolved. Over millions of years, we have inherited a wide range of individual and social behaviours that are programmed into our genetic make-up and over which we have little conscious control. These behaviours appear to satisfy a set of needs, some of which are quintessentially human and some more characteristic of our reptilian ancestors. In general, our more primitive instincts drive us to fear change while the more sophisticated help us see it as an opportunity to satisfy our curiosity and learn new things. In this way they often conflict. Whichever dominates at any point in time drives how willingly we embrace change. The challenge for firms is to tip the balance in favour of greater strategic intelligence.

But not all we do is hard-wired, driven by our genes. Much of our behaviour is learned, a function of nurture rather than nature; indeed, the human brain has an enormous capacity for learning. This is good news because change invariably means learning new knowledge and skills. But the way we learn is again driven by our genes, often making us blind to what we know and making it difficult to change, driving us to behave in foolish ways. We display a number of anti-learning skills, both as individuals and as groups, and we must learn to overcome them if we want to act smarter.

We must understand human nature if we are to turn it to our advantage. To do so, in **Chapter 3.2: What is a Mind?** we turn to evolutionary biology, neurology, behavioural psychology and social psychology to explain how nature and nurture drive us to behave the way we do. The objective is to identify the behaviours that help firms become strategically smarter and encourage them, and to pinpoint those that hold us back and look for ways to overcome them.

Hiring Smart Minds

We all like some change; too little causes boredom and too much causes stress. This is the never-ending fight between our need for security and our desire to learn something new. For each of us, the optimum lies somewhere in between. But some people are more open to change than others. They demonstrate **practical intelligence**, a curiosity about how the world works, constantly striving to deliver superior performance for themselves and the group they work with. Firms should seek these individuals out and hire them because they are the people who deliver superior strategic and Structural IQ.

In **Chapter 3.3: Hiring Smart Minds** we discuss how firms might systematically go about hiring people that are more open to change and learning.

When seeking the future leaders of strategic change, we take a broad view of the range of intelligence required.[1] We identify rational, creative, emotional and social intelligence as important elements of the mix because they increase capacity for individual and group learning. We also focus on commitment to learning; this requires curiosity, courage to see it through and a cast-iron will. It is the combination of capacity and commitment to learning that drives practical intelligence. Companies should test for these attributes, but they should also remember that, in the right context, we can all demonstrate more practical intelligence.

When firms recruit potential leaders, they look for "raw talent" and a set of knowledge and skills. For "novice" positions, such as new graduate intake, the primary focus is on raw talent. This is practical intelligence.

When companies hire for senior level management positions, they are also looking for candidates with experience, a demonstrated competence to do the job as illustrated by their past track record. The goal is to hire expertise that can immediately be put to work. But experience can be a handicap if we don't know what we know. If we want to build on our expertise and pass it on to others, we must be curious, questioning, always striving to improve and open to learning. We must also be willing to be questioned, ready to try to explain the causal logic behind what we do. In short, we must demonstrate practical intelligence.

Companies also test recruits for "fit", although this is often done informally rather than formally. Fit is important because new members of the firm must be able to work effectively with their colleagues. However, too much focus on fit can result in conformity, and conformity is dangerous because it blinds firms to the need to change.[2] Instead, firms should discipline themselves to hire diversely – people with different backgrounds and points of view. They will make better decisions as a result. But diversity can be disagreeable and it is then ignored. Companies should hire people who can express their point of view constructively, explaining their logic and reasoning and opening themselves to questioning in order to help everyone to learn. This too requires practical intelligence.

Addressing Basic Human Needs

Maslow first identified a hierarchy of human needs in 1943, long before neuroscience and evolutionary biology cast light on what drove them.[3] He observed physiological and security needs much in line with the more primeval, reptilian stages of human development, social and esteem needs more akin to the behaviour of small family groups of lesser mammals and high-level needs for self-fulfilment and purpose that are more closely associated with the advanced human brain. Maslow categorized the more basic needs as satiable and the higher needs as insatiable. However, the more basic needs must be met before we can think about higher needs.

The insatiable needs offer great potential to improve a firm's intelligence because they drive people to improve themselves and each other. But the basic needs must be met first, and if they are threatened by change, then people will resist fiercely. The challenge for a firm is to provide its people with a strong and secure base from which they can try new things.

In **Chapter 3.4: Addressing Basic Human Needs**, we revisit Maslow's hierarchy and discuss its relevance in business and society. We identify that employment plays a fundamental role in satisfying the full range of basic needs and provides the potential to satisfy many of our higher needs as well. But organizational change often threatens job security, leading to fierce resistance. So we look for ways to avoid layoffs in a changing world or make them less painful for both individuals and the firm.

We then turn to teamwork, which is fundamental to business success and also provides an important opportunity to meet our natural needs for belonging and esteem. Firms should aim to satisfy these natural needs while motivating their business teams to deliver great results and adapt to change. We discuss tools for supporting more fulfilling teamwork, and identify how team rewards can focus social pressure on continuous improvement.

We turn finally to the needs for individual and social esteem. To help satisfy them, we revisit **object-oriented architecture** (see **Chapter 2.3: Formal Architecture**) because it allows people more control over their work and strategic direction. We then look at how informal rewards can be used to compensate for the loss of office and associated social esteem that changes in the formal architecture often bring.

Harnessing Insatiable Human Needs

Once our basic needs are met, we dedicate ourselves to satisfying our insatiable higher needs. These represent a huge opportunity for firms striving to adapt to a fast-changing world. We are naturally curious and like to learn. We like to create things and seek out new experiences. We seek fulfilment that comes from achieving our very best; and when all this is done, we want to help others to do the same. And above all, we yearn for common purpose, to rise above our self-interests and serve the common good. These behaviours make us individually and collectively smarter, more able to adapt to change and shape the environment to our advantage. If the firm can harness these needs and provide the purpose we seek, then it too can become more intelligent.

In **Chapter 3.5: Harnessing Insatiable Human Needs**, we revisit Maslow's higher needs to identify those most likely to help raise the IQ of the firm.[4]

We highlight the importance of **learning** in driving company IQ, discuss how firms can encourage more learning and identify a number of anti-learning skills that humans demonstrate that we must overcome in order to be more effective learners. We also look at our natural drive to be creative and how this can be expanded to help create smarter organizations.

We then turn to **self-fulfilment** and examine the conditions that drive people to deliver their personal best.

We recognize the search for common **purpose**, and discuss how this can be translated into a vision and values that drive long-term competitiveness while harnessing the power of groups to work effectively together.

Finally, we touch upon our desire to help others to be fulfilled, identify how coaching and mentoring can meet these needs while driving performance and discuss the greatest gift of all – teaching people to learn.

Notes

1. See Howard Gardner's (1983) *Frames of Mind* for a discussion of the theory of multiple intelligences.
2. Irving Janis (1983) describes the dangers of conformity in his classic, *Groupthink*.
3. Maslow (1943).
4. Maslow (1969).

3.2

WHAT IS A MIND?

The Evolution of the Brain

The brain is a fascinating instrument, not well understood, although neuroscience has begun to unlock its mysteries. It is not, as once thought, a general purpose calculator, but made up of a set of highly localized functions added as it has evolved, with the more rudimentary located at the back of the neck at the top of the spine and the more complex toward the front of the skull, ending up with a large frontal cortex that allows us to reason consciously. We can think of our brain "growing" on the end of our spinal cord to meet ever more complex needs.[1]

Although it is very complex, the brain is organized into three major parts: the Archipallium, or primitive reptilian brain; the Paleopallium, or intermediate brain, typically found in simple mammals; and the Neopallium, or superior brain, found in primates including humans (Figure 29).

The Reptilian Brain

The Archipallium is responsible for basic reflexes and self-preservation. The behaviours triggered by the reptilian brain are without emotion and fiercely individualistic. Physiological needs such as food, water, shelter and sex are paramount. Humans also demonstrate such basic needs, and if they are not satisfied, higher-level needs are often ignored. When we are very hungry, we are in danger of reverting to our primeval ways!

We behave at our worst as a species when we are under the control of our reptilian brains, intent on satisfying our physiological and security needs. We are fiercely individualistic and actively resist change whenever it

Figure 29: The Human Brain

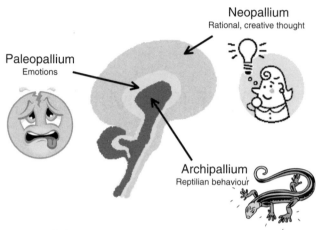

Derived from Rocha Amaral and Martins (2010)

threatens. Unless firms ensure that they satisfy these ancient, primeval needs, the human inertia they create can be fatal.

The Lesser Mammalian Brain

The Paleopallium commands a wide range of behaviours that help small group coordination and learning. Coordinated groups are more viable as species than individuals because they can bring down bigger game and protect each other. The wolf pack is a clear example – an extended family group under the control of an alpha male working together to increase their chances of survival. The Paleopallium drives behaviours that are critical to mammals, including nursing, protecting young and playing, which encourages experimentation and supports learning. It is made up of the structures of the limbic system which provides us with a wide range of emotions such as anger, fear, love, hate, joy and sadness, all of which help us to work cooperatively together and to learn.

Over time, as our brains grew in size, small-group coordination skills evolved to handle larger groups of up to 150 people (see **Chapter 2.4: Informal Architecture**).[2] In such groups a natural hierarchy forms. The alpha is helped by many lieutenants with specialized roles. Members derive their identity from the role they play, and superior performance creates a strong reputation which is highly valued amongst all group members. Specialization of tasks calls for the development of group processes and a means of exchange, a social currency to keep count of who did what. In large groups, a much broader set of social emotions is used to control behaviour. These include sympathy, embarrassment, shame, guilt, pride, jealousy, envy, gratitude, admiration, indignation and contempt. We express these through gesture, speech and facial expression.[3]

Trust is the critical glue that binds the group together. We like to trust. We derive chemical pleasure from it; it triggers dopamine in the brain that gives us a sense of well-being.[4] Humans are expert at detecting cheaters. There is a special region of the brain designed for this. When this is damaged, it is very difficult for the person to detect cheats.[5] When we sense cheating, we lose trust and feel uncomfortable. We do not like to be around people we do not trust.

Transparency, accountability, honesty and fairness promote trust and make the group more effective. We are genetically predisposed to be fair and honest to support group viability.

We are a social species, programmed to behave in quite predictable ways – social mechanics – to work effectively together for our own survival. Presented with a common interest, we are remarkably effective at self-organizing to pursue it in a highly efficient and effective manner. We put structures in place and establish values to guide behaviour which are strictly enforced.

When the common purpose is aligned with the firm, then social mechanics are a valuable ally. But when group survival is threatened, the full power of social mechanics will be brought to bear to resist the change and eliminate the source of the threat.

The Superior Brain

The superior brain, or frontal cortex, consists of a highly complex set of neural cells – 100 billion of them – supporting the development of symbolic language and reasoning skills. Symbolic representation allows for much more powerful communication, the generation of new ideas and rapid learning. These are all powerful tools for change. The superior brain also provides human self-awareness, raising tough questions of who we are and why we exist, driving the need for self-fulfilment and the search for greater purpose. The goal is to align these powerful needs to the long-term performance of the firm.

Neuroscience and Behavioural Psychology – The Individual Mind

The range of behaviours driven by the various layers of the brain was recognized long before neuroscience provided any answers. Behavioural psychologists have observed the behaviour of rats, monkeys and humans for over a century in an attempt to understand how the mind works. One of the most eminent was Abraham Maslow. While his predecessors, such as Sigmund Freud, focused on psychological deficiencies to understand the human mind, Maslow focused his attention on healthy individuals to try to build a fuller picture of the way the mind works. His ground-breaking ideas were first published in a 1943 paper entitled *A Theory of Human Motivation*.[6]

Maslow argued that, while individuals' behaviours might differ quite substantially, they are driven by the same basic underlying needs. Moreover, he postulated that humans have a hierarchy of needs (Figure 30), and that the most basic needs must be satisfied before the individual is concerned with those higher in the hierarchy. He wrote, "The urge to write poetry, the desire to acquire an automobile, the interest in American history, the desire for a new pair of shoes are, in the extreme case, forgotten or become of secondary importance." He also postulated that lower-level needs were deficiency needs – once satiated they were no longer of concern – but higher-level needs were insatiable.

Figure 30: Maslow's Hierarchy of Needs, 1943

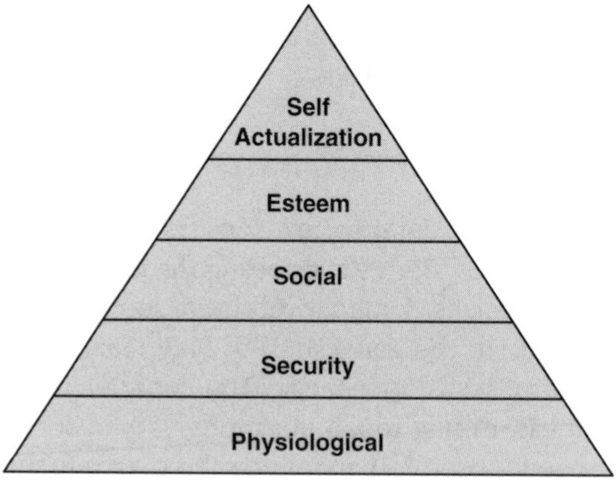

Source: Derived from Maslow, Abraham H., A Theory of Human Motivation, *Psychological Review* 50 (1943): 370–96

While there has been much academic debate over the last 65 years[7] on the veracity of Maslow's model, particularly the hierarchical nature of needs, his observations on the different levels of behaviour are remarkably consistent with the evolutionary layers of the brain and make his model all the more compelling.[8] His identification of basic and higher-level needs inspired work on different management styles.[9] A number of alternative models have also identified roughly the three same levels of needs.[10] And since the various layers of the brain are strongly interlinked rather than operating independently, it is not surprising that needs are not expressed as a strict hierarchy. However, intuition and personal observation suggest that hierarchy plays an important role. It is tough to think about learning new things if we are starving. We have the capacity to do so – people have starved themselves to death in pursuit of a higher purpose, but it takes a supreme act of will to ignore our primeval past when our basic needs are not met.

Basic Needs

Maslow identified the most basic class of human needs as physiological (Figure 31), very much in line with the reptilian brain. These needs include food, water, shelter, clothing and sex. Intuition suggests such needs are likely to override higher-level needs because the instinct for survival is very strong.

Figure 31: Maslow's Hierarchy of Needs and the Brain

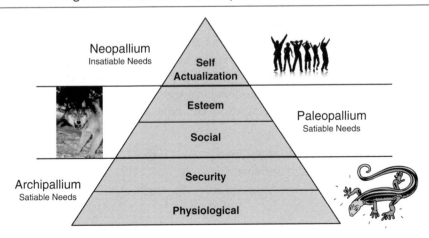

Source: Derived from Maslow

At the next level, Maslow identified the need for safety and security. The desire here is for freedom from fear, perhaps the first emotion of the developing intermediate brain. Stability, structure, routines, laws, borders, traditions and rituals are valued.

Above safety and security needs, Maslow placed love and belonging, behaviours very much driven by the old mammalian brain. Here, the focus is on fulfilling a sense of family and local community. The evolutionary power of the need for community is compelling. The ability to coordinate behaviour in small groups made for a much more viable species.

Next in Maslow's hierarchy, above belonging and love, is the need for esteem. Maslow identified two levels of esteem. The lower one is social esteem, received from others in the form of recognition, status or fame. The higher level is self-esteem in the form of feelings of inner competence, self-confidence, independence and freedom.

The need for social esteem is related to the evolution of more sophisti-cated social control mechanisms of the brain that support coordination in larger groups. Specialist roles are important in such groups and we need to feel good about adopting them. High performance in any of these roles creates a good reputation among all group members, and is highly valued. It is a measure of the esteem in which we are held. We subconsciously measure our reputation from the way people behave towards us and work to improve it. This drives us to perform our role even better and thereby make the group fitter to win the evolutionary race.

Self-esteem is on a higher level, and is driven by our desire to think ourselves a worthy member of the group. Indeed, some have suggested it is a skill that is required to enable individuals to measure their level of esteem within a group. However, the agonies of self-doubt with which many people with low self-esteem are burdened would suggest that the mechanism is far more powerful than this, driving us to continue to improve without group pressure.

According to Maslow, these needs are "deficit" needs; we strive to satisfy them but they are satiable.

Insatiable Needs

Above the deficit needs, Maslow puts an insatiable class of needs which he called self-actualization. These are largely a result of the work of the superior brain, which creates human self-awareness and drives the need for learning and self-fulfilment, curiosity and creativity, the desire to help others reach their full potential and the search for greater purpose.

This striving for self-improvement and the common good would obviously be very valuable to companies if it could be directed towards delivering long-term, sustainable performance. But based on Maslow's hierarchy, it is difficult for us to consider our higher needs when our more primeval needs are under threat. Our cognitive abilities are overwhelmed by emotions and reflex actions. However, if we understand why we do what we do and how we feel what we feel, then we are in a better position to exert conscious control, taking advantage of favourable emotions and reflexes and suppressing unfavourable ones.

What does this mean for our willingness as individuals to accept change? We have a real need for learning and feel excitement at something new, so we all like change to some degree. But these are high-level needs which we only welcome once our basic needs are met.

If physiological or security needs are threatened by change, those driving it will be resisted fiercely; people naturally fear losing their job, especially if it is hard to get another one. And when social groups are disrupted, the feeling of belonging is lost; when people lose their position in the structure and the reputation it bestows, social esteem is destroyed; when people are assigned to new tasks where they no longer feel competent, self-esteem is undermined. It is small wonder that humans do not relish reorganization. Instincts developed over millions of years warn us against it.

The challenge for a firm is to provide its people with a firm and secure base from which they can pursue self-actualization that supports constant strategic change.

Neuroscience and Social Psychology – The Collective Mind

Group Wisdom

The way the brain has evolved has a profound effect on the way we behave as groups. We are a social species, programmed to work effectively together for our own survival. Presented with a common interest, we are remarkably effective at self-organizing to pursue it in a highly efficient and effective manner. With the right motivation, groups are collectively much smarter than the individual members, make substantially better decisions on average than individuals[11] and, contrary to popular belief, can make decisions just as quickly. Groups learn to play more strategically,[12] and team performance is better on average than that of the best individuals playing alone.[13] We are more intelligent collectively. We have more knowledge, more curiosity and more commitment. Because we are sharing the risks, we have more courage. Because we have different frames of reference, we have more points of view. With many pairs of ears and eyes and many points of view, a group can be very knowledgeable and far more likely to see the need for change.

There is much wisdom in crowds if it is tapped wisely. Everyone knows something that is true but mixes it with personal bias and errors. As long as those biases and errors are not widely correlated, they will statistically cancel each other out in yielding robust solutions.[14] The danger in trying to tap such collective intelligence is that systematic biases and errors can be introduced into the process. For instance, if individuals are asked their opinions in front of others, what they say is likely to be influenced by those who are listening. And the listeners are likely to be biased by those who speak up early. Ideally, each person should be asked their view privately in order to seek out truth.

Group Biases

Group biases can be quite debilitating. Conformity drives them, either consciously or subconsciously. Subconscious conformity – groupthink – is the result of everyone seeing the world the same way, so potentially important variables are ignored. To avoid this, companies need to seek out diversity of perspective in their people. Conscious conformity arises when minority views are suppressed.[15] Here there is social pressure to "see things the right way". Some individuals will actually deny the truth to conform. To avoid this, it is important not only to hire people with diverse views, but make sure they have the courage to express them. Even a few dissenters are enough to give others the courage to speak out. However, they should be careful to express their divergent views in ways that help others learn or they simply will not be heard.

Group Stupidity

Groups can also appear remarkably stupid, displaying much less intelligence than any individual member. Unmotivated, they wander aimlessly, achieving nothing, or "head off to Abilene" – a direction in which it makes no real sense for anyone to go.[16] Poorly motivated, they sow the seeds of their own self-destruction, committing collective suicide.

Group behaviour is difficult to understand and to predict. It is dangerous to think of a group as "thinking" in the same way as an individual. Group behaviour is emergent; it is the sum total of the individual actions of the agents who are its members and the whole can appear to have quite different motivations from each of the parts. Douglas Hofstadter illustrated this beautifully when describing conversations between an ant eater and his best friend Aunt Hillary, an ant colony.[17] While individual ants might view the ant eater as an arch enemy, Aunt Hillary could see the sense of ant eating.

In the case of ants, the sophistication of the emergent behaviour of the ant colony compared to the relative simplicity of individual ants is quite stark. In companies, it often seems the other way round; individuals are very sensible but collectively, their behaviour appears foolish. However, we humans might reflect on the hugely complex social structures we create compared to our individual cognitive abilities. We are hard pressed to describe how a city works or an economy. Even the traffic jams that build up suddenly and for no apparent reason suddenly on highways, and then disappear equally quickly, are a mystery to most of us.

Emergent behaviour can be quite counter-intuitive, and so companies are now developing large-scale simulations of the behaviours of thousands of agents to try and predict likely outcomes.[18] Nasdaq did this when it was contemplating changing the tick size of trading from one-eighth of a dollar to one-sixteenth and eventually to one cent. The hypothesis was that this would reduce bid–ask spreads in the market and make it more efficient. However, a simulation of the likely reactions of thousands of market agents suggested that the opposite would be true. This led Nasdaq to adjust its plans.

Attributing logic to group decisions is dangerous.[19] Just because agents are logical, it doesn't mean that emergent behaviour will be so. Each individual might be acting in their own best interests (reptilian mode), but the outcome is likely to be political, depending on the relative power of the agents and their ability to influence outcomes.

Attributing logic to individual agent decisions is also dangerous when dealing with human beings. We are a collective species and this drives us to satisfy emotional and social needs that actually drive us to act in ways that protect our community. Ironically, this can make the group outcome appear more logical – individuals sacrificing themselves for group survival – but not always.

Groups can appear extremely smart and extremely foolish. The dramatic extremes are created by the amplification of individual needs by emotional and social ties. When some group members fear for their security, the emotion is catching, so we all feel their fear. We are driven instinctively to help because we are programmed to protect each other from external threats. We feel obliged to come to their aid because we have exchanged favours and are in their debt. And we hope that someone would also come to our aid in the same way if we were in the same position. In this way, the group behaves emotionally and socially as one, drawing on instinct to defend its members. Individuals will close ranks and make huge sacrifices for the group, but this does not always enhance group health. Sometimes, social units would rather commit suicide en masse than accept changes. This is not uncommon. Many firms have gone bankrupt as a result of industrial action by their employees against actions that were clearly essential for survival.

So how does a company counter this apparently irresistible force? It can only do so by appealing to emotions and instinct, not to logic. On the positive side, the change must be shown to create a more attractive, more fulfilling future for all who make it. On the other, the failure to change must be shown to threaten enough individuals to drive their reptilian instincts to sign up for their own survival, even at the cost of some other group members. They will then reluctantly bid their colleagues farewell.

The Brain as a Learning Machine

Not all of our behaviours are genetically inherited. Indeed, the human brain has a vast capacity for acquiring knowledge and skills and driving new behaviours which helps us to adapt intelligently to change, making us the powerful species we have become.

Adapting to change is a learning process. Sometimes we have seen a sequence of events before and know exactly what to do. But more often some aspects of the change are unfamiliar and we need to modify old responses to the new circumstances or even design completely new ones. As we discover new solutions, we add to our knowledge and skills and become more expert. In this way, intelligent behaviour builds on what we know – it is essential to the process of learning.

However, our inherited behaviours play an important role in how we acquire new ones, and subconscious emotional responses help us to learn. Understanding these processes helps to cast light on why we often resist change.

Conscious Processes of Learning

We learn in many ways. We understand our environment by touching it, tasting it, playing with it, as anyone who has watched a young infant would attest. We pull things apart to see how they are made. We build models in our minds of how they might work, predict outcomes and test them. We learn from our own experiences. We enquire of others and learn from theirs. As we learn, we build a model of the world – a personal frame – that represents our reality. And as we discover things, a positive emotion is triggered in our minds; we like to learn.[20]

Indeed, emotions are essential to learning. When we experience something, we react to it both physiologically and emotionally. When we face the same circumstances again, we feel the same emotions. If they are pleasant, we will attempt to repeat the behaviours; if not, we will seek to avoid them. In this way, we are programmed in the "pursuit of happiness".

Our pursuit of happiness often leads to procrastination. We put off tasks that we do not like, even though we know the consequences of failing to do them may eventually cause even more pain. It is not until the pain of taking no action is sufficiently close and certain that we are finally prepared to act.[21]

As we discover ways of doing things, we are parsimonious in our approach. The world is very complex, so we look to focus on the minimum number of variables we need to solve a problem. When we find an approach that works for us, we tend to accept this as the solution rather than seek out better solutions. We are satisficers rather than optimizers,[22] freeing up the frontal cortex of our brains to work on more novel problems. We thus build simplified models of the world that quickly identify what we consider to be relevant and act on them as if they are true. And the more often we succeed with our simple models, the more convinced we become that they are right.

Blind Expertise

The more we repeat past behaviour, the less we have to think consciously about it; the control of the process is slowly passed to another part of our brain until it becomes automatic, unconscious.[23] Most of us have experienced this when driving a car. When we are driving home on a familiar route, our brain switches off and we think of something else. It is only if something unfamiliar happens that we will consciously return to thinking about driving. We have become "blind" experts at what we do, and often the only way we can improve it is by learning all over again.

Few of us are concerned about improving our driving skills. Once we have attained a satisfactory level, we would rather spend our time doing something else. If we really wanted to be better drivers, we would need to return to first principles and work to unlearn certain behaviours, which is often a painful experience.

Many golfers have faced this problem when trying to improve their swing. In the first instance, it is hard work, feels awkward and is embarrassing, just as it was when they started playing; and in the process, scores drop before they increase. This is unpleasant, triggering negative emotions that our instincts tell us we should avoid. Learning the first time hurts and relearning hurts even more. As humans, we have to ask ourselves whether it is worth it. Is the promise of emotional satisfaction from learning something new sufficient to overcome the pain of getting there? As psychologists K. Warner Schaie and James Geiwitz observed, "old dogs rarely have difficulty learning new tricks; they more often have difficulty convincing themselves that it is worth the effort . . . "[24]

So, as blind experts, unless we can convince ourselves that we want to improve our expertise, we remain ignorant of what we know and simply repeat past behaviour.

Because we don't really know why we do things the way we do, we are also limited in the way we can help others to learn. We can encourage them to copy (see below), but when we are asked why we do it the way we do, we cannot explain. We may simply react defensively with expressions such as "in my experience" or "do as you are told". In this way, we pass on blind expertise.

Unconscious Learning through Metaphor

This blindness is an even bigger issue when we "learn" subconsciously how to solve a problem without ever really knowing what we are doing. Faced with a new challenge, the brain automatically searches through our subconscious for a solution to similar problems we have faced in the past. We then apply the solution and if it works, we automatically store it away as the "right" answer without ever knowing why. As Edward De Bono once remarked, *"The mind is a cliché making, cliché using machine."* [25]

Why does the brain operate this way? If we had to process every piece of information reaching our brains consciously, we would quickly reach overload. Hence, the brain acts as a very sophisticated filter, using past experience to prevent all but the most relevant information from reaching our consciousness, allowing us to focus all of our efforts on solving new problems. For instance, when sitting in a restaurant, we typically listen subconsciously to dozens of background conversations simultaneously, but we automatically filter out all those in which we have no interest and focus on the conversations that we want to hear. However, amid this cacophony, we might be able to pick out a familiar voice or unfamiliar sound. Similarly, as we drive along a highway, we observe thousands of objects subconsciously but note a change in the position of a road sign.

In a curious way, the human brain is designed *not* to work; it is always striving to avoid thinking consciously because this takes a lot of effort. Indeed, conscious thought burns up energy. Doing a crossword puzzle might use up to 40% of the total energy consumption of the human body – it is quite exhausting.[26] However, when we do something familiar, like driving home from work, an activity we might assume would require significantly more processing power, our brains go on to autopilot and we use up much less energy as a result.

Learning through Mimicry

Another way we learn is by copying experts, either by watching them or reading their sage advice. Unless they explain why they solve the problem in the way they do, we have no idea of the underlying logic of their approach: we simply copy and when it works for us, we then believe we know the answer. This works well until the problem changes a little and we don't know how to adjust our solution to solve it. If the expert is not around to revisit the original logic, we are in trouble. This is the **sorcerer's apprentice problem**, as so ably depicted in Disney's *Fantasia*.[27] Mickey Mouse was doing fine all the time he merely had to copy what the sorcerer did, but as soon as the sorcerer was no longer there to help, things started to go badly wrong.

Learning through Unconscious Mimicry

Learning through copying is much more prevalent than most of us would give it credit for. This is because we do it subconsciously all the time; we are genetically programmed to be expert mimics. We copy those we admire without even knowing. When we do so, mirror neurones[28] are triggered in our brains in very much the same way as if we were doing it ourselves. This helps us to learn solutions to problems without really knowing why.

Learning through Emotions

We can also learn and teach things subconsciously through our powerful ability to influence and be influenced by emotions. We signal our emotions to others through our tone of voice and through our body and facial movements. Indeed, we use 42 facial muscles to express happiness, sadness, surprise, fear, disgust and anger. This allows us to help others to learn. When we were children and our mothers shouted a warning – if, for instance, we were moving toward a swimming pool and didn't know how to swim – we sensed fear and did not repeat that behaviour, even though we never experienced the trauma of falling in. Later in life, we may feel the same fear whenever we approach water even though we don't know why. Having come from a family of non-swimmers for three generations, I am well aware of the powerful emotions involved.

The Learning Conundrum

Whether we forget what we learn or we acquire the knowledge subconsciously, we face the classic learning conundrum: we don't know what we know and we don't know what we don't know. Moreover, the emotional pain of learning hurts sufficiently for us to avoid trying to find out. It is only if we are driven by more powerful needs that we are prepared to make the effort. These may be more basic needs such as survival, or higher-level needs such as delivering our personal best.

Ironically, the limits on our ability to learn are created by the brain trying to be more efficient, to focus us on the critical new problems that affect our survival rather than what it interprets as being routine. We need to understand this in order to overcome it and consciously learn how to learn.

Anti-Learning Skills

To add to the learning conundrum, we develop highly effective anti-learning skills.[29]

We avoid accountability for our actions and play **blame games**. Our failure to accept responsibility in this way is partly a function of the emotional pain associated with failing, which we would rather avoid. It is also programmed into us by doting parents who think they are helping when they tell young children that it "isn't your fault" when the opposite is true. This undermines the child's ability to learn. If we are not willing to accept our errors, then we cannot learn from them.

When we explain our point of view, we make it forcefully to discourage anyone from questioning it and we do not provide any data or reasoning to back it up. This behaviour is often driven by fear that we don't really have an explanation for our advocacy and don't want to be embarrassed by questions that would prove this to be the case. If we are challenged, we defend ourselves with platitudes such as "in my experience" or "in my last company". This means that our models are never questioned so we have no way of discovering what they are or improving on them.

We fail to listen to the views of others, dismissing them as foolish because they do not reflect our own experiences. We are convinced that our model is correct and are too impatient to invest the time in finding out whether someone else may have a better approach. When we hear a model that we don't agree with, this triggers a negative emotion which we project onto those expressing the idea and assume they are stupid, and then dismiss everything they say. In this way, we guarantee that we will learn nothing from them.

If we want to learn as individuals and groups we must train ourselves to overcome these anti-learning behaviours. This requires coaching to help us learn what to do and what not to do, measurement to show progress (normally using instruments such as 360 degree feedback) and rewards that encourage the right behaviours and discourage the wrong ones.

We will discuss these issues in more detail in **Chapter 3.5: Harnessing Insatiable Human Needs**.

Group Learning Disabilities

The challenges of individual learning are also amplified in group learning processes. Because tasks are divided over many people, it is easy for groups to forget what they know. Only the process designer has an overview of how the whole process works, and if the designer moves on, the process continues on autopilot. Meanwhile, everyone involved becomes expert at their own task to the point that they themselves forget how they do what they do. Anyone wishing to change the process is faced with a large group of people, none of whom wants to learn to change. This is very challenging. It is only once the whole group is helped to rediscover the logic of the process that the members understand the need for change. And it is only once they believe that the personal benefits of the change exceed the costs of learning that they are prepared to consider it. But convincing everyone that change is good for them doesn't necessarily mean they will welcome it. Change causes pain, and groups will procrastinate until they are really pushed. Instilling a sense of urgency is essential. It is only when the cost of not changing is immediately felt that the group will embrace action.

Groups suffer other learning difficulties. As we have already discussed, biases and conformity blind groups to the need to change. Diversity of viewpoints helps to avoid this. We address this in **Chapter 3.3: Hiring Smart Minds**. Disparate interests prevent a collective point of view; members of the firm must be encouraged to align with company goals or this will always be a problem – to drive greater alignment and strategic intelligence, everyone should be rewarded for strategic success (see **Chapter 2.3: Formal Architecture – Navigating the Architecture Labyrinth**). Finally, individual frames of reference impede constructive dialogue. For this, individuals must be trained and encouraged to communicate to learn, which we cover in **Chapter 3.5: Harnessing Insatiable Human Needs**.

Summary

The human brain has evolved in ways that allow us to work very constructively together and to acquire huge volumes of knowledge. However, the way we are naturally programmed to behave and learn often gets in the way of strategic and structural change, creating human inertia. The ability of an organization to change its strategy and structure in an intelligent and purposeful way is thus ultimately limited by the willingness and ability of its people to do the same.

Figure 32: Climbing the Human IQ Ladder

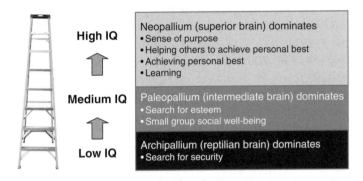

We behave at our worst as a species when we are under the control of our reptilian brains (Figure 32), intent on satisfying our physiological and security needs. We are fiercely individualistic and actively resist change whenever it threatens. Unless firms ensure that they satisfy these ancient, primeval needs, the human inertia they create can be fatal.

Once our reptilian needs are met, our lesser mammalian brain takes over and we become more effective as a species as we seek to satisfy our needs for belonging and our sense of esteem (Figure 32). This encourages team play and allows us to take on greater challenges. But these needs, too, are easily threatened by strategic and structural changes; when we reorganize, social cohesion is disrupted; when we lose a cherished role, our social esteem is dented; when jobs are redefined, our feelings of competence and self-esteem are lost; and if we face unemployment, both social and self-esteem are destroyed. Unless firms can mitigate these effects, change is most unwelcome.

But firms which manage to satisfy such basic needs in the face of change open up huge potential, since this frees up human beings to pursue their high-level needs (Figure 32). We become curious, want to try out new experiences and learn. We strive to do better, reach our full potential and help others to do the same. These behaviours make us individually and collectively smarter, more able to adapt to change and shape the environment to our advantage. And we seek to subordinate our own needs to a higher order, aligning around a common sense of purpose. If the firm can harness these needs and provide the purpose we seek, then it too can become more intelligent.

Notes

1. For a good online introduction to the structure of the brain, see Amaral and de Oliveira (2011).
2. Dunbar (1992).
3. Clippinger (1999; 2007).
4. Lehrer (2011).
5. Young (2002).
6. Maslow (1943).
7. Critics such as Mahmoud Wahba and Lawrence Bridwell have contended that, despite its wide acceptance, there is little evidence to support Maslow's hierarchy. See Wahba and Bridwell (1976).
8. I link the needs to the regions of the brain that have evolved in the human species. The regions of the brain are highly interlinked, so the needs they drive are unlikely to be expressed as a strict lexical utility function, but the structure of the brain as revealed by neuroscience casts useful light on the human behaviours observed by psychologists long before the secrets of the brain were exposed.
9. Douglas McGregor's (1960) work on Theory X (authoritarian, directive) and Theory Y (integrative, participative) management styles was a very influential practical application of Maslow's work. Theory X and Theory Y posited two different models of human behaviour: Theory X reflected Maslow's more basic needs; Theory Y, higher-level needs.
10. A number of studies by Clayton Alderfer (1972), Eugene Mathes (1981), Richard Ryan and Edward Deci (2000) and Michael Thompson, Catherine O'Neill Grace and Lawrence Cohen (2001) have posited three basic needs roughly in line with Maslow's major classes. Another study, by Nitin Nohria, Paul Lawrence and Edward Wilson (2001), uses a socio-biology theory to catalogue four needs. The Institute for Management Excellence has even weighed into the debate, proposing nine needs. The institute's work is discussed more fully by William Huitt (2004).
11. Blinder and Morgan (2000).
12. Cooper and Kagel (2005).
13. Lombardelli, Proudman and Talbot (2002).
14. Surowiecki (2004).
15. Asch (1951).
16. Harvey (1988).
17. Hofstadter (1979) *Prelude . . . Ant Fugue.*
18. Bonabeau (2002).

19. See Graham Allison's (1971) classic *Essence of Decision* for three perspectives on decision-making: rational actor, organizational and political.
20. See Garvin's (2000) framework for types of learning.
21. Procrastination leads to *Predictable Surprises*. See Bazerman and Watkins (2004).
22. See March and Simon's (1958) discussions on the limits of rationality and satisficing behaviours.
23. Rettner (2010).
24. Schaie and Geiwitz (1982).
25. De Bono (1977).
26. The brain uses more energy than any other human organ, accounting for about 20% of total consumption despite only being 2% of body weight. Research suggests that the brain uses more energy when we are thinking hard. See Larson, Haier, LaCasse and Hazen (1995).
27. *Fantasia* was released in 1942 by Walt Disney Productions. It consisted of eight animated segments set to music by Leopold Stokowski, one of which was Mickey Mouse as the Sorcerer's Apprentice.
28. Rizzolatti and Craighero (2004).
29. Argyris (1990).

3.3

HIRING SMART MINDS

Some people are more open to change than others. This depends on the balance of power between our basic and higher needs. Those in pursuit of learning and self-fulfilment, while suppressing more basic instincts, are more likely to welcome change. This is partly a function of age. As we develop as human beings, in our early years, much of our effort is directed at satisfying needs for security, belonging and esteem. It is only later in life that self-actualization becomes more important. But this is also a function of our environment; it is hard for human beings to mature in this way if they have lived a life of extreme deprivation. Instead they find themselves locked into a lower level of emotional development.

Individuals who are more open to change demonstrate what I call **practical intelligence** – a curiosity about how the world works – constantly striving to deliver superior performance for themselves and the group they work with. These are the individuals who help deliver superior strategic and Structural IQ.

Recruiting Raw Talent

When hiring "novices" with leadership potential, firms look for natural abilities that promise to help make them more effective executives. They should seek practical intelligence. This is a combination of rational, creative, emotional and social intelligence (Figure 33), and a strong sense of curiosity and a commitment to learning.[1]

Rational intelligence is the ability to solve problems in a logical fashion through reasoning. This requires pattern recognition and logical reasoning abilities, which are the focus of most IQ tests. At some level, apes demonstrate such capabilities, albeit that their scores are typically lower than humans. IQ

Figure 33: Types of Executive Intelligence

- Rational intelligence

- Creative intelligence

- Emotional intelligence

- Social intelligence

scores change little over an individual's lifetime – dumb is dumb for life – so it is important for firms looking for intelligent behaviour to select for high IQ.

Creative intelligence helps us "to think out of the box", "create" problems and seek out new knowledge. This requires curiosity, imagination and creativity, uniquely human attributes acquired later in the evolutionary process. These attributes are particularly valuable in promoting change. They are also correlated with standard IQ scores.

Reasoning and logical thinking are normally considered left brain activities, while creativity and imagination are considered right brain, although the latest neurological research shows this distinction to be a fallacy.[2] Nevertheless, in practice, some individuals are more predisposed to rational thinking and others to creative thinking. When rational and creative intelligence are separated, they are useful but limited. When combined, they are a powerful force, as Leonardo de Vinci demonstrated. A broad range of intellectual intelligence is required to identify new paths and make sound choices between them, to solve today's problems and imagine tomorrow's.

High IQ scores are an indicator of high rational and creative intelligence. However, they are no guarantee of effectiveness as an executive; many high IQ executives prove ineffective in organizations because of their lack of commitment or inability to understand either themselves or their co-workers. Effective executives also require *emotional* and *social* intelligence.

Emotional intelligence is a measure of psychological maturity: how self-aware individuals are, how comfortable they feel in themselves and how well they are able to manage their own emotional state. High emotional intelligence provides the right level of self-confidence, positive disposition, self-motivation, personal accountability and openness to learning. When combined with rational and creative intelligence, it creates high capacity for individual learning and change. There are many instruments that provide measures of an individual's emotional intelligence, and it makes sense for firms to test it in new recruits.[3]

Social intelligence is a measure of social maturity: how aware individuals are of their impact on others, how comfortable they feel in a group and how well they are able to manage other people's emotional states. High social intelligence provides good interpersonal skills, motivational skills – the ability to get things done through others – reputation for personal integrity and the capacity to be a good team member as well as a team leader. Those with high social intelligence have a high reputation in the informal architecture and demonstrate the behaviours that make social mechanics components effective (see **Chapter 2.4: Informal Architecture**).

Social intelligence combined with emotional, creative and rational intelligence provides an individual with the capacity to help drive effective organizational change and learning.[4]

Managing emotions is core to both emotional and social intelligence. Emotions, while subconscious, are quickly contagious, so the capacity to manage one's own emotions, a key measure of emotional intelligence, is the first step in managing those of others.

Rational and creative intelligence are centred in the frontal cortex of the brain, largely under our conscious control. They represent the most recent and most sophisticated stage of the evolution of the human brain. Emotional and social intelligence are more "hard-wired", more rapid thinking mechanisms added during our evolutionary past. Emotional thinking circuits are much faster than our ability to think logically about an issue and derive from signals generated deep in the amygdala of the brain. Indeed, much of our response to the world is emotional in nature, and much of our conscious thought is spent on rationalizing decisions we have reached emotionally.

In summary, a balance of rational, creative, emotional and social intelligence is a valuable driver of success in an executive expected not only to perform to a high level in a particular role but also to be open to change and able to drive necessary change in organizations. There are many instruments for assessing intelligence, all of which have their limitations, but they can provide a useful guide in making personnel selections.

While broad intelligence is important to success, it is not very useful if it isn't matched with commitment. However high a person's intelligence scores might be, if they are not motivated to act and committed to deliver superior results, they will not succeed. In many respects, commitment is a function of emotional intelligence. Commitment to learning needs an abundance of curiosity, courage to keep going when things get tough and a cast-iron will. Commitment from emotionally balanced individuals comes from an inherent human desire to grow personally, which helps them to overcome the pain of learning. But the right emotional balance is a difficult one to strike; those too satisfied and certain in themselves are often unwilling to strive; those too dissatisfied or uncertain are too afraid to act. When selecting recruits for consulting, I was always looking for those confident enough to build a model of the world they believed might be right but uncertain enough that they would test it rigorously before they would recommend it.

The combination of capacity and commitment to learning drives **practical intelligence** – the propensity of the individual to demonstrate intelligent behaviour to deliver ever-higher performance for themselves and the group they work with (Figure 34).

Figure 34: Practical Intelligence

Commitment to Learning
•Courage
•Curiosity
•Cast-Iron Will

Capacity for Learning
Rational, creative, emotional, social intelligence

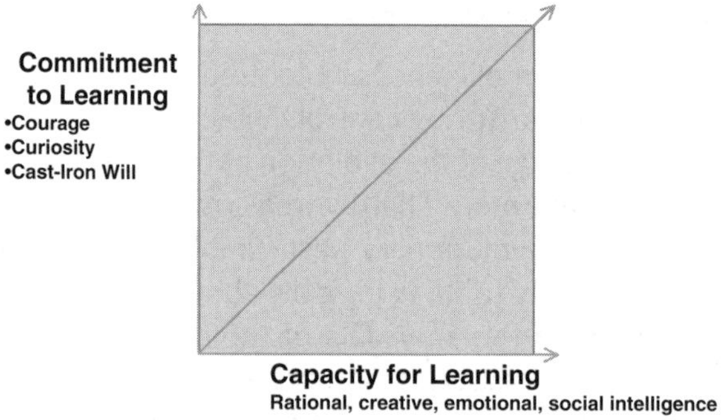

Selecting for Practical Intelligence

Psychographic and intelligence tests can be helpful in recruiting raw talent. Capital One, a leading credit card issuer in the USA, relies on them extensively to pick the right sort of individuals to support its business model of constant innovation. To apply such tests practically, it is best to select a sample of current employees of varying performance levels and ask them to take the tests, so that the results can be calibrated. Capital One uses a sample of 1,600 internal employees to do this.[5] The extent of the tests the firm employs actually discourages some candidates from applying to the company. Indeed, I have had MBA students in my classes over the years who have complained that the tests are demeaning. This, in itself, may form part of the selection process. Those who cannot demonstrate the emotional maturity to spend four or five hours on testing their suitability for a major career step may not be the sort of people Capital One wants.

Capital One finds testing in this way more predictive than interviews. As a recruiting device, interviews have a number of weaknesses, but a systematic approach to interviewing can help in the selection process. Twenty years ago, when recruiting new graduates as potential strategy consultants, I stumbled accidentally on an approach which, in retrospect, proved very effective; many of the young people that passed that test have gone on to become very effective leaders and entrepreneurs. My goal was to assess the candidates on four dimensions, comparing them with the best person I knew on any one dimension. The dimensions were reasoning and creative intelligence, which is key to strategic problem solving; charisma, which is key to convincing people of the need for change and leading its implementation; one-on-one interpersonal skills in interviewing and discussion, which are critical in so many aspects of consulting, from truly understanding a problem to collecting data to coaching individuals through the implementation process; and commitment, which is vital to seeing a tough problem through to a successful conclusion (Figure 35).

Figure 35: Four Dimensions of Talent

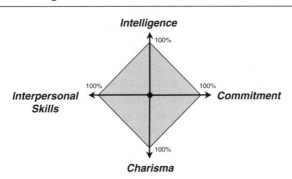

I tested for reasoning and creative intelligence using an unstructured case problem which required reasoning power and the ability to make assumptions and build models in the face of high uncertainty. I tested charisma by asking the candidate to stand up and present their findings in a large room. I tested interpersonal skills by presenting them with a very difficult "client" in a role play (me!). Finally, I tested commitment by observing their response to the interview. The whole process took about an hour and was, reportedly, highly stressful for the candidates. I displayed the results on a four-dimensional chart, assessing the candidate along each dimension relative to the best, who scored 100.

I was looking for the intelligence of Einstein and the charisma of Ronald Reagan (being careful not to confuse the two!). I was also looking for the one-on-one interpersonal skills of a priest and the commitment of a martyr. I sought candidates with a balanced skill-set, defining a diamond with a relatively large area rather than those that excelled on only one dimension. This I believed would make for successful change consultants. I was not disappointed. Those who scored well proved highly effective consultants and later went on to very successful business careers. As I reflect back on the process, although I didn't realize it at the time, I was testing for practical intelligence.

Encouraging Smarter Behaviour

Firms should hire individuals that score well on measures of rational, creative, emotional and social intelligence, but they cannot expect individuals to demonstrate behaviours that reflect these scores unless they are motivated to do so. Demotivated, even the smartest people do not do well. On the other hand, even those of modest ability can achieve a great deal when they push themselves to do so.

Take the example of young school children struggling with mathematics.[6] This is a subject that tests rational intelligence. A sample of school-children not performing well was separated into two groups. One group was told that their brain was like a muscle; the more they used it, the bigger and stronger it would get. The other group, the control group, was told nothing. The children in the first group improved significantly while those in the second group remained steadfastly at the bottom. Thus, with the right motivation, human beings can be encouraged to reason very effectively regardless of their intrinsic IQ scores. Equally, unmotivated individuals with high IQ scores seldom demonstrate any useful reasoning capacity.

As with rational intelligence, the ability of individuals to demonstrate creative intelligence can be increased significantly with the right training and motivation. All human beings are innately creative, but when we are asked to generate new ideas, we are our own worst critics. We generate an enormous number of options but we subconsciously compare these options with past experiences and eliminate most of them before they have surfaced in our consciousness. The challenge is to switch off our personal self-critic and allow more of these ideas to surface so that we can consider them more seriously. This is the aim of the many creativity tools and techniques.[7] They typically involve suspending judgment, allowing us to generate ideas before we start evaluating them for quality. For instance, simply by role-playing someone else, we can often free ourselves from self-criticism and allow ourselves to come up with many new and potentially useful ideas from a different perspective. Many years ago, I ran such a session for executives in the newly privatized British Airways. They were finding it difficult to come up with a clear view of BA's vulnerabilities until I asked them to role-play the senior management team of a major competitor and asked them to destroy BA. The list of weaknesses was long and very comprehensive.

Emotional and social intelligence can also be developed. Both are rooted in complex emotional response mechanisms, so the goal must be to help individuals understand the way their emotional responses impact their "rational" decisions and how their behaviour affects emotional responses of others. IMD in Switzerland, one of the world's leading business schools, provides extensive counselling and psychoanalysis to help its MBA students to understand their emotions and develop capacity to demonstrate higher levels of emotional and social intelligence.

Companies can also nurture their employees' innate curiosity and commitment to learning in the right context. We discuss this further in **Chapter 3.5: Harnessing Insatiable Human Needs**.

Recruiting Senior Executives

We turn now from recruiting novices to hiring senior personnel. This is a significant challenge, and failures are common. Archie Norman, Chairman of ITV, once told me of his "one-third" rule. One-third of senior executive hires are successful and add a lot of value; one-third are neutral; and one-third are a disaster and destroy value. The challenge, according to Archie, was to identify the failures fast and get rid of them.

When firms recruit senior executives, they are typically looking for "experience" and "fit". Experience is demonstrated competence to do the job, as illustrated by their past track record. Fit is ability to work effectively with others in the firm to get things done.

Experience is obviously important. It takes many years to acquire the knowledge and skills to operate in a particular knowledge domain at a senior level with a high degree of competence. It is also essential to be able to work effectively with colleagues to get things done. But there are dangers to both experience and fit unless combined with practical intelligence.

Beware Experience

Companies typically try to recruit senior executives who are already competent to do the job. They invest significant resources in assessing a candidate's past performance. They look for a track record of making successful decisions and having a significant positive impact in similar industries. This suggests the candidate has built up knowledge and skills in the right knowledge domain. The logic of this approach is that different types of industries operate under very different models, and knowledge of the right type of model is key to success. An executive with significant relevant experience is viewed as an expert and this expertise can immediately be put to work.

But it is often hard to corroborate the impact executives have had in their past roles. Moreover, expertise does not necessarily rise with experience. Some individuals work in an industry for only a few years and become quite expert while others spend decades and don't learn much at all. It all depends on their capacity and commitment to learning – their practical intelligence.

As we discussed in **Chapter 3.2: What is a Mind?**, expertise can also be "blind". We have faced the same problems so often in the past that we have forgotten the underlying logic of our solutions and simply apply them. The answers are "obvious". The danger here is that we are unable to adjust what we do if the logic changes.

Wild Oats, the number two organic food retailer in the US, suffered in this way. The company faced a formidable competitor in the number one player, Whole Foods Markets. Whole Foods set up a decentralized business model which allowed store employees to adapt rapidly to local market conditions and win against large grocers who were slow to make changes from the centre. When Wild Oats began attacking Whole Foods' core markets, profits suffered. The board pushed the founder-CEO aside and appointed a new management team with traditional grocery experience.[8]

True to type, the new leadership team at Wild Oats introduced a typical grocer business model with centralized purchasing and standardized merchandising planograms that specified exactly where each product should go on the shelf. This was ineffective against Whole Foods' fast-moving decentralized approach and was equally out-gunned by the large grocers who had much greater scale. Wild Oats continued its decline – all because it had hired "experience".

The danger of recruiting experience is that you get – experience! And if it is not the right experience it can destroy the firm.

Blind expertise poses several challenges. If we don't know the underlying causal logic for the solution to a problem, how can we improve on it? When the problem changes, how can we adapt our solution to fit the new circumstances? If we don't know why we do things, how do we train others and help them to learn? Telling people to "do as they are told" is no way to build organizational intelligence.

If we want to build on our expertise and pass it on to others, we must be curious, questioning, always striving to improve, open to learning; we must also be willing to be questioned, ready to try to explain the causal logic behind what we do. We must be prepared to be humble and relearn what we think we know. In short, we must demonstrate practical intelligence.

This is not to suggest that experience should be ignored. Business environments are extremely complex and it takes many years to really understand them. Senior executives with extensive experience of a particular knowledge domain have an obvious advantage. But their level of expertise in the knowledge domain is a function of their capacity and commitment to learning – their practical intelligence. Moreover, practical intelligence is essential in helping them address new problems effectively, build on their expertise and distribute intelligence throughout the organization. Therefore, it cannot be ignored.

Note that experienced blind "experts" may have been very successful in previous roles because their limitations didn't stand in the way of solving the problem at hand. This is particularly true of turnaround situations where the focus is typically on making rapid decisions to ensure short-term survival rather than building intelligence and long-term sustainability into the firm. Indeed, a person of limited rational, creative, emotional and social intelligence but the right domain expertise is likely to default to behaviour that is best suited to such situations – a willingness to rapidly dictate a prescribed set of actions in the face of crisis – because there is little time for going back to first principles and explaining to everyone why a particular action must be taken. However, once the short-term crisis is abated, it requires someone with more intelligence and openness to learning to build organizational capability.

Beware Fit

When looking to recruit senior executives, firms are rightly concerned about fit. New members of the firm must be able to work effectively with their colleagues. However, too much focus on fit can result in conformity and conformity is dangerous.

We are all naturally biased to hire "people like us"; people with the same background, education, interests, point of view. They think like us. They agree with us. They understand what we say. They are easy to get on with. They clearly fit! But this level of conformity leads to groupthink. Everybody sees the world the same way and so there is only one truth. The organization is blind to potential threats.[9] Sometimes the conformity is subconscious. No one is coerced in any way. At other times it is quite conscious. Everyone does what is expected of them and social pressure drives people to see things "the right way".[10] People will actually deny the truth to conform. When fit becomes conformity, it sows the seeds of failure.

Seek Diversity

Rather than insisting that everybody conforms, firms are healthier when they encourage diverse points of view. Diverse perspectives provide firms with greater capacity to identify problems and generate creative solutions. As James Surowiecki observed in *The Wisdom of Crowds*, "Individual judgment is not accurate enough or consistent enough; cognitive diversity is essential to good decision-making."[11] And it doesn't take that much diversity to avoid suppression of ideas; just one person with the courage to speak up will encourage others to do so.[12] Moreover, decision-making groups often fare better when they are not uniformly expert. The presence of a member who is prepared to ask "dumb questions" is enough to drive better decision-making. As James G. March noted, "The development of knowledge may depend on maintaining an influx of the naïve and the ignorant."[13]

Learning through Constructive Diversity

Diversity of views is good for learning, so firms should recruit people with different perspectives and the courage to share them with their colleagues. But diversity is sometimes disagreeable. And when people are disagreeable, we avoid them or ignore them. Thus, it is important for those with different points of view to state them in a way that does not threaten or create defensiveness and to support their conclusions with data and reasoning so that everyone understands.[14] Moreover, people should be encouraged to question the logic of others in order to learn for themselves and help others to learn. In this way, each member of the group discovers what they know and what they don't know; once-blind experts begin to see and to grow. Firms should not only be looking for people with diverse points of view but with the ability to state them in ways that help them and their colleagues to learn.

Diversity of Thinking, Not Action

Diversity of perspective can be very helpful when a firm is in "thinking" mode, assessing potential threats, identifying opportunities or creating and evaluating options for the future. However, there is a limit to the value of diversity. Decisions have to be made, and the organization must align behind the decisions to ensure effective execution. But if the diversity of views continues into the action phase and individuals pursue their own agendas, then this can have disastrous effects. The challenge is to recruit people who are not afraid to speak up during the thinking stage, but, once heard, are willing to commit to a decision that they may not agree with and execute in a disciplined way in the best interests of the firm.

Summary

When recruiting raw talent, it is important to look for practical intelligence: the sort of intelligence that leads to long-term business success. This is a balance of rational, creative, emotional and social intelligence and the commitment to apply them in the service of learning. There are many tests to choose from that help measure different forms of intelligence, and firms should calibrate these against a range of performers within their current employee base.

However, firms should not forget that if they provide the right training, reward systems and supportive environment within the firm, they can materially enhance the capacity of individuals of a given natural intelligence to demonstrate more intelligent behaviour.

When hiring senior executives, many firms focus on experience and fit, but practical intelligence remains very important.

The danger of fit is conformity, which can impede learning. Firms should look for diverse viewpoints and behaviours but ensure that the way they are expressed encourages everyone to learn.

Firms use experience as a surrogate for expertise, but it is not always a good indicator. However, practical intelligence combined with experience helps develop expertise. And practical intelligence provides the capacity to improve on that expertise and adapt it to different circumstances and changing times.

Notes

1. Howard Gardner (1983), in his book *Frames of Mind*, provides an extensive discourse on the theory of multiple intelligences.
2. Rose (2005).
3. Goleman (1996).
4. Goleman (2006).
5. Wells and Anand (2008).
6. Dweck (2007); Blackwell, Trzesniewski and Dweck (2007).
7. Glassman (1991).
8. Wells (2005; 2006).
9. Janis (1983).
10. Asch (1951).
11. Surowiecki (2004).
12. Asch (1951).
13. March (1991).
14. Argyris (1990).

3.4

ADDRESSING BASIC
HUMAN NEEDS

Introduction

Humans have a range of basic needs which can often be threatened by organizational change. When this is the case, they will resist fiercely, creating significant inertia. Firms must reduce this fear of change. Ideally, they should also try to meet their employees' basic needs as part of the process of change.

Basic Human Needs in Business and Society

Maslow identified a hierarchy of human needs (Figure 36), each of which must be satisfied before the next one becomes important.[1] Maslow's most basic class of needs was physiological, in which he included the need for sex, food, water, shelter and clothing. Today, we might also add healthcare.

In modern societies, employment typically provides us with sufficient income to satiate physiological needs, and when employment is not available, some societies provide a tax-funded social safety-net to do so. The welfare state that emerged in the UK after World War II is a case in point. Victorian England was very different from today, and enlightened business leaders attempted to fill the gap. For instance, William Hesketh Lever of Lever Brothers (later to become Unilever) built Port Sunlight, a model village complete with schools, libraries and public buildings for his workforce to alleviate the squalor and poverty of an industrializing England.[2] In the developing world, such needs remain important today. In 1996 when I became

Figure 36: Maslow's Hierarchy of Needs, 1943

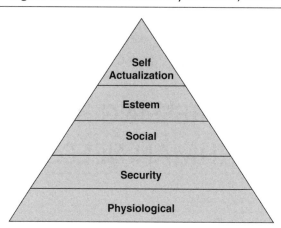

Source: Derived from Maslow, Abraham H., A Theory of Human Motivation, *Psychological Review* 50 (1943): 370–96

CEO of Wedel, Poland's leading chocolate maker, I found myself responsible not only for 3,000 employees and four factories, but also a hospital, two nurseries and an apartment building heated by the factory boiler. For an effective, functioning community, basic needs must be satisfied.

The next class of needs identified by Maslow was for safety and security, freedom from fear. Stability, structure, routines, laws, borders, traditions and rituals are valued. These are readily available in stable political environments but woefully lacking in some parts of the world. In more developed societies, the needs are typically expressed by the drive for regular income, savings and insurance. Religious and scientific beliefs also play an important role in "explaining" reality and reducing uncertainty. Overcoming threats to security is one of a leader's most challenging tasks in creating a context that welcomes change. Paradoxically, this often can be best done by making the impact of change appear more certain. Uncertainty breeds fear.

It is not surprising that a species with a heightened capacity for satisfying physiological and security needs proved more effective in the evolutionary race. But the implications of this evolutionary progression for driving change in an organization are significant. Any action which threatens our most basic needs will trigger fierce subconscious resistance. Employment is a major contributor to physiological and security needs, so threats to job security strike fear into any organization.

After safety and security needs, Maslow placed love and belonging. Here, the focus is on fulfilling a sense of family and local community. Prior to the industrialization and urbanization of societies, people typically lived close to their nuclear families in village communities, and love and belonging needs were readily met in this way. Access to the community was highly valued, and one of the greatest punishments the community could mete out was banishment.

The decline of the importance of the nuclear family and the rise in urbanization has changed all this. People move into huge cities, surrounded by millions of their own species and feel lonely. In modern urban societies, perhaps the greatest opportunity for us to satisfy our social needs is in the workplace, where we spend the majority of our waking lives. We naturally affiliate with others to form small groups, protect group members, expect to be protected by them and compete with other groups for resources. The bonds in such groups are powerful. Members do each other favours in return for social currency, which they can cash in later for future favours. Being seen to support the group is vital to membership; failure to do so results in a loss of standing and potential exclusion from the group. Armies have long used these social bonds to build strength in fighting units. The social currency that binds troops is very powerful. Soldiers seldom die for their country; they die for their comrades. Again, change can threaten social cohesion, and loss of employment is a form of banishment.

Firms can either be victims of such social behaviour or choose to take advantage of it. Business is teamwork; teams are essential to developing and executing strategic changes and to delivering results. In the process, if social needs are met, then strategic success is aligned with basic human needs. However, if the process of change threatens the social order, people will quite naturally resist.

Above belonging and love, Maslow placed the highest of basic human needs, that of esteem. Maslow identified two levels of esteem: social esteem, received from others in the form of recognition, status or fame; and self-esteem in the form of feelings of inner competence, self-confidence, independence and freedom. Self-esteem in the workplace comes from being able to perform well. Social esteem comes from our reputation amongst our peers in the role we play. We subconsciously measure our reputation from the way people behave towards us and work to improve it. This drives us to perform our role even better and thereby make the group fitter to win the evolutionary race.

Change threatens esteem. People fear being assigned new roles for which they lack competence. Any perceived reduction in rank in the formal hierarchy is a social disgrace; even sideways moves are considered signs of failure. Organizational change thus propagates fear.

Employment

In modern societies, employment is essential for meeting our physiological and security needs, and increasingly important in satisfying our needs for belonging and esteem. Moreover, it provides many of us with the best opportunity we are going to get of satisfying our higher needs. Loss of employment is thus a major blow; we value employment highly and when change threatens jobs, it strikes fear into the community.

Fear, like all powerful emotions, is catching; it spreads like wildfire throughout an organization. We instinctively act to protect each other, close ranks and resist the threat.

Those who have to fire people face a daunting task, especially if the victims are not at fault. We hate to fire people, as any executive who has done it knows. We defer the decision for far too long in the hope that it will go away. When we finally brace ourselves to do it, we feel their pain and our own guilt at what we do. These emotions travel fast too, shaping into a collective guilt at what has been allowed to pass. Now we are viewed with fear and suspicion by the rest of the community; trust is lost. These are natural reactions, programmed into us over eons, and they represent a powerful source of inertia.

In today's world, sadly layoffs are difficult to avoid. As the competitive environment evolves, the level of human resources and the skill-sets required must be adjusted to changing circumstances. This threat to employment creates a very real dilemma for the firm. Without job security, people find it difficult to pursue higher-level needs to satisfy their curiosity, learn from new experiences and stretch to reach their full potential. These are seldom demonstrated if people think they might lose their jobs. But the alternative, offering lifetime employment, seriously limits a firm's ability to change. Damned if you do and damned if you don't!

Commitment to the Core

One way to avoid laying people off is not to hire them in the first place – to play a human asset-lite game, as suggested in **Chapter 2.2: Smart Asset Management**. The logic here is to commit long term to a small core community – all firms need *some* people – and look to the marketplace for all other labour needs. Many seasonal businesses such as retailing, farming and the hospitality trade would not survive if they didn't take an asset-lite approach.

When operating human asset-lite, resisting headcount increases is absolutely essential or the core group will naturally expand in size. Even without the inflexibility it creates, the cost of maintaining an extra employee is far more than it first appears. When the extra capacity to resist change is factored in, the logic for avoiding headcount expansion becomes very compelling. A boss of mine at PepsiCo once said to me "beware of bums on seats, they cost a fortune". Curious, I calculated the full cost of an employee, taking into account all infrastructure and support, and the results were horrifying. The total cost "per seat" was more than double the direct labour costs at the administrative level and was a substantial part of total costs of even high-level executives when personal assistants, cars, etc. were taken into account. It was then that I began allocating all such costs to people to show the true cost of headcount.

The insidious thing about hiring more people is that it leads to hiring even more. I recall when I was running a professional service office that I put an arbitrary limit on the ratio of support staff to professionals of one-to-one. This resulted in many complaints of lack of support because the professionals felt that they were wasting valuable time on menial tasks rather than on providing professional services. After constant complaints, eventually I relaxed the constraint, whereupon, within a matter of twelve months, the ratio shot up to more than two-to-one. Now, we had not only more support staff, but supervisors to manage them and managers to manage the supervisors. Ironically, there was no material improvement in the perceived support received by the professionals. In the absence of clear targets and firm control, overhead grows!

Long-term commitment to the core group is made easier if employment costs are made more variable; everyone shares in the gains in the good times and the pain in the bad times. But the sharing must be fair or it will create resistance. Historically, in the United States, front-line manufacturing workers were typically laid off in downturns while executives maintained their jobs and even part of their bonuses. It is small wonder that the workforce often turned to unions and resisted change. It effectively created two communities at loggerheads with each other. In contrast, at Nucor, the most productive US steelmaker, the workforce was put on a three-day week when business turned down rather than being laid off, and managers took an 80% pay cut. With true sharing of the pain, costs were made more variable and the firm worked as one to deliver impressive increases in productivity.[3]

But all firms require at least some people so they should seek out highly productive, flexible ones. As with all things, the 80:20 rule applies with people, especially amongst the management ranks. 80% of the work is done by 20% of the people, so hiring great people pays huge dividends. And, pick more flexible ones that can try their hand at anything when times change. There is no substitute for recruiting the best, those with high practical intelligence and commitment to learning (See **Chapter 3.3: Hiring Smart Minds**.)

Strategic Positioning to Avoid Layoffs

The probability that a firm will face the need to fire people depends on the nature of the industry they choose to compete in and the strategic position they take. Firms in more volatile industries face greater risks and need to be more asset-lite to compensate for this. This is the beauty of Li & Fung's business model in the fast-moving fashion industry. They don't own any of their 15,000 manufacturers, so they can adjust their supply chain with a click of the mouse.[4]

Slow growth industries can also create an employment headache. If a business is not growing and requires 5% annual labour productivity improvements to stay competitive, then the labour force must fall 5% each year. While some of this can be achieved through natural turnover, this seldom delivers reductions where they are needed, so the firm must resort to firing some of its people as a matter of routine. Under such circumstances, productivity increases are bound to be resisted.

A few years ago, I discussed this issue with Tony Hapgood when he was chief executive of Bunzel, a portfolio of relatively low growth businesses. He was always making changes to drive productivity gains and I asked him how he dealt with this issue. His solution was simple: he focused on segments of the business that allowed above-average growth so that the productivity gains were not threatening.

Alleviating the Pain of Layoffs

However hard firms may try to avoid layoffs, from time to time they find they have no choice, so it is useful to find ways of making them less painful for both the individuals involved and the firm.

Making sure they only hire great people helps in this respect. If a firm only hires the very best, they have no concern for job security because they can always get a job elsewhere. Moreover, if the firm has a great reputation for developing its people, it makes them even more valuable in the marketplace. General Electric has an excellent track record of hiring and developing great people, and launching them on very successful careers when they move on from the company. Indeed, judged by the number of alumni occupying Fortune 500 CEO positions, GE is a better business school than Harvard. When it comes time for GE to part company with talented managers, there are fewer hard feelings all round.

GE provides a valuable career step for any ambitious executive, and this is the way companies should view it. They should aspire to become **preferred employers** (see discussion of human asset development in **Chapter 2.3: Formal Architecture**) because this creates a virtuous circle. Firms that offer the best career opportunities can attract the best people, those with the highest practical intelligence (see **Chapter 3.2**). These individuals deliver more value to the firm and learn faster, adding to their own value as well. And so, when it comes time to leave, they easily find good employment opportunities, making way for fresh new talent.

Many professional service firms would do well to run their human asset management in this way. Their business models do not normally allow for many new recruits to make it to partner, so the majority must leave and find alternative employment. In effect, these companies operate an up-or-out policy, so firing is a matter of routine. The key issue is how this is done.

They can follow the macho, investment-banking model – announcing layoffs over an intercom, handing out brown envelopes, emptying desks into black trash bags and marching the fallen to the exit door accompanied by security. This is close to Neanderthal.

Or they can follow the McKinsey approach. When it comes time to part ways, it is done with subtlety and respect; indeed, it is often triggered by individuals themselves. McKinsey then helps them to find new roles that they would never have reached without McKinsey experience and training; and these roles are often excellent positions from which to hire McKinsey in future. This business model helps McKinsey to attract the best, train them to be even better, pay them very well and launch them on to valuable careers as part of the McKinsey alumni network. This preferred employer approach makes people much more open to career changes.

Despite companies' best laid plans, sometimes they are faced with unforeseeable events that require a radical change in their human asset base. Adjusting under such circumstances takes significant courage. It is important that everyone sees the need for prompt action, but explaining the logic of the situation seldom works in these circumstances; the quickest and the most compelling way of creating alignment is to call upon the basic instincts for survival. Unless the community can be convinced that, unless some of its members are sacrificed, the whole community will die, they will continue to resist. Once the decision is taken, it is better to do it rapidly rather than piecemeal; death by a thousand cuts is very painful. Those leaving must be treated well and helped to find new employment; this is not only important for them but for those left behind who must overcome their own pain and guilt and rebuild the morale of the firm.

Teamwork

To satisfy our subconscious need for belonging, we like to work and play on teams and feel part of a larger community that respects our teamwork. We like to be on a winning team for the social esteem this creates. This is quite natural. The winning teams secure the best food supplies and have the best chance of survival in the evolutionary race. Thus, we would all rather associate with the winners, and we deliver higher personal performance when we are on winning teams. We strive hard to make a good personal contribution, not only for the social esteem that results but the personal esteem we feel at our accomplishments. We value the reputation we build in the community for the role we play and we work hard to maintain it. We are driven by the joy and pride of inclusion and the fear and indignity of exclusion. It is a fame and shame game.

If we are not presented with opportunities to satisfy these basic needs, we become frustrated and seek them out for ourselves. The implication for firms is clear; work designed to satisfy these basic instincts should produce high performance and a motivated workforce. In this respect, work cells make more sense than machine-paced production lines; team-based change initiatives create more commitment than command-and-control instructions from above. Moreover, once our basic needs are met, we look to satisfy higher needs, exercising our creativity to find better ways of doing things, stretching ourselves to meet new challenges and helping the firm to become much smarter. However, failure to satisfy the basic needs for belonging and esteem in the workplace opens the door for employees to build social structures and play games that distract them from the firm's main purpose or even conflict with it, undermining performance. Trade unions are a case in point.

If team objectives can be aligned with the objectives of the organization while meeting the fundamental social needs of the members, this can become a significant driver of competitive advantage. There are undoubtedly activities beyond the task itself that teams must engage in to fully meet their social needs, and firms should encourage this. It may be a night out bowling or a trip to the local ball-game, but firms need not worry about what exactly is required, since the teams will readily figure it out for themselves with only the smallest of encouragement (e.g. a small subsidy). The goal in supporting such behaviour is for the firm to deliver outstanding team experiences so that there is no need to look elsewhere for emotional satisfaction.[5]

Rewarding Teams for Change

To achieve greater strategic and Structural IQ, firms need their teams to strive for continuous improvement in productivity and to seek out new ways of doing things. But the teams must have an incentive to do this, and the firm must take both social and financial rewards into account. Effective teams will always be looking for productivity improvements, but, in the absence of an incentive to share them with the firm, they will act to capture the full benefits of the lower work hours for themselves in the form of extra leisure or social time. Indeed, it is very unlikely that the team will downsize itself and incur the social pain of doing so unless the financial rewards for the remaining members are substantial.

But financial reward systems can be used to align social currency with a firm's objectives, creating a powerful motivator. Nucor, for instance, uses a combination of financial and social currency to drive productivity in its mini-mills. It divides the work among a number of small teams and pays each team a substantial group bonus for productivity. If productivity targets are not met, no one gets a bonus so every member of the team works very hard to make sure they don't let the team down. Moreover, the teams have a very strong incentive to train new members and to discourage incapable members from staying. The objective of every team – increasing productivity – is strongly aligned with Nucor's objective of driving its primary competitive advantage: low-cost production.[6]

Given the power of team-based financial rewards, it is surprising that companies don't use them more often. What is even more surprising is that team activities involving change are often rewarded the least. Most executives with a specific functional role spend a large percentage of their time working on cross-functional teams executing change initiatives, but they are not rewarded for it. Instead, rewards are typically focused on their performance in running their departments and nothing accrues to them for the effort they spend on organizational change. In effect, they are being punished for investing in needed changes because, in doing so, they are neglecting their day-to-day operations. GE attempts to compensate for this by devoting a substantial proportion of annual performance bonuses to its change programmes. However, these are still individual rather than team bonuses. Businesses might be better off if they tracked the contribution of every team to long-term success and paid group rewards for achieving major milestones on the way.

Developing Team Skills

We are genetically programmed to work as teams but, as those who have had some terrible experiences would attest, they work more effectively together if they follow a few simple rules. Providing lists of what to do rarely motivates the right behaviour. Instead, it is better to allow teams to generate their own list. To really encourage engagement, ask the team for recommendations on how to run the team very badly. We are all well qualified to do this, and the exercise is a lot of fun which makes it easier to remember. Reversing the results then provides a useful checklist for chartering the team. Team members are more likely to comply with guidelines they have themselves generated and agreed to abide by.

Chartering is essential at the beginning of a team exercise, and it is important to revisit it on a regular basis to ensure that everything is on track. An ideal time for reflection is when a milestone is reached. Team members should celebrate what they've achieved and identify what they would do even better next time. They should then identify how they are going to adjust their game plan. Re-chartering is also required when anything material changes, such as resetting objectives or replacing a team member. Initial chartering may take some time, but after a while it can be achieved quickly.

Object-Oriented Architecture

The design of the formal hierarchy can have a significant impact on basic human needs. In **Chapter 2.3: Formal Architecture**, we discussed the benefits of breaking large hierarchies down into smaller, more flexible strategic business components (SBCs). By organizing their own work and responding to local strategic changes, they are more responsive than large, monolithic organizations. In **Chapter 2.4: Informal Architecture**, we identified how genetically inherited group behaviours – social mechanics – provided a very efficient and responsive informal architecture for coordinating work, just so long as the group size did not exceed the upper limit of a social mechanics component. By combining the two, creating SBCs of a size where social mechanics can complement formal architecture, we align the informal and formal organization.

Such structures not only make for more distributed strategic and Structural IQ; they satisfy needs for belonging as a result of the communities they create and esteem through the empowerment they provide. This empowerment comes from a sense of freedom and control employees have over their own destiny.

When creating SBCs and relying on social mechanics, firms must ensure that the conditions for healthy informal collaboration are met. The groups must have a clear objective and must be rewarded collectively for delivering on this. Trust must be promoted within the group; this takes legitimate leadership, transparency, accountability, honesty and fairness. These values must be reflected in the behaviours expected of people and the formal systems that regulate their work. When these conditions are met, social mechanics will thrive.

Rewarding Change-Makers Rather than Positions

Social esteem in the business context is related to the role individuals play in the organization and the respect they are shown. This is visible in the formal architecture in terms of title or rank. It is reflected in formal processes, such as the committees to which they belong and the meetings to which they are invited. It is also reflected in the way they are rewarded, although financial compensation is normally confidential. Any change in their title or responsibilities, any redesign of business process or any adjustments to rewards that do not communicate an improvement in status is thus seen as a threat. This creates inflexibility and inertia.

In the organization's informal architecture, esteem is measured by how individuals are treated by powerful leaders in the organization. When are individuals consulted? To whom does the chief executive say hello in the morning? Any changes in such behaviour on the part of powerful executives towards a member of the group are subconsciously detected and communicated very rapidly to all members of the group. Changes in status are measured in terms of symbolic rewards such as size and position of an office or brand of company car. They can also be manifested in awards schemes such as employee of the month.

Rather than allow measures of esteem to be driven solely by the formal roles in an organization, smart companies associate esteem with those most open to change. How can a business elevate the change-makers to heroes? One way is to bestow special privileges on those who sacrifice formal social status for the good of the organization.

For instance, a senior executive might be assigned to take on a lesser role in a developing market because he or she has the ideal skills to perform that role, but this would be seen by the organization as a reduction in formal status. But if the individual was asked personally by the chief executive to perform this role and to report back to the chief executive on a regular basis, then the informal status this arrangement conveys might be enough to overcome any issues of formal status. In this instance, the company is using the informal structure to compensate for the inertia of the formal structure.

I recall such a mechanism at PepsiCo. Each year, a small number of executives were chosen to spend the weekend with Chairman Roger Enrico at his ranch to discuss with him their plans for a breakthrough idea for the company. The picture taken during the weekend with Roger, conspicuously placed on executive desks, was one of the most valuable symbols of success within the company, and spurred many to seek out breakthrough ideas.

Summary

Humans have a number of fundamental basic needs that must be satisfied before they can think about change. And often these basic needs are threatened by change, so change never gets onto the agenda; change-makers are faced with fierce resistance buried deep in our genes.

In modern societies, employment plays a critical role in satisfying our basic needs. It helps pay for our food, drink and clothing, provides us with security, a sense of belonging and a source of self and social esteem. In this respect, employment is a fundamental human need. Threats to job security are an anathema; firms must work towards providing security to core members of their community and helping those who must leave through no fault of their own to find another home. Becoming a preferred employer helps in this respect because it makes employees more valuable in the marketplace, so the fear of leaving is reduced.

Employment also provides a great opportunity to satisfy our needs for belonging and esteem. Companies that shape the work environment to satisfy these human needs while meeting the firms' own needs for continuous change stand to benefit from superior motivation and higher performance. Those that ignore these issues face the possibility that employees will find other ways to find fulfilment, which may distract them from their daily work or even bring them into direct conflict with the firm.

When basic needs are not satiated, humans give little thought to higher-level needs. But once firms have met basic needs, they are ready to begin tapping into the infinite desire people have to learn and achieve their personal best and to drive up strategic and structural intelligence. This is the subject of the next chapter.

Notes

1. Maslow (1943).
2. http://www.portsunlight.org.uk/ Accessed January 4, 2008.
3. Ghemawat and Stander (1992).
4. Fung and Magretta (1998); Fung, Fung and Wind (2008).
5. For a detailed discussion of how to improve business team performance, see Ancona and Bresman (2007). For an analysis of some very famous teams, see Boynton and Fischer (2005).
6. Ghemawat and Stander (1992).

3.5

HARNESSING INSATIABLE HUMAN NEEDS

Introduction

Once our basic needs are met, we dedicate ourselves to satisfying our insatiable need for what Maslow termed self-actualization. We are naturally curious and like to learn. We like to create things and seek out new experiences. We seek fulfilment that comes from achieving our very best; after doing so, we want to help others to do the same. Above all, we yearn for common purpose, to rise above our self-interests and serve the common good. In this chapter, we examine the nature of these needs and investigate how firms can harness them to develop higher strategic intelligence.

Maslow's Higher Needs

The highest level of fundamental human needs identified in Maslow's 1943 schema was the need for self-actualization. He described this as the drive for personal growth and self-fulfilment. In his later work, Maslow expanded self-actualization into four categories:

- **Cognitive:** the need to **learn**, understand and discover. Since change always involves some level of learning, firms seeking to adapt quickly to the competitive environment must tap into their members' desire to learn. We all love to learn as long as we can overcome the pain that this often involves. We must also overcome some of the anti-learning skills we often exhibit.

- **Aesthetic:** the need for symmetry and beauty. Aesthetic needs do not appear to have much bearing on a firm's adaptive capacity, although beauty and simplicity in solutions to problems may make them more effective and easier to implement. It has also been argued that Design Management which bridges the disciplines of product aesthetics and disciplined innovation processes can contribute to competitive advantage. Balance in workplace design also has a significant impact on productivity and morale, as those who practise Feng Shui would attest.

- **Self-actualization:** to realize one's full potential. At its simplest, self-actualization is the desire to **deliver our personal best**. Firms which manage to align this individual drive for personal improvement to continuous improvement in the firm are increasing their capacity to adapt.

- **Self-transcendence:** the desire to **help others to realize their full potential** and to seek out common purpose. People actually get emotional satisfaction from helping others. Firms must encourage their employees to help others to help the firm. Common purpose is a powerful facilitator. Those firms with a strategic vision that shapes common purpose create powerful alignment.

In his later work Maslow described a wide range of behaviours demonstrated by self-actualizers. They are objective in their judgment, not influenced by personal biases or social pressures and emotionally mature enough not to be overwhelmed by their basic need for belonging. They hold themselves accountable for their actions, which helps them to learn rather than blame others for their failings. They are accepting and respectful of others, and embrace a wide range of personal styles, races and cultures. This makes them open to a diversity of viewpoints which helps them to learn. They are curious and excited by everything; creative and inventive. They see problems as opportunities to discover new solutions; they are keen to involve themselves in extraordinary experiences with lasting impact.

The behaviours described by Maslow as self-actualizing are the same behaviours that help senior executives keep their companies on the leading edge strategically. They are demonstrations of practical intelligence, which is necessary to help firms to adapt and learn.

Self-actualization is about individuals looking to fulfil their own potential; **self-transcendence** is about helping others to do so. It is about **teaching** rather than learning; "giving back", coaching and mentoring others, developing the next generation. Self-transcenders seek **purpose**. They need to be on a mission. They need to have a clear and inspiring vision of where they are headed which contributes to the common good and be guided by a set of values on the way that distinguishes right from wrong. Mission equals vision plus values. To take advantage of their enormous talents, companies must provide self-transcenders with a vision and values that align with the firm's need to drive greater strategic and structural intelligence.

Maslow reserved self-transcendence for those who reached the highest level of emotional maturity. Self-transcendence concerns itself with spiritual awakening and liberation from egocentricity. Although it is unusual to discuss spirituality in a business book, businesspeople are human and human beings of countless races and cultures have demonstrated a consistent need for spirituality for thousands of years. Moreover, close examination of the major religions of the world indicates that the fundamental values they espouse are remarkably similar. Evolutionary biology would argue that these universal needs have contributed to our strength as a species, driving cooperative behaviours and subordinating self-interest to the common good. Firms that can identify in the minds of their employees with the common good have much to gain from these instincts.

Maslow described some of the characteristics of self-transcendence in his landmark 1969 article *Theory Z*.[1] Self-transcenders are motivated by values such as truth and goodness, by a selfless cause rather than by material rewards. They seek a sense of purpose and are visionary innovators with a clear sense of the ideal. They take a very holistic view of the world rather than dividing it up with nationalism or religion. They look for the win–win solutions rather than play zero-sum games. According to Maslow, everything is sacred to them; there are no classes or discrimination; hence their compassion for the weak and less fortunate. The more they learn, the more the mystery increases for them and the greater their humility and reverence. They do not put themselves up on a pedestal and yet they are inspiring, godlike, saintly, revered.

Below, we will discuss Maslow's higher needs and how companies can harness them to drive strategic intelligence in more detail.

Learning

Aligning Learning Needs with Greater Competitive Advantage

Learning is essential for companies committed to driving up their strategic intelligence. To build capacity for strategic change they need to involve everyone in the process, which is itself a huge learning exercise. They must encourage their people to constantly question the current business model and look for improvements. They also want employees to seek out and test completely new business models. They need their people to work fast and effectively together, learning from each other as they shape new strategic options and execute them in the marketplace. Continuous improvement requires continuous learning.

The good news is that we all like to learn, so as long as we are learning by driving superior competitiveness, the needs of employees and the firm are aligned. But learning is also painful. We must force ourselves to take the initial pain to reach the rewards that we will later enjoy. Firms can help to address the balance between pain and gain, rewarding learning behaviours and encouraging their people to experiment. They can also help their people to overcome the anti-learning skills described in **Chapter 3.2: What is a Mind?** that get in the way of learning and work more constructively with their colleagues to learn from each other.

Modifying Learning Behaviours

What we are discussing here is changing behaviours so that we are more effective learners and we also help others to learn. Modifying behaviours is no easy task, but the good news is that when people are committed, they can retrain themselves to do so. First they need to know what they are doing wrong and be shown how to do it right. An expert coach helps here. They must also see the payoff from correcting their current behaviours to drive them to change. Firms can help in this respect by providing appropriate rewards and punishments. Finally, there must be a way of measuring the behaviour to check progress. Many firms use regular 360° feedback to measure behaviours – when they back it up with rewards, then it really has teeth!

Overcoming Blind Expertise and Anti-Learning Skills

When we learn, we build simplified models of the world to help solve problems. We identify what we believe to be relevant and act on it. If it works for us, we believe our model to be true. The more it works, the more we believe it to be true. And the more we use it, the more our responses become automatic, so we forget the underlying model. We become blind experts. We don't know what we know and we don't know what we don't know. And unless we are prepared to allow our expertise to be questioned, we will remain blind.

This is a common problem in business. Two executives from different backgrounds, when presented with the same information, select what they consider to be relevant. They then infer meaning from the selected data and draw "expert" conclusions that are quite "obvious" to them with little conscious thought. They each advocate their solution as if it were the truth and assume that the other person is an idiot because what they are saying doesn't seem to make sense. Moreover, they resent the fact that their expertise is being challenged. As a result, they simply "talk" at each other rather make any attempt to understand each other's point of view.

I recall an example to illustrate the point. I was facilitating a cross-functional workshop in a major consumer products company to develop strategy in a product category where the market leaders had approximately the same market share and were aggressively competing away profits. There was a strong implicit hierarchy in the firm; marketing executives were revered as gods, the sales executives were mere mortals, and manufacturing executives were lower life forms. However, it was my role to improve cross-functional learning and ensure that everybody contributed to the discussion. On this particular day, the representative from the manufacturing function was new to the company and did not understand the implicit hierarchy. This led to some very interesting interchanges.

After a few opening pleasantries, I explained that the objective was to find an effective way of competing in the category and that everyone should come forward with ideas. A number of people raised questions and points of clarification but no one seemed to want to come forward with an idea until finally the head of marketing spoke. She said that "share of voice leadership" was the answer. Everybody looked at each other and nodded affirmatively, suggesting that we had found a solution. It was then that the manufacturing executive upset the flow of the meeting by asking, "What's share of voice leadership?" There were raised eyebrows all around, and the odd intake of breath. A number of the team members looked at the manufacturing executive with disdain as if to suggest that everybody knew what share of voice leadership was. However, the body language seemed somewhat over played and I suspected that the manufacturing executive was not the only one in the room who didn't understand. Certainly no one chose to answer until the head of marketing impatiently explained that by out-spending competition by 20% on advertising we would gain share and thereby build a clear leadership position.

The explanation quickly relieved the tension in the room and the affirmative nodding began again. However, the manufacturing executive, curiosity piqued, continued undaunted, asking, "But what will the competi-tion do?" The room went silent again. Disdain beamed once more upon the manufacturing executive from the majority, but a minority group was indicating that this might be a good question. At this stage, the head of marketing was a little more than irritated. Face flushing, she snapped, "They won't do anything because they won't get the Nielsen data for nine months so they won't know what we're up to." "But what will they do when they get the Nielsen data?" the manufacturing executive countered. Now a significant percentage of the crowd swung back to look at the head of marketing. "They'll probably increase advertising," she reluctantly admitted.

By now, everyone in the room was engrossed in the debate, and the body language suggested that a fair proportion were siding with the manufacturing executive, who nonchalantly asked, "So what will we do then?" The response was dismissive from the head of marketing. "We'll up our advertising spend straight away; that's what share of voice leadership's about." And it was then that the manufacturing executive volleyed back a winner. "But how can we? We won't get the Nielsen data for nine months!"

It was at this stage that the shouting started and I lost control of the meeting. My cross-functional facilitation had been a disaster. We adjourned for coffee and then came back to review what we had learned. The simple conclusion of the discussion was that starting an advertising war with the main competitor was not going to be a very effective strategy, since it would simply drive profit out of the category. We had to find a better way. However, more interesting to me was the learning process that had taken place.

The manufacturing executive, unconstrained by the implicit communi-cation protocols in the organization, had demonstrated the courage to ask a question of the marketing expert. While the marketing expert, in the first instance, was defensive at being asked to explain herself to a representative from manufacturing, she was eventually obliged to lay out her data and reasoning in support of a recommendation and allow others to test it. In the process, the manufacturing executive might have learned a little bit about marketing, but more importantly, the marketing expert became more expert in her field.

Communicating to Learn

Too often, when we communicate with colleagues, we aggressively advocate our position to win rather than seek the truth. However, if we encourage people to enquire about our data and reasoning, we are more likely to discover what we know and be able to build on it, increasing our expertise. Moreover, we are also helping others to learn because we make them aware of the underlying model that we are using and they can build on it themselves.

When providing explanations, we must beware of using the phrase "in my experience" to justify a recommendation, unless we relate a specific experience and explain how it is relevant. Otherwise, this response provides our colleagues with no useful information, allows us to lazily avoid reflecting on our experiences and tells them not to challenge us.

When questioned, we should also suspend judgment and look for insight from the line of inquiry, however illogical it may first appear. We should use it like any other creativity tool or technique to help encourage our learning. We can learn from fools as well as geniuses. As the late Sir Yehudi Menuhin said, *"Open mindedness, tolerance and generosity are the very conditions for learning . . . We must be humbly ready and equally prepared to learn from an idiot as from an ant."*

In the same way that we should encourage others to enquire of us, we must have the courage to enquire of others. This means constructive questioning to understand how they are framing the problem and to identify the data and reasoning they are using to reach a solution. Again, this requires patience and suspending judgment. The goal is to discover their model, not argue with it every step of the way.

The challenge is to balance advocacy with enquiry (Figure 37). Advocacy without enquiry is merely forcing our views on others rather than testing them

Figure 37: Learning Skills – Balancing Advocacy with Enquiry

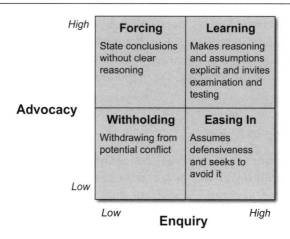

Source: Derived from Argyris (1990)

for ourselves and helping others to learn. Enquiry without advocacy doesn't allow others to learn from us; nor does it force us to take a position or draw conclusions from our analysis, so we fail to find coherent solutions. We need to develop skills in both advocacy and enquiry to learn and help others to learn. Different personality types demonstrate different biases when it comes to advocacy and enquiry. Promoters tend to be strong advocates while analysts are closer to the enquiry end of the spectrum. If we want to learn and want to help our colleagues to learn, we must develop skills that allow us to gravitate towards the centre of the scale.[2]

Listening to Learn

In many respects, enquiry skills are the skills of a good listener. The fascinating thing about listening effectively is this: it can often help people to solve their own problems. It is tempting when somebody asks a question to answer it. However, it is often more effective to turn the question back on the questioner or ask them to identify possible options to the problem. By simply listening and encouraging them to address their challenge, they very often come up with their own answer or solution and learn from the experience. What is remarkable is that they cannot do this alone. The presence of another human being encouraging them and helping them to reflect is sufficient to boost their ability to resolve difficult issues significantly. There is probably more than an element of truth in the jest that psychiatrists are paid $500 an hour just to listen!

Even those of us who supposedly know better yield to the temptation to talk. My default response to a request for help is to begin providing an answer before the questioner has even completed the question. The obvious danger here is that the solutions I might provide are poor because I have not fully understood the problem. In the long run, there is an even bigger problem: I have undermined the questioner's abilities to develop the skills to deal with the questions for themselves. A little listening takes more patience but ultimately has a much higher payoff.

Of course, it is important to apply the right sort of listening. **Negative listening** does very little to help facilitate learning. The negative listener questions everything the speaker says in a way that suggests that the speaker is wrong or in some way misguided. It is very hard for the speaker to reflect on the issues at hand under such a barrage of negative judgment. It is easy to demonstrate the impact of negative listening by asking a colleague to explain a project to you. Simply by frowning, looking confused and asking every now and then questions such as "what's the point of that?" is sufficient to drain the energy of the speaker and bring them slowly to a halt.

Neutral listening can be just as challenging. I used to have a boss who would sit there making copious notes when I went to see him. He had no expression on his face and he would simply sit there writing while I tried to explain my problem or my proposal. In the face of this blank wall, it was very difficult to maintain enthusiasm.

What we all seek in a good listener is **positive listening**, someone who shows a genuine interest in our problem, asks non-threatening, clarifying questions and encourages us to explain, while making us feel valued. Positive body language such as nodding is a big help, as long as we really mean it – human beings are expert at detecting disingenuous behaviour. With a good listener, we can talk through our problems and often solve them ourselves.

The Role of Personal Accountability in Learning

Personal accountability accelerates learning. We cannot learn from mistakes if we blame others for them. While others may have played a part, it makes more sense to focus on areas that we can influence than waste time and effort being concerned about what we have very little impact on. By identifying how we contributed to the error, it helps us to avoid repeating it in the future. If we focus on our areas of influence, they will grow. If we focus our effort on areas of concern that are beyond our area of influence, our area of influence will shrink.

The challenge of accountability is that many of us have become expert at avoiding it. Politicians have taken this to an art form. Many parents make the mistake of telling their young children that their palpable errors are "not their fault". This allows them to pass the blame onto others. What might be considered an attempt to comfort young children at an early age actually undermines their capacity to learn. Firms must do the opposite; they must encourage their members to develop their natural capacity for personal accountability, which will make them feel better about themselves and learn more effectively into the bargain.

Positive Thinking to Learn

Positive thinking is another valuable self-actualization behaviour that accelerates learning. William James, an eminent American psychologist, recognized its ability to shape our lives over a century ago. He is said to have remarked, "*The greatest discovery of our generation is that a human being can alter his life by altering his attitudes.*"[3] Since then, many have made their fortune espousing its benefits. Positive thinkers see opportunities to be exploited where negative thinkers see problems to be avoided. A positive frame of mind can have a significant impact on our ability to perform, and we can shape this for ourselves. To demonstrate this, all we have to do is to smile. This physical act under our conscious control triggers a response in our brain that tells us we are happy, creating a more positive frame of mind. If we want to reinforce this effect, we only need to look into a mirror while we are doing it. When someone smiles at us, we automatically smile back; we catch the positive emotion like a virus. The same goes for our reflected image. When it smiles at us, we smile in return, reinforcing the positive attitude.

Positive thinking is positively correlated with luck. It's common to hear the argument that some people are luckier than others, but there was little rigorous support for this view until 2003 when research was published in the UK by psychologist Richard Wiseman.[4] Wiseman's work demonstrated that some people are systematically luckier than others, but it has less to do with Lady Luck smiling on them than their attitude of mind.[5] Positive thinkers are more likely to see opportunities and be more open to improvement, which means they perform systematically better. The role of luck in business success has become quite a popular research topic, most recently addressed by Malcolm Gladwell[6] and Jim Collins.[7]

Given the viral nature of emotions, one way of maintaining a positive frame of mind is to avoid negative thinkers and spend time with those more positively inclined. There are winners and whiners in most firms and they seldom mix.

Creativity to Learn

The frontal cortex of the brain provides humans with enormous capacity for addressing and resolving new problems. However, what probably distinguishes us the most as a species from other animals is our innate curiosity and imagination, our ability to create alternative futures. Nobel Laureate Albert Szent-Gyorgi once commented, *"Discovery consists of looking at the same thing as everyone else and thinking of something different."* As long as our basic needs are not threatened, we have a passion for creating problems, not just solving them. We take what works well and try to improve it; we then destroy it, looking for a much better way. We are essentially a creative species constantly battling to break free from what we have already learned in order to learn more. And, as Pablo Picasso said, *"Every act of creation is first an act of destruction."*

Everyone has a remarkably creative brain. We have the capacity to generate an enormous number of ideas, but we have an equal capacity for eliminating these ideas as unsound before we even have the chance to consciously evaluate them. Our brains act as very powerful censors, deleting the suggestions inconsistent with our past experience. The challenge is to suppress our capacity for self-censorship, to suspend judgment and allow the ideas to reach our conscious minds. We must discipline ourselves to consciously separate the idea generation process from the evaluation process.

There are a plethora of creativity tools and techniques to help in this process. They work on the principle of suspending self-judgment and the judgment of our colleagues in order to generate a richer set of options. I have listed a few of the more well-known ones below.

Brainstorming is very familiar to most of us. It is a group work session where everyone is encouraged to generate ideas without fear of critique because no one else is allowed to comment on them until the brainstorming is complete. **Brainwriting** is similar, but requires everyone in the group to write down their ideas. This encourages quieter members to come up with more suggestions. There is seldom a correlation between the quality of an idea and the conviction with which it is expressed – and the anonimity encourages more creativity.

Using **random stimuli** is a rather a curious approach to generating ideas. The process requires taking a random object such as a stone and trying to relate it to the issue in question to see what ideas might come up. I've not found this particularly effective in generating creative approaches to strategic problems, but this may say more about me than about the technique!

Metaphors and analogies are powerful because the brain thinks in metaphors. The group takes an example as a metaphor and identifies what it might mean for strategy. For instance, what would we expect the "the **Wal-Mart** of financial services" to be?

The **contrarian** identifies conventional wisdom and does the opposite. I typically ask myself what is the dumbest way to compete in a particular business and then work hard to find a business model that would make it profitable. For instance, in the auto insurance business, conventional wisdom argues that firms should insure the safest drivers because they have the fewest accidents. However, Progressive Insurance managed to make very good money out of focusing on just the opposite. They sought out high-risk drivers that were not as bad as most and provided high-priced insurance. As one analyst observed, they "pick the best of the worst and make a ton".[8]

The objective of **attribute listing** is to identify as many attributes as possible associated with a particular product or service and then try to picture how to enhance it or reconfigure the attributes to create new product ideas. For example, the very successful Cirque du Soleil combines the least costly elements of a stage musical and a circus; the very expensive animals and star performers have been eliminated while the dramatic trapeze acts, gymnastics and music have remained.[9]

Prospective hindsight involves going forward into the future and building a number of scenarios for how the world might look, both favourable and unfavourable for the firm. Working backwards, the goal is to identify the critical events that might have led to these scenarios. This helps the firm to identify actions that reduce the probability of the pessimistic scenarios and increase the probability of the optimistic ones. I have found this to be a particularly useful technique in helping management teams to develop strategy under uncertainty.

Role-playing is a simple but powerful approach in which individuals are asked to play a role other than their own. This gives them the licence to come up with ideas that they do not have to take responsibility for. They may play the role of a competitor assessing the strengths, weaknesses, opportunities and threats of their firm. Many years ago, I ran such a session for executives in the newly privatized British Airways. They were finding it difficult to list BA's vulnerabilities until I asked them to role-play the senior management team of a major competitor and asked them to destroy BA. They were quickly able to generate a long and comprehensive list.

Another effective role-play is to ask people to step out of their normal function and look at the issues from the point of view of another function. This provides them with a cross-functional perspective and helps them to generate many more ideas than if they just viewed the problem from their own frame of reference.

Creativity tools and techniques boost our natural ability to come up with creative solutions to problems. If we are willing to suspend judgment, we can become individually and collectively smarter as a result.

Self-Fulfilment – Delivering Our Personal Best

The difference between average performance and delivering our personal best is quite significant. Performing at our highest level triggers strong positive emotions from the self-fulfilment it provides. Firms would do well to provide more opportunities for their members to perform at this level; the firm gets extraordinary results and the members get a deep-felt sense of satisfaction from delivering them.

I have asked many groups of executives to recall occasions when they delivered their personal best and they have no difficulty in doing so. When they do, they feel good – almost as if they are reliving the experience. Firms can harness the benefits of personal best performance by replicating the conditions that led to it. When asked to reflect back, executives identified a number of common characteristics:

Stretch. They were asked to deliver on a task that was well beyond their normal comfort zone. This drove them to learn new things but created a certain level of risk for the team, and extra work for the team leader. The natural inclination when we lead a team is to take the safe route and assign individuals tasks well within their capabilities. But this does not motivate individuals to deliver extraordinary performance. We must take more risk and be prepared for the extra coaching and support this requires.

High profile. The team's task had high visibility within the organization and so did its members. The risk of individual and collective failure was therefore high. This suggests that if we want the teams we lead to deliver at their best, we must raise the stakes and bear the extra risks involved. We must take on tasks that are critical to the firm's success, provide team members with exposure at the highest levels of the organization and give them full credit where it is due.

Great team. Most executives report working with great team members and building strong relationships that often endured throughout their careers. They recalled strong mutual support and having fun together, celebrating successes and confronting failures along the way as a team. Clearly this satisfied more basic needs for affiliation, but the social pressure to deliver combined with the support to help them do so drove extraordinary performance.

Commitment. The level of personal commitment to deliver on the task was very high. Executives recall long hours and personal sacrifice. They worked hard not because they were asked to but because of the stretch nature of the task, the high profile associated with it and their commitment to other team members. While they agree that it would not be possible to deliver at such levels on a regular basis, they would prefer short bursts of such experiences rather than routine tasks.

Many drivers of personal best behaviour require leaders to take on more risk and work harder to develop their people. Why might we expect them to do this? Part of the reward is material; it comes from delivering better results. But much is emotional; there is a sense of self-fulfilment from leading a winning team, and of transcendence in helping others to reach their full potential.

Mission – Vision and Values

We seek purpose; it helps us to fulfil our highest need for self-transcendence. A strong sense of a common purpose builds morale and creates alignment across huge organizations, helping tribes to become nations. It drives superior performance; with purpose, we can deliver more output over a longer period of time and still feel better for it. It makes us more willing to change, as long as we believe the change is necessary for our purpose to be met. But if we lack purpose, we quickly become dispirited, unproductive and dysfunctional.

Firms may try to provide purpose through mission statements, but it is not mission statements that we crave but a sense of mission; those on a mission have purpose. They have a clear vision of where they would like to be and a set of values that guide them on their journey. Mission is vision plus values.

Vision

Firms often set goals like increasing profits by 15% each year. But where does this lead? Why should employees care? It is tough to convert this into missionary zeal. Companies must develop a more motivational vision. They must also ensure it builds greater strategic intelligence, driving the firm forward to improve the current strategy and seek new ones in the quest for greater competitive advantage.

We discussed the design rules in **Chapter 1.5: High Strategic Intelligence**. The vision must motivate, it must stretch and it must seek greater advantage.

A motivating vision paints a picture of the future that everyone would be proud to reach. It inspires each of us to make the journey. It promises that everybody in the firm will be better off, but it promises more than this. Motivating visions call for a contribution to the greater good, to help humanity. Progressive Insurance aims "to take the trauma out of road accidents". This is a much worthier goal than making money from selling insurance policies.

To be effective, visions are a stretch; they go well beyond where the company currently operates and force us to imagine new futures. When Wal-Mart was only a $20 billion company, Sam Walton's exciting challenge to create a $100+ billion business was well beyond what appeared possible. Indeed Wal-Mart's business model at the time would not have allowed it to reach such a scale, but the challenge encouraged the firm to find new formats and try different business models. Wal-Mart has now passed through the $400 billion mark.[10]

A good vision also drives firms towards building superior performance and greater competitive advantage. Firms should make no apology for this since it is critical to their survival and health. Progressive aims to take the trauma out of road accidents, but in profitable ways!

An effective vision resonates throughout a firm. Merely presenting employees with senior management's views seldom has impact. The challenge is to really understand what is likely to inspire everyone, and this involves much discussion and debate. Once it is identified, it is then important to communicate it time and again to get it to resonate throughout the organization.

Values

Values are the rules that guide us on the way to reaching the vision. They are reflected in the way we believe we should behave towards each other. These behaviours are respected, admired, mimicked and rewarded. They also define behaviours that are not acceptable. These are reviled and punished, distinguishing right from wrong. Values are reflected in many of the organization's formal systems and processes. What gets rewarded? Who gets promoted?

Firms often claim they live by a set of values but actually follow a different set. Many firms espouse a good work–life balance and yet it is the workaholics in the organization who are mimicked, admired, lauded and rewarded. Beware the gap! When leaders espouse one set of values but demonstrate behaviours that suggest another set, then they undermine their credibility and are viewed as hypocrites.

So what values should a firm aim for? The surprising thing to many firms is that they go through a lengthy exercise to identify the values they feel they identify with and discover that they end up with pretty much the same list as every other firm. At this point, they express disappointment and murmur that they were hoping for something a little more differentiated. But they miss the point. There is a set of universal human values that make groups of humans working in collaboration more effective. They are the genetically inherited rules of social mechanics (see **Chapter 2.4: Informal Architecture**). The system is based on trust. Trust requires honesty, integrity, fairness (justice), transparency and accountability. People are expected to respect each other and help each other. These are the core values of a healthy community. The origins of virtue are in our genes.[11] To these we must add those behaviours that drive adaptability and capacity for learning to ensure that the community remains healthy in the long term: curiosity, courage and commitment.

These values drive behaviours that lead to long-term sustainable performance; behaviours that encourage people to work cooperatively together to deliver higher performance for the firm while meeting their social needs; behaviours that encourage constant innovation and learning to drive greater competitiveness; behaviours that encourage objectivity in making decisions in the best interests of the firm and accountability for results. In short, a firm's values should encourage behaviours that align people's higher-level psychological needs with the firm's long-term success.

What distinguishes firms is not the list of values they espouse but the degree to which they live by them. The values of a firm are expressed in the behaviours of its members. And the behaviours of each individual are an expression of their individual values. It is hard to change a person's values, so firms should take care to test for the ones they seek in the recruiting process.

However, it is possible to change individual behaviours to some degree, as long as they can be measured. The challenge is that it is difficult for us to "see" our own behaviours, so we need processes such as personal coaching and 360° feedback to open our eyes. If our good behaviours are rewarded, financially or with social esteem, and our bad behaviours censured, then we learn to adapt. We are all capable of modifying our behaviours when we have the incentive to do so. Initially, we act to "live" the new values even though, we may not be emotionally predisposed to do so. But as we get positive feedback and pratice, we become better at it and shape our emotions into alignment to the point we actually begin to believe the values we are expressing.

Teaching

Self-transcenders get emotional satisfaction from helping others to fulfil their full potential and help firms to increase their collective intelligence. Mentoring and coaching are the most common ways of doing this in firms. Coaching is designed to help individuals improve their performance by providing critical feedback. Mentoring goes beyond coaching; it provides personal sponsorship to help individuals establish an effective social network and find suitable roles in the organization.

There are few executives who do not believe coaching is a good idea, but there seem to be equally few that actually practice it successfully on a regular basis. I often ask groups of executives whether they have coached their subordinates in the last few weeks. They invariably respond in the affirmative. However, when I then ask them whether they have been coached by their bosses during the same period, they typically say no. I then ask them to reflect on this strange asymmetry. Perhaps their subordinates hadn't recognized that they had been coached? Or they might have perceived it not as coaching but as criticism. The challenge is not just to coach but to coach effectively, so that the person being coached learns from it. If they merely think they are being criticized, they are probably not learning.

Most of us are not naturally good at coaching. Indeed, many of us actually avoid such difficult conversations. But by following a few simple guidelines and practising, we can all become quite good at it. As with so many things, the initial learning is painful, so we must convince ourselves that the effort is worthwhile. If we are coaching our own people, we get an immediate payback in performance. But we must also remember that it helps to satisfy a fundamental need we have to develop our people. We can expect tremendous personal satisfaction from a successful coaching experience.

Figure 38 Coaching Rules of The Road

- Ask permission
- Little and regular
- Close to the event
- Have a positive attitude
- Balance constructive and appreciative feedback
- Be specific
- Talk about the behaviour not the person
- Offer alternatives
- Use simple direct statements
- Prepare
- Care about the person

Typically, we think of coaching as coming from our supervisors. Indeed most people expect to be coached by their boss. It is more of a challenge for a subordinate to coach upwards, but it is very useful for the supervisor to create a context which allows this to happen. The trick here is to shut up and listen rather than argue – it is hard to give feedback to your boss – and to encourage the subordinate to follow the guidelines.

If coaching is such an effective way of helping people to learn, then why doesn't it happen more often in organizations? The common excuse is that it takes too much time, but this is not borne out by the facts. However, it does take preparation and careful thinking, and therefore an investment on the part of both the coach and the coached. Too often, both would rather avoid this work and the discomfort of confronting failure. Members of the top management team can set an example by coaching their subordinates on a regular basis, and if they do this, the propensity to coach will typically cascade down through the organization. Moreover, coaching can be integrated into a 360° feedback form for performance evaluation. It is remarkable how much harder we will try to improve our coaching skills if we are rewarded for it.

Formal training sessions are another way in which executives can help teach their organizations. While rarer than coaching, teaching can be a highly effective way of transferring specialized expertise to a group of executives. Danaher, one of the fastest growing and successful conglomerates in the USA, has been doing this to good effect for many years. It has developed a wide curriculum of courses that are taught by line executives with significant skills and experience in the topic. The approach is normally action learning; on-the-job training where participants actually solve a real problem as they learn. In effect, Danaher has created a virtual business school where the faculty consists of experienced executives and the students are business teams. The participants gain relevant knowledge from the programmes just when they need it, and the faculty members grow more expert as they teach; there is no better way of actually learning something than to have to teach it.

Teaching Organizations to Learn – Leadership Behaviour

Ultimately, in a complex and changing world, our highest purpose must be to help people to learn. Many of the behaviours we have discussed in this chapter boost learning capacity, so programmes that develop skills in these behaviours are important. But there is one more that deserves special mention.

We learn by watching people we admire and love, and mimicking them. Indeed, we are powerful mimics and copy without realizing it. Just ask yourself whether, as an adult, you have ever suddenly realized that you sounded just like your mother or your father sounded when you were a child. As American novelist James Arthur Baldwin remarked, *"Children have never been very good at listening to their elders, but they never fail to imitate them"*. Hence the saying "like father, like son" and the admonishment "set an example". The power of humans to mimic the people they look up to is high.

The implications for leadership are clear. If we want our people to demonstrate certain behaviours, then we must set an example and demonstrate them ourselves. Our subordinates will then mimic these behaviours and, in turn, their subordinates will do likewise. In this way, the behaviours cascade down through the organization. As leaders, we cast a long shadow.

This means we must become fully aware of our own behaviours. We are always on duty, and our behaviour will be amplified, regardless of our intent. Indeed we may find ourselves frustrated by behaviour patterns we see in subordinates when we are unwittingly demonstrating those very same behaviours ourselves. It is essential that we develop clear awareness of what we are doing and how it impacts the behaviour of others. If in doubt, then a personal coach to heighten awareness makes a lot of sense.

There is also a danger that we ask our people to demonstrate behaviours and fail to do likewise. This undermines our credibility and legitimacy to lead. We must "practice what we preach" if we wish to remain effective. Leadership is a message backed by action.

Summary

The high-level needs described by Maslow can generate the power to drive intelligent companies toward long-term sustainable success. Human beings are curious and want to learn and experience new things. We drive ourselves to deliver our personal best – achieve our full potential – and we want to help others to do the same. We need a sense of purpose that goes beyond personal gain. We need to be guided by a universal set of human values like honesty, integrity and fairness. These needs drive us to perform better for our community and as a community. They also help us to become individually and collectively smarter, more able to respond to change and better able to shape the competitive environment to the firm's advantage. With a clear understanding of these needs, firms can design work to satisfy them, harnessing the natural intelligence of the human species to become strategically smarter.

Notes

1. Maslow's landmark 1969 article, *Theory Z* (reprinted in Maslow's basic text on Transpersonal Psychology, *The Farther Reaches of Human Nature*, NY: Viking, 1972).
2. Argyris (1990).
3. This is one of William James's most famous quotations, but I cannot identify the source of the quote. The meaning, however, is well taken.
4. Wiseman (2003).
5. Professor Wiseman cites four characteristics of lucky people: they make the most of their opportunities, they listen to their intuition, they think positively and they turn bad luck into good.
6. Gladwell (2008).
7. Collins (2001).
8. Wells, Lutova and Sender (2008).
9. Kim and Mauborgne (2005).
10. Ortega (1998).
11. Ridley (1996).

Bibliography

Alberts, D.S. and Hayes, R.E. (2003) *Power to the Edge: Command Control in the Information Age*. Department of Defence, Command and Control Research Program.

Alderfer, C. (1972) *Existence, Relatedness, & Growth*. New York, NY: Free Press.

Allison, G.T. (1971) *Essence of Decision: Explaining the Cuban Missile Crisis.* Little Brown.

Amaral, J.R. and de Oliveira, J.M. (2011) *Limbic System: The Center of Emotions*. The Healing Center on-Line. Retrieved September 30, 2011 from http://www.healing-arts.org/n-r-limbic.htm

Anand, B.N., Collis, D.J. and Hood, S. (2008) *Danaher Corporation*. Harvard Business School case 708-445.

Ancona, D. and Bresman, H. (2007) *X-Teams. How to Build Teams that Lead, Innovate and Succeed*. Boston, MA: Harvard Business School Press.

Ansoff, I. and McDonnel, E. (1990) *Implanting Strategic Management*. Hemel Hempstead, England: Prentice Hall.

Argyris, C. (1990) *Overcoming Organizational Defences: Facilitating Organizational Learning*. Boston, MA: Allyn and Bacon.

Argyris, C. (1993) *Knowledge for Action*. San Francisco, CA: Jossey-Bass.

Argyris, C. (2000) *Flawed Advice and the Management Trap: How Managers Can Know When They're Getting Good Advice and When They're Not*. New York, NY: Oxford University Press.

Argyris, C. (2004) *Reasons and Rationalizations: The Limits to Organizational Knowledge*. New York, NY: Oxford University Press.

Argyris, C. and Schön, D.A. (1978) *Organizational Learning: A Theory of Action Perspective*. Reading, MA: Addison-Wesley.

Asch, S.E. (1951) "Effects of Group Pressure upon the Modification and Distortion of Judgment." In H. Guetzkow (Ed.) *Groups, Leadership and Men*. Pittsburgh, PA: Carnegie Press.

Austin, R.D. and Nolan, R.L. (2000) *IBM Corp. Turnaround*. Harvard Business School case 600-098.

Baldwin, C.Y. and Clark, K.B. (2000) *Design Rules: The Power of Modularity*. Cambridge, MA: MIT Press.

Bang-yan, F. (2007) *100 Years of Li & Fung: Rise from Family Business to Multinational*. Singapore: Thomson.

Barnard, C.I. (1938) *The Functions of the Executive*. Cambridge, MA: Harvard University Press.

Baron, D.P., Barlow, D.S., Barlow, A.M. and Yurday, E. (2004) *Anatomy of a Corporate Campaign: Rainforest Action Network and Citigroup (A)*. Stanford Graduate School of Business, June 01, 2004.

Bartlett, C.A. (1999). *GE's Two-Decade Transformation: Jack Welch's Leadership*. Harvard Business School case 399-150.

Bazerman, M.H. and Watkins, M.D. (2004) *Predictable Surprises: The Disasters You Should Have Seen Coming and How to Prevent Them*. Boston, MA: Harvard Business School Press.

BBC News (2004) "Super ant colony hits Australia." Posted Saturday, 14 August, 2004. Retrieved December 8, 2010 from http://news.bbc.co.uk/2/hi/science/nature/3561352.stm

Beinhocker, E.D. (2006). *The Origin of Wealth: The Radical Remaking of Economics and What it Means for Business and Society*. Boston, MA: Harvard Business School Press.

Blackwell, L., Trzesniewski, K. and Dweck, C.S. (2007) Implicit theories of intelligence predict achievement across an adolescent transition: A longitudinal study and intervention. *Child Development*, **78**, 246–263.

Blenko, M., Mankins, M. and Rogers, P. (2010) *Decide & Deliver: 5 Steps to Breakthrough Performance in Your Organization*. Boston, MA: Harvard Business School Press.

Blinder, A.S. and Morgan, J. (2000) *Are two heads better than one: an experimental analysis of group vs individual decision making*. NBER Working Paper, No. 7909, September.

Bonabeau, E. (2002) Predicting the Unpredictable. *Harvard Business Review*, March 2002.

Bower, J.L. (2007) *CEO Within: Why Inside Outsiders Are the Key to Succession Planning*. Cambridge, MA: Harvard Business School Press.

Boynton, A. and Fischer, B. (2005) *Virtuoso Teams: Lessons from Teams that Changed Their Worlds*. Harlow, England: Prentice Hall.

Brandenburger, A.M. and Nalebuff, B. (1996) *Co-Opetition: A Revolution Mindset that Combines Competition and Cooperation*. New York, NY: Doubleday.

Brosnan, S.F. and Waal, F.B.M. (2003) Monkeys Reject Unequal Pay. *Nature*, **425**, 297–299.

Brown, A.W. (2000) *Large Scale, Component-Based Development*. Upper Saddle River, NJ: Prentice Hall.

Brown, S.L. and Eisenhardt, K.M. (1998) *Competing on the Edge: Strategy as Structured Chaos*. Boston, MA: Harvard Business School Press.

Burns, T. and Stalker, G.M. (1966) *The Management of Innovation*. London: Tavistock Publications.

Carroll, L. (1865) *Alice's Adventures in Wonderland*, London: Macmillan.

Casadesus-Masanell, R. and Larson, T. (2010) *Competing through Business Models (B)*. Harvard Business School Module Note 710-410.

Casadesus-Masanell, R. and Ricart, J.E. (2007) *Competing through Business Models (A)*. Harvard Business School Module Note 708-452.

Casadesus-Masanell, R., Tarzijan, J. and Mitchell, J. (2005) *Arauco (A): Forward Integration or Horizontal Expansion?* Harvard Business School case 705-474.

Chandler, A.D. (1962) *Strategy and Structure: Chapters in the History of the American Industrial Enterprise*. Cambridge, MA: MIT Press.

Chesborough, H. (2006) *Open Business Models: How to Thrive in the New Innovation Landscape*. Boston, MA: Harvard Business School Press.

Christensen, C.M. (1997) *The Innovator's Dilemma: When New Technologies Cause Great Firms to Fail*. Boston, MA: Harvard Business School Press.

Cisco Corporate Overview (2011) Retrieved October 23, 2011 from http://newsroom.cisco.com/documents/10157/1204766/Public_Corporate_Overview_FY11_Q3.pdf

Clippinger, J. (1999) *The Biology of Business: Decoding the Natural Laws of Enterprise*. New York, NY: Jossey-Bass.

Clippinger, J. (2007) *A Crowd of One: The Future of Individual Identity*. New York, NY: Public Affairs.

Cockburn, A. (2002) *Agile Software Development*. Arlington, MA: Pearson Education.

Collins, J. (2001) *Good to Great: Why Some Companies Make the Leap and Others Don't*. New York: Harper Business.

Collins, J. and Hansen, M.T. (2011) What's Luck Got To Do With It? *New York Times*, October 29, 2011.

Collins, J. and Porras, J.I. (1994) *Built to Last: Successful Habits of Visionary Companies*. New York, NY: Harper Business.

Collis, D.J. (2011) *Quantitative Analysis of Competitive Position: Customer Demand and Willingness to Pay*. Harvard Business School Module Note 711-495.

Collis, D.J. and Conrad, M.B. (1996) *Ben & Jerry's Homemade Ice Cream, Inc.: A Period of Transition*. Harvard Business School case 703-755.

Collis, D.J. and Ruckstad, M.G. (2008) Can You Say What Your Strategy Is? *Harvard Business Review*, April 01, 2008.

Cooper D.J. and Kagel, J.H. (2005) Are Two Heads Better than One? Team versus Individual Play in Signaling Games. *American Economic Review*, **95** (3),477–509.

Corts, K.S. and Wells, J.R. (2003) *Alusaf Hillside Project*. Harvard Business School case 704-458.

Cosby, P.B. (1979) *Quality Is Free: The Art of Making Quality Certain*. New York, NY: McGraw-Hill.

Covey, S.M.R. (2006) *The Speed of Trust: The One Thing That Changes Everything*. New York, NY: Free Press.

Cyert, R.M. and March, J.G. (1963). *A Behavioral Theory of the Firm*. Englewood Cliffs, NJ: Prentice Hall.

De Bono, E. (1973) *Lateral Thinking: Creativity Step by Step*. Perennial Library.

De Bono, E. (1977) *Lateral Thinking: A Textbook of Creativity*. Pelican Books.

DeMarco, T. (2001) *Slack*. New York, NY: Broadway Books.

D'Innocenzio, A. (2011) "Target's blunder with designer continues". Associated Press, September 22, 2011.

Dunbar, R.I.M. (1992) Neocortex size as a constraint on group size in primates. *Journal of Human Evolution*, **22**(6), 469–493.

Dunbar, R. (2004) *The Human Story: A New History of Mankind's Evolution*. London: Faber and Faber.

Dweck, C.S. (2007) *Mindset: The New Psychology of Success*. New York, NY: Ballantine Books.

Econimides, N. and Salop, S.S. (1992) Competition and Integration Among Complements, and Network Structure. *Journal of Industrial Economics*, **XL**(1), 105–123.

Eesley, C. and Lenox, M.J. (2005) *Secondary Stakeholder Actions and the Selection of Firm Targets*. Draft Working Paper, Fuqua School of Business, Duke University.

Fairtlough, G. (1994) *Creative Compartments: A Design for Future Organiza-tion*. Covent Garden, London: Adamantine Press.

Feng, B-Y. (2007) *100 years of Li & Fung: Rise From Family Business to Multinational*. Singapore: Thomson.

Fernandez-Araoz, C., Groysberg, B. and Nohria, N. (2009) The Definitive Guide to Recruiting in Good Times and Bad. *Harvard Business Review*, **87** (5),74–84.

Fong, A. (2006) Survey of the literature at http://eview.anu.au/cross-sec-tions/vol2/pdf/ch06.pdf.

Foster, R. and Kaplan, S. (2001) *Creative Destruction: Why Companies That are Built to Last Underperform the Market – and How to Successfully Transform Them*. New York, NY: DoubleDay/Random House.

Fung, V. and Magretta, J. (1998) Fast, Global, and Entrepreneurial: Supply Chain Management, Hong Kong Style; An Interview with Victor Fung. *Harvard Business Review*, September 1, 1998.

Fung, V.K., Fung, W.K. and Wind, Y. (2008) *Competing in a Flat World: Building Enterprises for a Borderless World*. Upper Saddle River, NJ: Wharton School Publishing.

Gaines-Ross, L. (2010) Reputation Warfare. *Harvard Business Review*, December 2010.

Galbraith, J.R. (1973) *Designing Complex Organizations*. Reading, MA: Addison-Wesley.

Galbraith, J.R. (1977) *Organization Design*. Reading, MA: Addison-Wesley.

Gardner, H. (1983) *Frames of Mind: The Theory of Multiple Intelligences*. New York, NY: Basic Books.

Gardner, H. (2006) *Changing Minds: The Art of Changing Our Own and Other People's Mind*. Boston, MA: Harvard Business School Press.

Garvin, D.A. (2000) *Learning in Action*. Boston, MA: Harvard Business School Press.

Gavetti, G. (2003) Strategy Formulation and Inertia. Harvard Business School Note 703-515.

Gavetti, G. and Rivkin, J.W. (2001) Complexity, Cognition and Adaptation: Toward a Grounded Theory of the Origins of Strategies. HBS Working Paper.

Gavetti, G., Henderson, R. and Giorgi, S. (2004) Kodak and the Digital Revolution. Harvard Business School case 705-448.

Gerstner, L.V. (2002) *Who Says Elephants Can't Dance? Inside IBM's Historic Turnaround.* New York, NY: HarperCollins.

Ghemawat, P. (1991) *Commitment, the Dynamic of Strategy,* New York: The Free Press.

Ghemawat, P. (1999) *Strategy and the Business Landscape.* Upper Saddle River, NJ: Pearson Prentice Hall.

Ghemawat, P. and Nueno, J.L. (2003) ZARA: Fast Fashion. Harvard Business School case 703-497.

Ghemawat, P. and Stander, H.J. III (1992) Nucor at a Crossroads. Harvard Business School case 793-039.

Ghoshal, S. and Bartlett, C.A. (1997) *The Individualized Corporation.* New York: Harper Business.

Gladwell, M. (2008) *Outliers.* New York, NY: Little, Brown and Company.

Glassman, E. (1991) *The Creativity Factor: Unlocking the Potential of Your Team.* San Diego, CA: Pfeiffer & Company.

Goleman, D. (1996) *Emotional Intelligence: Why it Can Matter More than IQ.* London: Bloomsbury Publishing.

Goleman, D. (2006) *Social Intelligence: The New Science of Human Relationships.* New York, NY: Random House.

Graham, J.R., Harvey, C.R. and Rajgopal, S. (2005) The Economic Implications of Corporate Financial Reporting. *Journal of Accounting and Economics,* **40**(1–3), 3–73.

Grove, A.S. (1996) *Only The Paranoid Survive: How to Exploit the Crisis Points that Challenge Every Company.* New York, NY: Bantam DoubleDay Dell.

Gulati, R. (2007) Silo Busting: How to Execute on the Promise of Customer Focus. *Harvard Business Review,* May 1.

Hall, R.H. (1972) *Organizations: Structure and Process.* Englewood Cliffs, NJ: Prentice Hall.

Hamel, G. (2000) *Leading the Revolution.* Boston, MA: Harvard University Press.

Hamel, G. and Prahalad, C.K. (1989) Strategic Intent. *Harvard Business Review,* May–June.

Hammer, M. (1990) Reengineering Work: Don't Automate, Obliterate. *Harvard Business Review,* July 1.

Hammer, M. and Champy, J.A. (1993) *Reengineering the Corporation: A Manifesto for Business Revolution.* New York, NY: Harper.

Hammermesh, R.G., Gordan, K. and Reed, J.P. (1987) *Crown Cork and Seal Co., Inc.* Harvard Business School case 378-024.

Harreld, J., O'Reilly, B.C.A. III and Tushman, M.L. (2007) Dynamic Capabilities at IBM: Driving Strategy into Action. *California Management Review*, **49** (4),Summer.

Harvey, J.B. (1988) *The Abilene Paradox and other Meditations on Management*. San Diego, CA: Lexington Books.

Henderson, R.M. (2006) The Innovator's Dilemma as a Problem of Organizational Competence. *Journal of Product Innovation Management*, **23**, 5–11.

Henderson, R.M. and Kaplan, S. (2005) Inertia and Incentives: Bridging Organizational Economics and Organizational Competence. *Organization Science*, **16**(5), 509–521.

Heywood, J. (1546) *Dialogue of Proverbs* ii. ix. K4.

Hofstadter, D.R. (1979) *Gödel, Escher, Bach: an Eternal Golden Braid*. New York, NY: Basic Books.

Holland, J.H. (1995) *Hidden Order: How Adaption Builds Complexity*. Reading, MA: Addison-Wesley.

Huawei Corporate Information (2011) Retrieved October 23, 2011 from http://www.huawei.com/en/about-huawei/corporate-info/research-development/index.htm Research & Development.

Huitt, W. (2004) Maslow's hierarchy of needs. *Educational Psychology Interactive*. Valdosta, GA: Valdosta State University. Retrieved September 30, 2011 from http://www.edpsycinteractive.org/topics/conation/maslow.

IDEO Inc. (2011) IDEO History. Retrieved October 1, 2011 from http://www.fundinguniverse.com/company-histories/IDEO-Inc-Company-History.html

Itami, H. with Roehl, T.W. (1987) *Mobilizing Invisible Assets*. Cambridge MA; Harvard University Press.

Iverson, K. (1998) *Plain Talk: Lessons from a Business Maverick*. New York, NY: John Wiley & Sons, Inc.

Janis, I.L. (1983) *Groupthink: Psychological Studies of Policy Decisions and Fiascos*. Boston, MA: Houghton Mifflin.

Joni, S.A. and Beyer, D. (2009) How to Pick a Good Fight. *Harvard Business Review*, December.

Joyce, W.F., Nohria, N. and Roberson, B. (2003) *What Really Works: The 4+2 Formula for Sustained Business Success*. New York: Harper Business.

Kagel, J.H. and Roth, A.E. (1995) *The Handbook of Experimental Economics*. Princeton, NJ: Princeton University Press.

Kanter, R.M. (1982) *The Change Masters: Corporate Entrepreneurs at Work*. London: George Allen and Unwin.

Kanter, R.M., Stein, B. and Jick, T.D. (1992) *The Challenge of Organizational Change: How Companies Experience It and Leaders Guide It*. New York, NY: Free Press.

Kaplan, R.S. (2010) Leading Change with the Strategy Execution System. Harvard Business Publishing Newsletters, November 15.

Kaplan, R.S. and Norton, D.P. (2000) *The Strategy-Focused Organization: How Balanced Scorecard Companies Thrive in the New Business Environment*. Boston, MA: Harvard Business School Press.

Kaplan, R.S. and Norton, D.P. (2004) *Strategy Maps: Converting Intangible Assets into Tangible Outcomes*. Boston, MA: Harvard Business School Press.

Katz, M.L. and Shapiro, C. (1985) Network Externalities, Competition and Compatibility. *The American Economic Review*, **75**(3), c424–440.

Khanna, T., Gulati, R. and Nohria, N. (2000) The Economic Modeling of Strategy Process: Clean Models and Dirty Hands. *Strategic Management Journal*, **21**, 781–790.

Kidder, T. (1981) *The Soul of a New Machine*. New York, NY: Little, Brown and Company in association with The Atlantic Monthly Press.

Kim, W.C. and Mauborgne, R. (2005) *Blue Ocean Strategy: How to Create Uncontested Market Space and Make the Competition Irrelevant*. Boston, MA: Harvard Business School Press.

Koch, R. (1998) *The 80/20 Principle: The Secret to Achieving More with Less*. New York, NY: Doubleday.

Koch, R. (2002) *The 80/20 Individual: How to Build on the 20% of What You Do Best*. New York, NY: Doubleday.

Koch, R. (2004) *Living the 80/20 Way: Work Less, Worry Less, Succeed More, Enjoy More*. Clerkenwell, London: Nicholas Brealey.

Kotter, J.P. (1996) *Leading Change*. Boston, MA: Harvard Business School Press.

Kuhn, T.S. (1962) *The Structure of Scientific Revolutions*. Chicago, IL: University of Chicago Press.

Larson, G.E., Haier, R.J., LaCasse, L. and Hazen, K. (1995) Evaluation of a "mental effort" hypothesis for correlations between cortical metabolism and intelligence. *Intelligence*, **31**(3), 267–278.

Laseter, T. and Cross, R. (2006) The Craft of Connection. *Strategy+Business*, Autumn, Issue 44: August 28. Retrieved on October 31, 2011 from http://www.strategy-business.com/article/06302?pg=all&tid=27782251

Lawrence, P.R. and Lorsch, J.W. (1967) *Organization and Environment: Managing Differentiations and Integration.* Boston, MA: Graduate School of Business Administration, Harvard University.

Lehrer, J. (2011) A New State of Mind. Seedmagazine.com, October 5, 2011. Retrieved October 5, 2011 from http://seedmagazine.com/content/article/a_new_state_of_mind/

Liedtka, J.M. (2011) Beyond Strategic Thinking: Strategy as Experienced. Rotman School of Management, January 1, 2011.

Lombardelli, C., Proudman, J. and Talbot, J. (2002) Committees versus individuals: an experimental analysis of monetary policy decision-making. Bank of England Working paper No. 165.

Luehrman, T.A. (1998) Strategy as a Portfolio of Real Options. *Harvard Business Review,* September 1.

Magrath, L. and Weld, L.G. (2002) Abusive Management and Early Warning Signs. *The CPA Journal,* August 2002. Retrieved October 31, 2011 from http://www.nysscpa.org/cpajournal/2002/0802/features/f085002.htm

Magretta, J. (2002) Why Business Models Matter. *Harvard Business Review,* May 1.

March, J.G. (1991) Exploration and Exploitation in Organizational Learning. *Organizational Science,* **2**(1), 71–87.

March, J.G. and Simon, H.A. (1958) *Organizations.* New York, NY: John Wiley & Sons, Inc.

Martin, R.L. (2010) The Execution Trap. *Harvard Business Review,* July 1.

Maslow, A.H. (1943) A Theory of Human Motivation. *Psychological Review,* **50**, 370–396.

Maslow, A.H. (1969) Theory Z. *Journal of Transpersonal Psychology,* **1**(2), 31–47.

Mathes, E. (1981) Maslow's hierarchy of needs as a guide for living. *Journal of Humanistic Psychology,* **21**, 69–72.

McGregor, D. (1960) *The Human Side of the Enterprise.* New York, NY: McGraw-Hill.

McNichols, M.F. and Stubben, S.R. (2008) Does Earnings Management Affect Firms' Investment Decisions? *The Accounting Review,* **83**(6), 1571–1603.

Meyerson, M. (1996) Everything I Thought I Knew About Leadership Is Wrong. *Fast Company,* April/May, 5–11.

Miles, R.E. and Snow, C.C. (1978) *Organizational Strategy, Structure and Process.* New York, NY: McGraw-Hill.

Millward Brown Optimor (2011) *The BrandZ Top 100 Most Valuable Global Brands.* Retrieved October 1, 2011 from http://www.millwardbrown.

com/Libraries/Optimor_BrandZ_Files/2011_BrandZ_Top100_Chart.sflb.
ashx

Mintzberg, H. (1979) *The Structuring of Organizations*. Englewood Cliffs, NJ: Prentice Hall.

Moingeon, B. and Edmondson, A. (1996) *Organizational Learning and Competitive Advantage*. London: Sage Publications.

Moll, J., Krueger, F., Zahn, R., Pardini, M., de Oliveira-Souza, R. and Grafman, J. (2006) Human fronto–mesolimbic networks guide decisions about charitable donation. *PNAS*, **103**(42), 15623–15628.

Montgomery, C.A. (ed.) (1995) *Resource-Based and Evolutionary Theories of the Firm: Towards a Synthesis*. Norwell, MA: Kluwer Academic Publishers.

Montgomery, C.A. and Collis, D.J. (1998) *Corporate Strategy: A Resource-Based Approach*. Boston, MA: Irwin/McGraw-Hill.

Moreno, J.L. (1986) *Who Shall Survive? A New Approach to the Problem of Human Interrelations*. Washington, DC: Nervous and Mental Diseases Publishing.

Morgan, G. (1986) *Images of Organization*. Beverly Hills, CA: Sage Publications.

Nadler, D.A. and Tushman, M.L. (1997) *Competing by Design: The Power of Organizational Architecture*. New York, NY: Oxford University Press.

Newstead, B. and Lanzerotti, L. (2010) Can you open source your strategy? *Harvard Business Review*, October 1.

Nohria, N. (2006) Survival of the Adaptive. Forethought. *Harvard Business Review*, **84**(5), 23.

Nohria, N. and Gulati, R. (1996) Is slack good or bad for innovation? *Academy of Management Journal*, **39**(5), 1245–1264.

Nohria, N., Joyce, W.F. and Roberson, B. (2003) What Really Works. *Harvard Business Review*, **81**(7), 42–52.

Nohria, N., Lawrence, P. and Wilson, E. (2001) *Driven: How human nature shapes our choices*. San Francisco, CA: Jossey-Bass.

Norton, D.P. and Russell, R.H. (2011) The Office of Strategy Management – The State of the Art, 2011. *Harvard Business Review*, January 14.

Oberholzer-Gee, F. and Wulf, J.M. (2009) *Alibaba's Taobao (A)*. Harvard Business School case 709-456.

Oberholzer-Gee, F. and Wulf, J.M. (2009) *Alibaba's Taobao (B)*. Harvard Business School case 709-457.

Ortega, B. (1998) *In Sam we Trust: The Untold Story of Sam Walton and How Wal-Mart is Devouring America*. New York, NY: Times.

Ouchi, W.G. (1981) *Theory Z*. New York, NY: Avon Books.

Pande, P.S., Neuman, R.P. and Cavanagh, R.R. (2000) *The Six Sigma Way. How GE, Motorola and Other Top Companies are Honing Their Performance.* New York, NY: McGraw-Hill.

Paparone, C.R. and Crupi, J.A. (2002) Janusian Thinking and Acting. *Military Review,* January–February, pp. 38–47.

Penrose, E.T. (1959) *The Theory of the Growth of the Firm.* Oxford: Basil Blackwell.

Pinker, S. (1997) *How the Mind Works.* New York, NY: W.W. Norton and Company.

Piskorski, M.J. (2006) *LinkedIn (A).* Harvard Business School case 707-406.

Piskorski, M.J. (2007) *I am not on the market, I am here with friends: Finding a job or a spouse on-line.* Boston, MA: Working Paper, Harvard Business School.

Piskorski, M.J. (2011). Social Strategies that Work. *Harvard Business Review,* November 1.

Piskorski, M.J. and Knoop, C.-I. (2006) *Friendster (A).* Harvard Business School case 707-409.

Piskorski, M.J., Eisenmann, T.R., Chen, D. and Feinstein, B. (2008) *Facebook's Platforms.* Harvard Business School case 808-128.

Porter, M.E. (1980) *Competitive Strategy: Techniques for Analyzing Industries and Competitors.* New York, NY: The Free Press.

Porter, M.E. (1996) What is Strategy? *Harvard Business Review,* November 1.

Porter, M.E. (2004) *Competitive Advantage: Creating and Sustaining Superior Performance.* New York, NY: Free Press.

Porter, M.E. (2008) The Five Competitive Forces that Shape Strategy? *Harvard Business Review,* January 1.

Prahalad, C.K. and Hamel, G. (1990) Core Competence of the Corporation. *Harvard Business Review,* May 1.

Pugh, D.S. (Ed.) (1971) *Organization Theory.* London: Penguin Books.

Quinn, J.B. (1980) *Strategies for Change: Logical Incrementalism.* Georgetown, Ontario: Richard D. Irwin.

Rettner, R. (2010) How your brain works on autopilot. *Live Science.* Retrieved September 9, 2010 from http://www.msnbc.msn.com/id/37603247/ns/health-behavior/

Ridley, M. (1996) *The Origins of Virtue.* London: Viking.

Rivkin, J.W. (1998) *Airbourne Express.* Harvard Business School case 703-751.

Rivkin, J.W. and Halaburda, H. (2007) *Analyzing Relative Costs.* Harvard Business School Module Note 708-462.

Rivkin, J.W. and Porter, M.E. (1999) *Matching Dell.* Harvard Business School case 799-158.

Rizzolatti, G. and Craighero, L. (2004) The mirror-neuron system. *Annual Review of Neuroscience*, **27**, 169–192.

Rose, S. (2005) *The 21st Century Brain: Explaining, Mending and Manipulating the Mind.* London: Vintage Books.

Rosenfeld, J.R. (2011) An MCI Friends and Family mailing is a poignant reflection of the'90s decade and the epitome of database marketing. *AllBusiness.com.* Retrieved October 17, 2011 from http://www.allbusiness.com/marketing/direct-marketing/342093-1.html

Ruckstad, M.G., Collis, D.J. and Levine, T. (2001) *Walt Disney Co.: The Entertainment King.* Harvard Business School case 701-035.

Rumelt, R.P. (1995) Inertia and Transformation. in C. Montgomery (Ed.) *Resource-based and Evolutionary Theories of the Firm: Towards a Synthesis.* Norwell, MA: Kluwer Academic Publishers.

Ryan, R. and Deci, E. (2000) Self-determination theory and the facilitation of intrinsic motivation, social development, and well-being. *American Psychologist*, **55**(1), 68–78.

Schaie, K.W. and Geiwitz, J. (1982) *Adult Development and Aging.* New York, NY: Little Brown.

Scherer, F.M. (2001) The Link Between Gross Profitability and Pharmaceutical R&D Spending. *Health Affairs*, **20**(5), 219.

Schwartz, P. (1991) *The Art of the Long View: Planning for the Future in an Uncertain World.* New York, NY: Doubleday.

Selznick, P. (1948) Foundations of the Theory of Organization. *American Sociological Review*, **13**, 25–35.

Senge, P. (1990) *The Fifth Discipline: The Art and Practice of the Learning Organization.* New York, NY: Doubleday.

Seth, J.N. (2007) *The Self-Destructive Habits of Good Companies and How to Break Them.* Harlow, England: Pearson.

Siegel, J. and Chang, J.J. (2005) *Samsung Electronics.* Harvard Business School case 705-508.

Simons, R. (2000) *Performance Measurement and Control Systems for Implementing Strategy.* Englewood Cliffs, NJ: Prentice Hall.

Simons, R. (2010) Stress-Test Your Strategy: The 7 Questions to Ask. *Harvard Business Review*, November 1.

Simpson, J. and Speake, J. (2009) *The Oxford Dictionary of Proverbs.* Oxford: Oxford University Press.

Stalk, Jr., G. and Hout, T.M. (1990) *Competing Against Time: How Time-based Competition is Reshaping Global Markets*. New York, NY: The Free Press.

Sull, D.N. (2003) *Why Good Companies Go Bad and How Great Managers Remake Them*. Boston, MA: Harvard Business School Press.

Surowiecki, J. (2004) *The Wisdom of Crowds*. New York, NY: Anchor Books/ Random House.

Taleb, N.N. (2007) *The Black Swan: The Impact of the Highly Improbable*. London: Penguin.

Taylor, D.A. (1995) *Business Engineering with Object Technology*. New York, NY: John Wiley & Sons, Inc.

Taylor, D.A. (1998) *Object-Oriented Technology: A Manager's Guide*. Upper Saddle River, NJ: Addison Wesley.

Taylor, F. (1911) *Principles of Scientific Management*. New York and London: Harper & Brothers.

Teece, D., Pisano, G. and Shuen, A. (1997) Dynamic Capabilities and Strategic Management. *Strategic Management Journal*, **18**(7), 509–533.

Tennyson, A. (1854) The Charge of the Light Brigade. *The Examiner*, December 9.

Thompson, J.D. (1967) *Organizations in Action*. New York, NY: McGraw-Hill.

Thompson, M., Grace, C. and Cohen, L. (2001) *Best Friends, Worst Enemies: Understanding the social lives of children*. New York, NY: Ballantine Books.

Tripsas, M. and Gavetti, G. (2000) Capabilities, Cognition and Inertia: Evidence from Digital Imaging. *Strategic Management Journal*, **21**, 1147–1161.

Tushman, M.L. and O'Reilly, C.A. III (1996) Ambidextrous Organizations: Managing Evolutionary and Revolutionary Change. *California Management Review*, **38**(4), 8–30.

Tushman, M.L. and O'Reilly, C.A. III (1997) *Winning through Innovation: A Practical Guide to Leading Organizational Change and Renewal*. Boston, MA: Harvard Business School Press.

Van der Heijden, K. (1996) *Scenarios: The Art of Strategic Conversation*. Chichester, West Sussex: John Wiley & Sons, Ltd.

Veryard, R. (2001) *The Component-Based Business: Plug and Play*. London: Springer.

Vom Brocke, J. and Rosemann, M. (eds) (2010) *Handbook on Business Process Management 1: Introduction, Methods, and Information Systems*. Berlin, Heidelberg: Springer.

Wahba, A. and Bridwell, L. (1976) Maslow reconsidered: A review of research on the need hierarchy theory. *Organizational Behavior and Human Performance*, **15**, 212–240.

Wells, J.R. (2003) *Energis (A)*. Harvard Business School case 703-505.

Wells, J.R. (2005) *Best Buy Co., Inc.: Competing on the Edge.* Harvard Business School case 706-417.

Wells, J.R. (2005) *Whole Foods Market, Inc.* Harvard Business School case 705-476.

Wells, J.R. (2005) *Circuit City Stores, Inc.: Strategic Dilemmas.* Harvard Business School case 706-419.

Wells, J.R. (2005) *Providian Financial Corporation.* Harvard Business School case 707-446.

Wells, J.R. (2006) *Wild Oats Markets, Inc.* Harvard Business School case 707-438.

Wells, J.R. (2008) *The Allstate Corporation.* Harvard Business School case 708-485.

Wells, J.R. and Anand, B. (2008) *Capital One Financial Corporation, 2006.* Harvard Business School case 708-489.

Wells, J.R. and Haglock, T. (2005) *The Rise of Kmart Corporation 1962–1987.* Harvard Business School case 706-403.

Wells, J.R. and Haglock, T. (2006) *The Rise of Wal-Mart Stores Inc. 1962–1987.* Harvard Business School case 707-439.

Wells, J.R. and Raabe, E. (2005) *Bally Total Fitness.* Harvard Business School case 706-450 [19].

Wells, J.R. and Raabe, E. (2005) *24 Hour Fitness.* Harvard Business School case 706-404.

Wells, J.R. and Raabe, E. (2006) *Gap Inc.* Harvard Business School case 706-402.

Wells, J.R. and Raabe, E. (2007) *Update: The Music Industry in 2006.* Harvard Business School case 707-531.

Wells, J.R., Dessain, V. and Stachowiak, M. (2005) *JCDecaux.* Harvard Business School case 705-458.

Wells, J.R., Hazlett, S. and Mukhopadhyay, N. (2006) *Riding with the Blackhorse (A).* Harvard Business School case 706-484.

Wells, J.R., Hazlett, S. and Mukhopadhyay, N. (2006) *Riding with the Blackhorse (B).* Harvard Business School case supplement 706-509.

Wells, J.R., Lutova, M. and Sender, I. (2008) *The Progressive Corporation.* Harvard Business School case 707-433.

Williamson, O.E. (1975) *Markets and Hierarchies: Analysis and Antitrust Implications*. New York, NY: The Free Press.

Wiseman, R. (2003) *The Luck Factor: The Four Essential Principles*. New York, NY: Hyperion.

Wright, T.P. (1936) Factors Affecting the Cost of Airplanes. *Journal of Aeronautical Sciences*, **3**(4), 122–128.

Yoffie, D.B. and Kwak, M. (2001) *Judo Strategy: Turning Your Competitors' Strength to Your Advantage*, Boston, MA: Harvard Business School Press.

Yoffie, D.B., Casadesus-Masanell, R. and Mattu, S. (2003) *Wintel (A): Cooperation or Conflict*. Harvard Business School case 704-419.

Young, E. (2002) Brain's Cheat Detector is Revealed. *New Scientist*, August 12, 2002. Retrieved October 5, 2011 from http://www.newscientist.com/article/dn2663-brains-cheat-detector-is-revealed.html

Zich, J. (1997) Ambidextrous Organizations. *Stanford News Service*, June 26. Retrieved October 4, 2011 from http://news.stanford.edu/pr/97/970626oreilly.html

Index

Index compiled by Annette Musker